International Economic
Organisations and the
Third World

International Economic Organisations and the Third World

Marc Williams
*School of African and Asian Studies,
University of Sussex*

HARVESTER
WHEATSHEAF

New York · London · Toronto · Sydney · Tokyo · Singapore

First published 1994 by
Harvester Wheatsheaf
Campus 400, Maylands Avenue
Hemel Hempstead
Hertfordshire, HP2 7EZ
A division of
Simon & Schuster International Group

Typeset in 10/12 pt Times
by Photoprint, Torquay, Devon

Printed in Great Britain by BPC   Wheatons Ltd, Exeter

British Library Cataloguing in Publication Data

A catalogue record for this book is available from the
British Library

ISBN 0–7450–1432–1

2   3   4   5   98 97 96 95 94

Contents

List of tables

Preface

The economic crisis of the 1980s brought increased prominence to the activities of the main international economic organisations in the Third World. At the same time, the increasing differentiation among Third World countries led many to question the very validity of the term. This book sets out to examine the relationship between the Third World and the main international economic organisations. I have chosen to concentrate on the activities of the International Monetary Fund, the World Bank, the General Agreement on Tariffs and Trade and the United Nations Conference on Trade and Development. The influence of the first three organisations mentioned is evident, and indeed it is their activities which sparked the controversies. UNCTAD was created as a result of the pressures by the Third World in the United Nations and represented the hope for a New International Economic Order. It thus seemed fitting to examine the fortunes of this organisation alongside the hegemonic Bretton Woods trio.

I do not see the Third World as an economic expression, but rather as a coalition of developing countries in the international system. I am concerned with the collective expression of Third World demands and the deviations from group behaviour. It is clear that the Third World coalition is still in existence, even if more developing countries are prepared to seek accommodation rather than confrontation with the industrialised countries. In one sense, then, this book is about the limits of Third World unity.

Although the book addresses the events of the last decade it is not exclusively about them. It adopts an historical perspective so that recent events can be placed in a better context. I recognise the existence of competing perspectives on the subjects under review and one of my themes is the conflicting interpretations of the activities of the international economic organisations. These issues are far too often discussed as though only one perspective mattered. In placing emphasis on the importance of ideas and theories in structuring expectations and action, I try to show that conflicts of values are internal to the operations of international organisations. Many writers on the role of international economic organisations tend to omit consideration of the institutional aspects: one way in which I hope this book will contribute to a better understanding of development diplomacy is through the linking of institutional features with the outcomes of international economic organisations.

This book would not have been possible without the help of a number of individuals and institutions. I would like to thank David Harrison and Mahvash Alerassool who read and commented on parts of the text. Katrin Ostertag and Jessica Rowlands provided research assistance at crucial stages in the evolution of this project and I am grateful for their help. I have discussed the ideas in the book with a large number of individuals and it is not possible to thank them all, but Rachel Fletcher deserves special mention for listening to the ideas advanced here at an early stage and for helping me to sharpen my thinking and discussions with Julie Fox on a wide range of theoretical issues were helpful. I owe a special debt to the graduate students taking my Politics of International Economic Organisations course, especially Claudia Deane, Nadia Osman, Colette Boughton, David Parry, Ian Scott and Camille Bonora. Earlier versions of some of these chapters were presented at seminars at the London School of Economics and Political Science, the University of Southampton and the University of Sussex. I am grateful to all who took part in the discussions on those occasions.

I would like to thank my family for the support and encouragement they give to me in my work. Finally, I would like to thank everyone at Harvester Wheatsheaf for their patience and gentle prodding and support throughout the time it has taken to get this book to press.

List of acronyms

ACP	African, Caribbean and Pacific countries
AIC	advanced industrial country
BSFF	Buffer Stock Financing Facility
C-20	Committee of 20
CAP	Common Agricultural Policy
CCFF	Compensatory and Contingency Financing Facility
CF	Common Fund
CFF	Compensatory Financing Facility
DFC	development finance company
DFI	direct foreign investment
EAP	Enlarged Access Policy
ECLA	Economic Commission for Latin America
ECOSOC	Economic and Social Council
EFF	Extended Fund Facility
EIP	Environmental Issue Paper
ESAF	Enhanced Structural Adjustment Facility
FAO	Food and Agriculture Organization
FOG	functioning of the GATT system
FY	financial year
G7	Group of 7
G10	Group of 10
G24	Group of 24
G77	Group of 77
GAB	General Arrangements to Borrow
GATT	General Agreement on Tariffs and Trade
GEF	Global Environmental Facility
GNG	Group of Negotiations on Goods

GDP	gross domestic product
GNP	gross national product
GNS	Group of Negotiations on Services
GSP	Generalised System of Preferences
IAEA	International Atomic Energy Agency
IBRD	International Bank for Reconstruction and Development
ICA	International Commodity Agreement
IDA	International Development Association
IEO	international economic organisation
IFC	International Finance Corporation
IO	international organisation
ILO	International Labour Organization
IMF	International Monetary Fund
IPC	Integrated Programme for Commodities
ISI	import substitution industrialisation
ITO	International Trade Organisation
IUCN	International Union for the Conservation of Nature and Natural Resources
LDC	less developed country
LTA	Long-term Arrangement Regarding International Trade in Cotton Textiles
MFA	Multi-fibre Arrangement
MFN	most-favoured nation
MIGA	Multilateral Investment Guarantee Agency
MTN	Multilateral Trade Negotiations
MTO	Multilateral Trade Organisation
NAM	Non-Aligned Movement
NGO	Non-Governmental Organization
NIC	newly industrialising country
NIEO	New International Economic Order
NTB	non-tariff barrier
ODA	official development assistance
OECD	Organization for Economic Cooperation and Development
OESA	Office or Environmental and Scientific Affairs
OF	Oil Facility
PFP	policy framework paper
SAF	Structural Adjustment Facility
SAL	structural adjustment loan
SAP	Special Action Programme
SDR	Special Drawing Rights
SECAL	sectoral adjustment loans

SFF	Supplementary Financing Facility
STA	Short-Term Arrangement
SUNFED	Special United Nations Fund for Economic Development
TDB	Trade and Development Board
TNC	transnational corporation
TRIMs	trade-related investment measures
TRIPs	trade-related aspects of intellectual property rights
UNCTAD	United Nations Conference on Trade and Development
UNDP	United Nations Development Programme
UNEP	United Nations Environment Programme
UNESCO	United Nations Educational, Scientific and Cultural Organization
VER	voluntary exports restraint
WHO	World Health Organization
WRI	World Resources Institute
WWF	World Wide Fund for Nature

1

Introduction

The purpose of this book

In the last decade the relationship between international economic
organisations (IEOs) and the Third World has been the focus of
extensive scrutiny. In particular, the Bretton Woods institutions, the
World Bank and the International Monetary Fund (IMF), have been
criticised for their roles in reorganising and restructuring the economies
of their Third World members. Most of this criticism has emanated from
left-wing critics, as they perceived an increased rightward drift in the
policies and advice of the Bretton Woods institutions. However,
dissatisfaction with the performance of IEOs is not confined to radical
writers on the left. In this book, various criticisms of the performance of
IEOs are assessed in relation to the two central concerns of the book.

The first issue to be addressed is that of the demands made by Third
World states of the IEOs. The relationship between the 'needs' of the
Third World and the 'demands' of their spokespersons in international
organisations raises a number of problems for analysis. If it is accepted
that the various government officials are acting in the national interest,
the positions taken by the representatives of Third World countries in
international organisations will reflect the 'needs' of these countries. If,
on the other hand, it is recognised that governments need not always act
in the national interest or the concept is rejected as a useful analytical
tool,[1] then 'demands' and 'needs' will not be synonymous. In what
follows, I will not assume that 'demands' and 'needs' can be equated.

The second issue discussed in the book is the response of the IEOs to
the demands of the Third World states. These two issues are, of course,
intimately connected. The impact of IEOs on the economies and

1

societies of poor countries can be investigated from a number of perspectives. This book analyses one dimension of this complex topic but does not exhaust the possible approaches that could be taken to the subject. Much of the debate on the activities of the IEOs tends to take place without explicit reference to the perspectives of Third World governments. In this book the demands of these governments are treated as the starting point of the investigation but not as the only perspective from which to assess the impact of the IEOs.

At the outset it is necessary for me to define the way in which I will be using the term Third World, since it is becoming increasingly difficult to use the term without running into objections. The collapse of the Second World of Soviet-style communism and the increasing economic differentiation among the poorer economies is calling into question the nomenclature of the Cold War era in world politics. After examining the term Third World I will discuss the thorny problem of the classification of countries, and other terms frequently used in an interchangeable manner to describe the less developed economies in the world.

The Third World as a political concept

The use of the term, Third World, to describe a group of countries in the international system is both widespread and to some extent insecure. The French phrase 'tiers monde' entered the vocabulary of political scientists in the 1950s and since then it has been defined in a number of ways. Among writers who employ the term no agreement exists on its meaning. On the other hand, a number of scholars question the usefulness of the concept. I think that, notwithstanding the controversy surrounding the concept, it is possible to demonstrate that it is not redundant.

Those analysts who argue that the Third World is a myth do so from three different positions. The first, is that the group of countries which is often identified as the Third World lacks sufficient unity and cohesion to be conceived as an independent and distinct grouping in world politics. In this perspective, if a Third World existed it would display an effective degree of unity and its pronouncements and actions in world politics would have some significance. To J. D. B. Miller writing in 1966, the Third World is a myth since at that time the relevant degree of unity was absent and he did not foresee it occurring. He concluded his survey of the politics of the Third World with the assertion that, 'A Third World characterized by unity, purpose and effective tactics is . . . a chimera.'[2]

Some critics argue that the Third World only exists because it was created by the practice of foreign aid. As Bauer asserts, 'The Third

World is the creation of foreign aid: without foreign aid there is no Third World.'[3] No real ties of interests bind these diverse countries together and the ending of foreign aid would cause this spurious unity to disappear. In this conservative approach the deep and fundamental divisions among these countries are obscured by a false sense of solidarity which enables them to wrest concessions from the West.

A radical version of this critique rejects the use of the term because it masks the real struggle in the world between oppressed peoples and international capitalism. A false unity among the elites of a number of countries cannot hide the deep ideological divisions which exist in the global system. Pierre Jalée argues that, 'the so-called Third World is no more than the backyard of imperialism, which does not mean that it does not belong to the system – quite the contrary. The expression Third World, does however tend to conceal this reality and it serves objectively to cause confusion.'[4]

Despite these criticisms the term is used by politicians and academics in at least three different ways. In the first approach, the Third World pertains to a group of countries united by adherence to a set of common cultural values. According to this view the Third World is that part of the globe which either has rejected Western values, is in the process of rejecting Western values, or has never concerned itself with Western values. A common anti-Western system unites these countries even though no cultural homogeneity binds them together. This approach underlines the work of Frantz Fanon.[5] And Peter Worsley, in excluding communist countries from his definition of the Third World because they 'do not constitute a distinctly different set of political cultures',[6] gives prominence to cultural characteristics. Other observers detail cultural difference rather than unity among these countries. The problem with the cultural approach lies in the difficulty of showing the existence of unity across diverse cultural traditions and separate histories. These countries differ in tradition, culture and religion and a cultural unity is difficult to demonstrate.

It is as an economic concept that the term has gained most acceptance. In this approach, the Third World is the term given to the poorer countries in the world. The Third World is used interchangeably with other terms which signify the level of economic development attained by a country, e.g. developing, less developed, underdeveloped. The defining condition of the Third World is shared underdevelopment. This standpoint was put succinctly by John Goldthorpe when he wrote, 'If the affluent industrial countries of the modern world are grouped into those of the "West" and "East", capitalist and communist, then the poor countries constitute a "Third World" whose small command over resources distinguishes them from both.'[7] The problem with this definition, however, arises from the absence of any agreed criteria on what constitutes a developing country. If we use per capita income (perhaps the most simple measure), we immediately face the problem of deciding on the relevant cut-off point. The wide economic diversity among developing countries which gathered increased pace in the 1980s suggests not a simple category for all developing countries but rather a proliferation of categories. In other words, if the Third World is defined solely in economic terms then distinctions between middle-income, oil-exporters, heavily indebted, least developed, land-locked, etc, seem more pertinent than some all-embracing category. And indeed, as a consequence of increased differentiation among developing countries in the 1970s, some writers began talking about Fourth and Fifth Worlds.[8]

The Third World, if anything, is a political and ideological and not an economic concept. Indeed, from the outset it referred to more than shared economic characteristics. The Third World is not reducible to a category of countries sharing similar economic characteristics. It is an expression of the perception and consciousness of a certain degree of powerlessness in world politics. The Third World is the symbolic expression of political difference in international relations. It consists of those countries which consciously think of themselves as such and whose foreign policies are affected by this consideration. In this political perspective, the concept of the Third World signifies a major shift in the self-conception of the countries in question. The Third World comprises those countries which identify common interests and have forged a diplomatic unity.

At the global level, the Third World coalition consists of two separate groupings – the Non-Aligned Movement (NAM) and the Group of 77 (G77). Historically, the origins of the Third World can be traced to two important developments in post-war international relations: the Cold War and decolonisation. The division of the world between the East and West and the struggle for supremacy seemed an irrelevance to the leaders of many newly independent countries. The NAM was an attempt to develop a 'third way' in international relations. Rejecting both East and West and refusing to follow accepted practices of neutrality the ex-colonial territories tried to forge a unity based on opposition to great power blocs. The NAM also shared common objectives in relation to issues such as decolonisation, the role of the United Nations and economic development.[9] The G77 created at the first United Nations Conference on Trade and Development (UNCTAD) in 1964 became the chief instrument through which the Third World expressed its dissatisfaction with the international economic order.

The Third World coalition is based on an acceptance of the diversity of its membership. The member countries do not share a common ideology or political philosophy, and exhibit widely different levels of development. They differ in political culture, political systems and economic organisation. Nevertheless, they have created a caucasing bloc in international organisations and created a platform from which to bargain for changes in the international political economy.[10] In this book, the term Third World will for the most part refer to this diplomatic solidarity. In the IEOs discussed, the Third World has presented common positions and negotiated both individually and collectively. The coalition is not static and the degree of unity attained is affected by changes in the international system. The approach adopted here recognises the existence of unity in diversity. In other words it treats the Third World as a political entity and neither assumes that the unity attained is organic or misguided, natural nor false. The extent to which the Third World is able to speak collectively is a function of the internal resolution of differences among the membership. Moreover, I do not assume that the policies campaigned for by the Third World coalition will automatically benefit all of its members.

A note on the classification of countries

The classification of countries according to economic criteria is not an unproblematic exercise. Nevertheless, academics, governmental officials and the staff of international organisations do undertake this exercise. In the absence of agreed criteria on which to base judgements, controversy will surround this task and there will be room for debate on the groupings to which certain countries are assigned. The simplest and most often used criterion for dividing one group of countries from another is gross national product (GNP) per capita. The inadequacy of this measure has led to attempts to use a variety of other criteria. These include the level of industrialisation, the percentage of manufactured exports, levels of literacy, the rate of infant mortality, life expectancy, and basic sanitation and clean water facilities.

Classification schemas can be as simple as a twofold division between developed and developing countries or one which distinguishes between high-income, middle-income and low-income countries. Countries can be classified in relation to their population, resource base, whether they are oil-importing or oil-exporting, etc. The standard division between developed and developing countries is a legacy of the era of decolonisation. This broad categorisation has always hidden huge disparities in economic performance within each grouping. Moreover, a number of marginal countries have persistently created problems in classification.

The labelling of a country as developed or developing is not the outcome of some strictly scientific enterprise but the product of political and economic considerations.

The developing countries do not constitute a homogeneous group. These countries vary enormously in size, population and population density, natural resource endowment, industrial development and GNP per capita. The variation in economic performance among developing countries became more marked following the oil price rise of 1973–74, and accelerated in the wake of the debt crisis from 1982 onwards. The success of, particularly, the East Asian newly industrialising countries (NICs), in pursuing successful growth strategies further increased the differentiation among the developing countries. Table 1.1 on the distribution of income among developing regions shows that contrary to a widely held belief, the distribution of income among developing regions was never equal. It also shows the widening gap in income levels in the 1980s.

The changed share of developing country income resulted from diverging growth rates in the 1970s and 1980s. The East Asian share increased from 22 per cent to 37 per cent because by the 1980s, per capita GDP growth in East Asia reached 6.7 per cent, but fell in Sub-Saharan Africa and Latin America (see Table 1.2).

The terminology used to describe countries at different stages of development has changed over time. The language of development responds to changing perceptions concerning the appropriateness of particular words. Terms such as backward, poor and underdeveloped were discarded because of their negative connotations, implicit cultural bias and racist undertones. The phrase less developed country (LDC) came into fashion in the mid-1960s and remains the preference of some writers. I use the term developing countries because that is the usage of the United Nations and it is also the preferred terminology of the representatives of this group of countries. The positive connotation of

Table 1.1 Changes in the distribution of income in the developing world

Region	1960–65 (Average)	1988–89 (Average)
Sub-Saharan Africa	12	7
East Asia	22	37
South Asia	15	12
Middle East, North Africa and Europe	19	17
Latin America and the Caribbean	33	37

Source: World Bank, *World Development Report 1990* p. 10.

Table 1.2 Performance indicators, by developing region, selected periods

Region	Growth of real per capita GDP (per cent)		
	1965–73	1973–80	1980–89
Sub-Saharan Africa	3.2	0.1	−2.2
East Asia	5.1	4.7	6.7
South Asia	1.2	1.7	3.2
Middle East, North Africa and Europe	5.5	2.1	0.8
Latin America and the Caribbean	3.7	2.6	−0.6

Source: World Bank, *World Development Report 1990* p. 11.

developing country is the main reason why it is so widely used. One can, of course, object to calling these countries developing on the grounds that many countries in this category are economically stagnant and record negative growth rates. Andre Gunder Frank's striking phrase, 'the development of underdevelopment' highlighted not only the fact that international inequality is an historically created process but also the reality of the absence of positive economic development in many poor countries. But the alternative terms are also subject to objection. To call one group of countries underdeveloped implies that these are the only countries with undeveloped resources. It has been argued that less developed country is a more appropriate term because poverty is a relative concept.[11] But with no agreement on the international poverty datum line this term is not as neutral as it first appears. In the absence of a satisfactory answer to the problem of appropriate terminology I have chosen the most widely used term and the one which is less offensive than others.

In this book I will be using Third World and developing countries synonymously because for the most part these categories do overlap and membership of the Third World is based on the level of economic development reached by a country. But as I have indicated, the use of these terms is compatible with a recognition of the diversity of the groupings. The International Relations literature has long distinguished between great powers and small states. Such classifications are based on an analysis of the relative power of states in a stratified international society and they do not imply that all small states are the same. The usefulness of categories depends on their descriptive and analytical powers. It is possible to approach the global power structure and international stratification and inequality from a number of different perspectives. A division into developed and developing countries recognises the existence of a global dominance system in which the developing countries are marginalised. It does not assume that these countries will always lose in any confrontation with developed countries but recognises that as a result of the superior resources held by other actors and the operation of structural power they lack the ability to determine outcomes on the majority of issues.

Contending perspectives on development cooperation

The view taken of the impact of IEOs on the developing world depends on the perspective taken. Each perspective comprises a set of values, beliefs and assumptions concerning development, the international economy and international cooperation. These perspectives do not conform to a specific theory and neither are they coherent bodies of thought. Perspective is being used here to denote a broad intellectual framework with a common core set of assumptions concerning the relevant objects of study and the proper methods to be employed in such tasks.

Judgements about the roles and functions of IEOs cannot be divorced from the values and beliefs of the analyst. Assessment of the success or failure of collective action to address the problems faced by developing countries in the global economy is inseparable from the perspective taken on the causes of underdevelopment, the operation of the contemporary international economic system and the limitations and possibilities of international economic cooperation. Writers on international political economy have discerned the existence of three perspectives – liberalism, realism/mercantilism and Marxism.[12] Writers on development have, similarly, elaborated a number of competing perspectives or paradigms in the study of development.[13] Attitudes to development cooperation arise from a mix of the international political economy perspectives and development paradigms. The liberal, reformist and radical perspectives on development cooperation are based on conflicting perceptions on the causes of international inequality, the international economic order and proposals for change.

The liberal perspective is based on classical and neo-classical economic theory. Liberal theories of economic development concentrate on the internal obstacles to growth. In this view the current developed countries underwent a process of modern economic growth which transformed their production structures and raised standards of living. Development consists in the successful diffusion of this process to the poor countries. The failure to develop arises from domestic market imperfections, inefficient and unproductive factor markets, low levels of education, poor infrastructure, and social and political attitudes and institutions harmful to the pursuit of economic growth. The key to development lies in market-oriented policies which remove internal impediments to growth and free the productive forces of production.

Writers in this perspective believe that the international economy exercises a benign influence on a country's efforts to develop. International specialisation, trade and capital movements lead to a more efficient allocation of global resources and benefit individual countries. Thus the unrestricted operation of market forces results in an optimal international division of labour and although the gains from trade may not be equitably distributed, trade expands the production-possibility frontier and therefore the nation will benefit. Liberal theorists with their commitment to the market and the price mechanism believe that increased integration into the international economy is beneficial for developing countries. Foreign trade provides an engine of growth and improves the productivity and efficiency of local firms. Foreign investment increases productivity through the transmission of technical and managerial skills and helps to improve local savings. Foreign aid provides much needed capital, especially to fund products without a high rate of return in the short run.

From the liberal viewpoint international cooperation can assist poor countries to acquire capital, technology and relevant skills in order to foster development. The aim of development cooperation is to remove barriers to the free movement of goods and services domestically and internationally. Primarily, intergovernmental agreements should increase reliance on the market mechanism and private enterprise. The IMF, GATT and the World Bank are based on liberal principles.

The reformist perspective lies somewhere between the liberal and radical approaches. Writers in this perspective use a variety of economic theories. They share with the liberals an appreciation of the success of market-oriented policies in promoting development, but argue that market imperfections prevent the diffusion of growth from rich to poor nations. For reformist theorists, the liberal model is divorced from reality and fails to take sufficient account of economic power and historical changes which have created conditions in which liberal prescriptions are unlikely to be successful Reformists argue that once major disparities in income exist, the market ceases to function either efficiently or equitably. They contend that development will not arise simply through the diffusion of modern economic growth from the rich countries. In this perspective underdevelopment is caused by structural rigidities at the domestic and international levels. Reformists question the assumptions concerning the benevolent workings of the market.

The reformist argument recognises that free trade and the free movement of capital need not act as an engine of growth for developing countries. The purchasing power of the rich results in a skewing of the benefits of economic intercourse in their favour. The unregulated operation of market forces leads to an excessive degree of specialisation in developing countries in the production and export of primary commodities. Since primary commodities suffer from chronic instability and deteriorating terms of trade, international specialisation in the absence of corrective intervention will not lead to development. Although foreign investment can increase incomes in the developing world, it can also retard economic growth. Transnational corporations with their control over production and marketing, and activities such as transfer pricing, export restriction and the use of patents can have negative impacts on employment levels and the balance of payments of the developing countries. And foreign aid, although in theory capable of achieving the twin goals of economic growth and poverty alleviation, is too often subject to political and economic restrictions which reduce its effectiveness.

From the reformist perspective international cooperation is therefore necessary to assist the efforts of the developing countries through correcting the distortions caused by the unfettered operation of market forces. A redistributivist and interventionist approach to the international economy is the best way to overcome the obstacles to Third World development. UNCTAD was founded on such reformist principles. And the proposals for a New International Economic Order (NIEO) took as their starting point the reformist critique of the liberal order.

The radical perspective tends to be based on some variant of Marxism and adopts a critical perspective on the workings of the capitalist world economy. From this standpoint underdevelopment arises from the operation of the law of value under capitalism. Any attempts to remedy the poverty of the developing countries is destined to fail as long as capitalism remains the dominant social and economic system. Underdevelopment is not simply the result of low incomes, low savings and domestic market imperfections. It is the consequence of centuries of exploitation, first through colonialism and latterly through imperialism.

International trade, far from providing an engine of growth is inherently a process of unequal exchange. Trade and investment extract surplus from the developing countries and transfer it to the core countries in the international system. Capitalism, by its very nature, creates wealth and poverty, development and underdevelopment. Thus, the division of the world into economically wealthy and impoverished countries is not accidental but the outcome of a process of uneven development central to capitalism. Foreign investment and aid create and perpetuate dependence and retard the development of autonomous and self-sustaining growth.

Given that for radical theorists, capitalist production and exchange creates underdevelopment and subjugates the needs of the majority in the Third World to the interests of foreign capital and local comprador classes, development cooperation is a contradiction in terms. Any attempt to promote increased integration into the capitalist world economy is, according to this view, likely to reinforce economic and political dependence. The radical perspective leads to the conclusion that the four IEOs analysed in this book cannot promote development and are more likely to increase internal inequality and maintain the control exerted by the major capitalist states over the Third World.

The structure of the book

The purpose of this book is to describe and explain the interactions between the Third World and international economic organisations. It takes as its starting point the demands by developing countries for the reform of existing IEOs. It investigates the extent to which international economic organisations have responded to the concerns and interests of the Third World countries. It discusses the developing countries' dissatisfaction with the performance of the IEOs and their proposals for change and then assesses the response of the IEOs to the Third World challenge.

Chapter 2 deals briefly with the developing countries and the world economy. It presents an overview of some relevant economic indicators and discusses contrasting explanations of the economic performance of the Third World. Chapter 3 focuses on international economic organisations and international cooperation; it provides an account of the strengths and weaknesses of regime theory as an approach to the study of international cooperation. The following four chapters examine in detail the relationship between the Third World and four IEOs. They are: the International Monetary Fund (Chapter 4); the World Bank (Chapter 5); the General Agreement on Tariffs and Trade (Chapter 6) and the United Nations Conference on Trade and Development (Chapter 7). The campaign by the Third World has often been couched in terms of economic justice. The final chapter examines the applicability of economic justice to the issues discussed in the book.

Notes

1. On the national interest as a concept see Joseph Frankel, *The National Interest* (London: Pall Mall 1970) and James N. Rosenau, 'The National

Interest' in his *The Scientific Study of Foreign Policy* rev. ed. (London: Frances Pinter 1980) pp. 283–93.

2. J. D. B. Miller, *The Politics of the Third World* (Oxford: Oxford University Press 1966) p. 126.

3. P. T. Bauer, *Equality, the Third World and Economic Delusion* (London: Methuen 1981) p. 87.

4. Pierre Jalee, *The Pillage of the Third World* (New York: Monthly Review Press 1968) p. 3.

5. See Frantz Fanon, *The Wretched of the Earth* (Harmondsworth: Penguin Books 1967).

6. Peter Worsley, *The Third World* (London: Weidenfeld & Nicolson 1964) p. x.

7. J. E. Goldthorpe, *The Sociology of the Third World: Disparity and Involvement* (Cambridge: Cambridge University Press 1975) p. 1.

8. See, for example, C. Fred Bergsten, 'The Response to the Third World', *Foreign Policy* (Winter 1974–75) pp. 9–11; and George W. Ball, *Diplomacy for a Crowded World* (London: Bodley Head 1976) pp. 278–98.

9. Numerous studies of the NAM are in print. For discussions of the principles of non-alignment and the evolution of the movement see Hans Kochler (ed.), *The Principles of Non-Alignment* (Vienna: International Progress Publishers 1982); and A. W. Singham & Shirley Hune, *Non-Alignment in an Age of Alignments* (London: Zed Books 1986).

10. See Robert Mortimer, *The Third World Coalition in World Politics* (New York: Praeger 1980).

11. Salvatore Schiavo-Campo and Hans W. Singer, *Perspectives of Economic Development* (Boston: Houghton Mifflin 1970) p. 18.

12. See, for example, Robert Gilpin, *The Political Economy of International Relations* (Princeton, NJ: Princeton University Press 1987) ch. 2; and Stephen Gill & David Law, *Global Political Economy* (Hemel Hempstead: Harvester Wheatsheaf 1988) chs. 3–5.

13. See, for example, Diana Hunt, Economic Theories of Development: An Analysis of Competing Paradigms (Hemel Hempstead: Harvester Wheatsheaf 1989); David Harrison, *The Sociology of Modernization and Development* (London: Unwin Hyman 1988); and Ankie M. Hoogvelt, *The Sociology of Developing Societies* 2nd ed. (London: Macmillan 1978).

2

The Third World in the world economy

The Third World's campaign for reform of the international economic order is shaped by changes in the global economic environment and perceptions of the impact of these transformations on the development process. It is not the intention of this chapter to review the literature on trade and development or to elaborate on the three perspectives on the relationship between the international economy and the developing countries outlined in the previous chapter. This chapter will review changes in the world economy and the growing integration of the developing countries into an increasingly interdependent system of international trade and payments. The Third World is linked to the global economy through flows of trade, investment and aid and this chapter will review broad trends in these three areas with a special focus on developments since 1980.

The history of the world economy since 1945 can be divided into two broad periods. Between the end of World War II and 1971–73 the international economy experienced a long period of economic growth. The end of the post-war boom in the mid-1970s ushered in a period of crisis and instability. The political and economic shocks of the 1980s exacerbated the turbulence and uncertainty in the international economy, and the high growth rates attained in the 1950s and 1960s have not been achieved in the 1990s.

Considerable disagreement exists over whether the Third World, as a whole, has benefited from participation in the international economy. Opposing theoretical perspectives, competing sources of data and variations in the time period covered lead to widely divergent conclusions. What seems certain is that world economic growth has oscillated over time and the performance of the developing countries has been uneven. The economic differentiation of the Third World, which always existed in reality, if not in the elegant theories of economists and political scientists, became more pronounced and therefore any attempt to examine these countries' performance in the international economic order must take cognisance of differences among developing countries.

The growth rates of the developing countries as a group has been higher than that achieved by the industrial countries for most of the post-war period. Between 1950 and 1975 the developing countries achieved average annual growth rates of 5.6 per cent and the industrial countries 4.7 per cent.[1] The onset of global recession and the less favourable conditions in the world economy reduced these rates in the period, 1980–89 to 3.8 and 3.0 per cent respectively.[2] These aggregates conceal wide regional and country variations and some groups of countries have fared much better than others. Tables 2.1 and 2.2 provide data on growth in gross domestic product and gross national income per capita, on the basis of the level of development of the economy.

In regional terms, the variations among the different developing regions were even more stark. East Asia performed best while Sub-Saharan Africa and Latin America have fared less well. Per capita incomes in Sub-Saharan Africa have fallen, in real terms, since 1973. As a percentage of the average industrial country income the region's per capita income declined from 11 per cent in 1950 to 5 per cent in 1991.[3] If one compares average annual per capita growth rates in the 1980s, the uneven growth in the developing world is clearly revealed. The East Asian region recorded 6.3 per cent growth, South Asia reached 2.9 per

Table 2.1 Average annual growth of GDP, 1965–89

Country group	1965–73	1973–80	1980–89
Low- and middle-income economies	6.5	4.7	3.8
Low-income economies	5.3	4.5	6.2
Middle-income economies	7.0	4.7	2.9
High-income economies	4.8	3.1	3.0
World	5.0	3.3	3.1

Note: In the World Bank classification Hong Kong, Kuwait, Saudi Arabia, Singapore and the United Arab Emirates are included in the 'high-income economy category'.

Source: *World Development Report 1991* p. 186.

Table 2.2   Average annual growth of GDP, 1965–90

Country group	1965–73	1973–80	1980–90
Low- and middle-income economies	4.3	2.6	1.5
Low-income economies	2.4	2.7	4.0
Middle-income economies	5.3	2.4	0.4
High-income economies	3.7	2.1	2.4
World	2.8	1.3	1.4

Source: *World Development Report 1992* p. 186.

cent, and Latin America 0.5 per cent. But Sub-Saharan Africa and the Middle East and North African regions both recorded negative growth rates of −1.1 per cent and −1.5 per cent respectively.[4]

Trade

These overall trends are also reflected in the trading performance of the developing countries. World trade has expanded faster than world output in the post-war period and the developing countries' fortunes have been distinctly mixed. The developing countries' share of world trade fell from 31 per cent in 1950 to 21.4 per cent in 1960, rose to 27.9 per cent in 1980 but declined to 20.4 per cent in 1990. At the same time, the developed countries increased their share of world trade from 60.4 percent in 1950 to 66.8 percent in 1960, registered a slight decline to 63.1 per cent in 1980 but rose again to 69.9 in 1990. The developing countries' ability to benefit from this expansion in world trade is determined by three main factors: (i) the structural determinants of trade flows; (ii) the political and economic dominance of the industrial countries over the international trading system; and (iii) the trade strategies of the developing countries.

World trade has grown consistently in the post-war period, with manufacturing proving the most dynamic sector. Between 1950 and 1985, trade in manufactures increased more than twice as fast as manufactured output. Trade in other commodities has grown at a much slower pace. Between 1950 and 1983, trade in minerals grew at approximately the same pace as the growth in world output, but has grown more slowly since. Trade in agricultural products has grown more slowly than world output.[5] The poor export performance of many developing countries arises from a concentration of exports in primary commodities, i.e. the products with the most sluggish demand in world markets.[6] The share of primary commodities in world trade has stagnated or declined for a number of reasons. The two most important are their low income elasticity of demand and their vulnerability to substitution from synthetic fibres and other materials as a result of technological innovation in the developed world.

The poor performance of primary commodities in world trade has led to a debate on the terms of trade. No agreement exists on whether there is a persistent tendency for the terms of trade of the Third World as a whole to deteriorate relative to those of the industrial countries. Competing and conflicting theoretical and methodological approaches make it difficult to compare the various findings. John Spraos conducted a survey of a number of studies and came to the conclusion that, 'while the deteriorating tendency cannot be decisively refuted, it is open to doubt when the record up to the 1970s is taken into account.'[7] Although a persistent tendency for the terms of trade of primary commodities to deteriorate *vis-à-vis* manufactured products cannot be proven, nevertheless, the prices of primary products are more unstable. And since 1974, with the exception of 1979–80, prices of primary commodities have fallen steadily. In the 1980s, prices of many primary commodities plummeted, recording the lowest levels since the end of World War II. At the close of the decade, average commodity prices were 33 per cent lower than at the beginning of the 1980s.[8] This decline in prices affected the poorest countries which had not diversified their structures of production. The two regions with the largest terms of trade losses were Sub-Saharan Africa and Latin America. Declining terms of trade cost Sub-Saharan Africa and Latin America, 13 and 15 per cent respectively of their purchasing power in real terms relative to the 1970s.[9] It is arguable that for Third World exporters with a heavy dependence on the export of specific commodities the international trading system has been unfavourable, not only in the 1980s but for most of the post-war period.

For the Third World, as a whole, the impact of falling commodity prices has been offset by an expansion in manufactured exports. The developing countries, as a group, increased their share of world trade in manufactures from 4.3 per cent in 1963 to 12.4 per cent by the mid-1980s.[10] From 1965 to 1988, the share of manufactured goods in exports from the developing countries increased fourfold, from 16 to 64 per cent.[11] This shift in the commodity composition of the Third World's exports was more pronounced in East Asia and South Asia than in Africa. According to World Bank calculations, the share of primary commodities in Africa's merchandise exports declined by only 1 per cent between 1965 and 1992, from 93 to 92 per cent. For the Middle East and North Africa region the share of primary commodities in total exports declined from 98 to 87 per cent.[12]

This tremendous increase in manufactured exports athough not confined to a handful of countries mainly benefited the NICs, particularly the four 'Asian tigers' of Hong Kong, Singapore, South Korea and Taiwan which account for approximately 33 per cent of the Third World's manufactured exports. The more developed of the developing countries were thus not caught in the trap of dependence on a limited number of primary commodities. The successful industrialisation strategies of these countries enabled them to diversify their production base and to increase, significantly, their exports of manufactured goods.

The expansion in Third World manufactured exports has, to a considerable extent, been achieved against the defensive policies of the advanced industrial countries (AICs). The political and economic dominance of the developed countries in the international trading system enables them to mount effective protectionist barriers against the manufactured exports of the developing countries. Powerful political forces have successfully persuaded Northern governments to enact protectionist measures against Southern exports as the developing countries became more competitive. Perhaps, the classic example of Northern protectionism is the Multi-fibre Arrangement (MFA).

The Third World comparative advantage in textiles and successful export of textiles and clothing has been met with Northern protectionism masquerading as orderly market arrangements. As early as 1962, with the Long-Term Arrangement Regarding International Trade in Cotton Textiles (LTA) developed countries reacted to Third World competitiveness with restrictive measures. The MFA, first concluded in 1974 and subsequently renewed, extended and increased restrictions on developing countries' exports of textiles and clothing. Even Bangladesh, one of the world's poorest countries, was subjected to MFA quotas when it developed an efficient textile industry in the 1980s.

The practice of tariff escalation also harms the export prospects of the developing countries. A central feature of AICs' tariff structures is that duties generally increase according to the degree of processing. Duties on imported raw materials tend to be low or even nil, but duties escalate the higher the degree of processing in the final product. The effect of this tariff regime is to discourage processing of commodities in developing countries and to inhibit their exports of manufactured products.

Developed countries also employ a number of non-tariff barriers against the manufactured exports of the developing countries. Health and safety measures, customs valuation procedures and so-called voluntary exports restraints are examples of some of these non-tariff barriers used to restrict the access of Third World countries to the markets of the AICs.

The political and economic dominance of the AICs also has a negative impact on the agricultural trade of the Third World. Agricultural support policies in the United States, the European Community, Japan and other industrial countries protect the incomes of domestic farmers through price support, direct payments and other policies but harm Third World exporters. The farm trade policies of the industrial countries result in overproduction thus reducing imports into the North, increasing exports and lowering world prices. Moreover, about one-third of the agricultural exports of the developing countries are affected by non-tariff barriers.[13]

A country's ability to gain from international trade is to some extent dependent on the foreign trade regime it operates. Liberal theorists argue that one of the main reasons for the poor export performance of the developing countries arises from inappropriate trade strategies. The primary strategy of the developing countries from the end of World War II until the 1980s was import substitution industrialisation (ISI). ISI policies were based on a pessimism about the export prospects of the developing countries. In this context, protection to promote domestic industries through high tariff barriers, multiple exchange rates, import licensing arrangements and subsidies was not seen as detrimental to trade and development.

It is now widely agreed that prolonged application of ISI is a mistake. ISI did encourage industrialisation but at severe costs to the local economy. The balance of payments did not improve because the capital-intensive components needed to produce the finished products increased import costs, and the reallocation of resources in favour of the manufacturing sector reduced traditional agricultural exports and curtailed efforts to foster export-oriented industrialisation. Moreover, capital-intensive technologies had a negative impact on employment and shifted income in favour of capital. In addition, the concentration on domestic industry shifted the internal terms of trade against agriculture. Declining profits in agriculture led to reduced investment in the agricultural sector, further increasing the income inequalities between agriculture and industry. Industrialisation through import substitution required the creation of an institutional framework conducive to capital accumulation and the efficient allocation of resources, but these conditions were not met. Inefficient economic management by the companies established to promote ISI and the inability of the state to create regulatory frameworks that limited waste and corruption increased the costliness of the ISI experiment.[14]

The success of the Asian NICs in promoting export-led growth has been an important factor in the movement towards more open trading policies in the developing world in the 1980s. Liberal theorists argue that the rapid economic growth and successful industrialisation of the Asian NICs is due to pursuit of liberal, market-oriented policies.[15] A number of studies have challenged this argument and provide convincing evidence that the success of the NICs cannot be attributed primarily to the adoption of export-led, market-oriented policies, but to close state control of the domestic economy and foreign trade.[16]

The debate between state intervention on the one hand, and market policies on the other, is in many respects a false one. The crucial variable is not the presence or absence of state intervention but the ways in which the state mediates between foreign economic actors and local actors. The foreign trade regime adopted by a particular state will affect its ability to gain from participation in the international economy. The flows of capital and investment and successful export promotion strategies will be conditioned by the interaction of global and local forces.

Investment

Considerable disagreement exists over whether the Third World benefits from foreign investment in general, and the activities of transnational corporations (TNC) in particular. The standard debate between liberal theorists and dependency theorists on the impact of foreign investment on developing countries reproduces the central assumptions held by the two groups concerning the consequences of capitalist development. The liberal paradigm stresses the potential beneficial effects of direct foreign investment (DFI). These include, apart from the provision of capital, a positive contribution to the balance of payments, improved access to technology, increased employment, the transfer of managerial skills and access to foreign markets. The radical critics argue that TNCs increase political and economic dependence. For these critics any development arising from DFI constitutes 'distorted development'. Instead of contributing to capital inflow, they insist that TNCs are responsible for a net outflow of capital through the repatriation of profits, transfer pricing and other activities. In this perspective TNCs fail to increase employment, stifle local business and transfer inappropriate technology.[17]

Third World governments appeared to share many of the assumptions of the radical paradigm and the prevailing approach to TNCs in the 1960s and 1970s was one of suspicion. The demand for 'permanent sovereignty over natural resources' voiced in the UN and elsewhere and the nationalisation and expropriation of foreign assets were indicative of this mood which reached its apogee with the attempt to establish a code of conduct for transnational corporations during the NIEO negotiations. The influence of neo-liberalism, the impact of the debt crisis and a decline in TNC investment led to a shift towards a more cooperative and less confrontational stance by many Third World governments in the 1980s.[18] Whether the impact is positive or negative, there is no escaping the crucial role played by TNCs in the global economy. The globalisation of economic activity through the internationalisation of production and the growth of intrafirm trade is an inescapable feature of contemporary international relations.[19] The challenges of development and efforts at international cooperation are profoundly affected by these changes. The developing countries' access to DFI is therefore important in determining their growth prospects.

Direct foreign investment is unevenly distributed among the developing countries. In the 1980s, 10 countries alone accounted for three-quarters of total DFI flows ($16 billion) to the Third World.[20] Tables 2.3 and 2.4 illustrate the uneven distribution of direct foreign investment to developing countries.

At the beginning of the decade the largest volume of DFI was in Latin America, but the rapid rates of increase in Asia saw the Asian share

Table 2.3 Major destination of direct investment to developing countries, 1982–92

Country group	1982	1989	1990	1991	1992
Low-income	1,760	7,717	6,601	7,383	9,212
Middle-income	9,392	15,604	17,606	26,524	29,040
All countries	11,158	23,321	24,008	33,907	38,252

Source: World Bank, *World Debt Tables 1992–93* p. 16.

Table 2.4 Direct investment to developing countries, by region, 1980–89

	Annual average inflows	
	(US $ billion)	
Region	1980–84	1985–89
Africa	1.2	2.6
Asia	4.7	10.7
Latin America & the Caribbean	6.1	8.3

Source: UNTC, *World Investment Report 1991* (Table 4).

Table 2.5 Aggregate long-term net resource flows to developing countries, 1980–92

	1980	1985	1990	1991	1992
Net flows	82.8	73.4	98.0	115.2	134.3
Official grants	12.5	16.1	28.2	31.3	31.1
Official loans (net)	20.1	24.6	30.6	28.2	30.9
Bilateral	12.2	11.8	15.8	13.8	13.4
Multilateral	7.9	12.8	14.8	14.4	17.5
Private flows	50.2	32.8	35.4	48.1	64.2
Private loans	41.1	21.8	11.4	14.2	25.9
Direct foreign investment	9.1	11.0	24.0	33.9	38.3

Source: *World Development Report 1991* p. 24 and *World Debt Tables 1992–93* p. 16.

overtake Latin America by the end of the 1980s. Increased investment in Hong Kong, Malaysia, Singapore and Thailand was most responsible for the increase in Asia's share of world DFI from 5.3 per cent in 1975 to 8.8 per cent in 1989. Asia's rise has been matched by Africa's decline. Africa's share of world DFI fell from 6.7 per cent in 1975 to 1.9 per cent in 1989. The flows of DFI in the 1980s went increasingly to the more developed and fastest growing economies. The least developed countries experienced both an absolute and relative decline in direct investment from abroad. These trends have continued in the 1990s with Asia and Latin America enjoying strong increases in private sector financial flows.

The globalisation of economic activity and the creation of a new international division of labour further marginalises the majority of developing countries. Contrary to myth, the AICs are the major recipient as well as the prime source of DFI. The rapid increase in worldwide DFI since 1983 has been unequally distributed between developed and developing countries. By the end of the 1980s, the developed world accounted for 75 per cent of the world's DFI flows. Conversely, the developing countries' share fell from 26 to 21 per cent in the 1980s. Given the uneven distribution of DFI among the developing countries detailed above, one consequence of this trend is that the most dynamic developments in the world economy are bypassing the majority of Third World nations.

DFI became more important to developing countries in the 1980s as other sources of lending declined. Commercial bank lending fell dramatically in the 1980s and official development assistance also declined. In 1989, DFI surpassed all other sources of lending as a source of foreign capital and this development has been repeated in the 1990s (see Table 2.5).

The increase in DFI has been accompanied by a greater contribution of DFI to domestic capital formation.[21] The impact of DFI on the local economy is not something that can be determined in advance. Under certain conditions, foreign investment will not make a positive contribution to the balance of payments, and will result in net losses to the economy. A different mix of domestic policies can, on the other hand, lead to significant gains for the local economy. The political economy of direct foreign investment is the result of the interplay of governmental policies, the actions of firms and market structure. The scope for bargaining and the efficacy of tax and regulatory policies will vary from country to country but are unlikely to fit either of the broad scenarios painted by the liberal or dependency paradigms.

Aid

The developing countries have consistently campaigned for increases in official development assistance (ODA). Flows of ODA are affected as much by political considerations as by economic rationale. The quantity, terms and conditions and geographical distribution of aid are the result of the interplay of political, strategic and economic considerations.

Aid flows increased in the 1950s and early 1960s in response to the demands of the newly independent countries and Cold War rivalry. In the mid-1960s, reduced support in the United States for aid led to a diminution of US foreign aid and a slight fall in total aid flows. Until the early 1970s, aid flows stabilised at this new level as other countries increased their aid. Aid flows then increased in the mid-1970s in response to the worsening external environment faced by the developing countries.[22] Aggregate ODA flows increased in the 1980s annually, with the exception of 1989. In 1990, aggregate ODA from members of the Organization for Economic Cooperation and Development (OECD) increased by 4.1 per cent in real terms, from $46.7 billion to $55.6 billion. But as a percentage of GNP, ODA increased only marginally from 0.33 to 0.36 per cent.[23] The UN target of 0.7 per cent of GNP was reached by only three OECD donors in 1990.[24]

The potential contribution of aid to development is reduced by the practice of aid 'tying' where the recipient is required to buy goods and services from the donor country. Furthermore, where the primary motivation for aid giving is the commercial and political interests of the donor the value to the recipient is significantly reduced. Two recent trends in official development assistance may increase the positive impact of aid. First, in 1991 and 1992, grant aid exceeded loans. Secondly, multilateral aid increased considerably (see Table 2.5). This shift to multilateral lending is not always welcomed by the developing countries since multilateral institutions, especially the World Bank and the IMF have been in the forefront of the practice of using resource flows to exercise leverage over domestic economic policy. From the perspective of the developing countries the attachment of policy conditions to aid, by both bilateral and multilateral donors, is a continued infringement of economic sovereignty. The explosion of borrowing from private capital markets in the 1970s was a reaction to the perceived political dependence attached to aid.

The role of aid in promoting growth and alleviating poverty varies from country to country and has changed over time. Not only is there an absence of consensus on the role played by aid in the development process, pro-aid theorists cannot agree on the reasons for variations in the performance of aid. In other words, no clear standards exist by which to measure aid effectiveness and to determine under what conditions aid is likely to promote growth.[25]

External sources of finance whether private or public (except in the case of grants) incur interest payments. The onset of the debt crisis in 1982 was a stark reminder of the dangers inherent in heavy borrowing from external sources. The origins of the debt crisis lie in international and domestic structures and policies. A combination of changing interest rates, declining terms of trade, changing structure of credit and the unproductive use of borrowed capital all contributed to the debt crisis with its economic and financial ramifications.[26] For the heavily indebted countries, debt repayment and debt management have consumed their energies for the past 12 years.[27] The impact of the debt crisis and relevant solutions differ from country to country, although a broad distinction can be made between the low-income heavily indebted countries and the middle-income heavily indebted countries.

Conclusion

This account of the interactions between the developing countries and the international economy has highlighted two main features. First, the record is one of uneven development. Some developing countries have successfully embarked on growth and industrialisation in the context of a liberal international economic order. Other countries have fared less well, with some even experiencing a decline in standards of living in the post-independence period. Secondly, the impact of the international economic order on developing countries is always mediated by particular local factors. The impact of a favourable or adverse international economic climate cannot be determined solely through an examination of structural variables. An adequate explanation of the Third World's performance must be based on an analysis which integrates the inter-actions between domestic policies and international structural con-straints. It is beyond the scope of this chapter, and this book, to examine in detail the contribution of domestic variables to economic develop-ment.

The changing global economy provides both opportunities and con-straints for the developing countries. Differential rates of growth create cleavages among the developing countries and presents an obstacle to unity which brings into question the economic justification of a strategy for the entire Third World. The uneven development of capitalism and the diverging economic fortunes of Third World states suggests that members of the coalition should pursue individual interests rather than bloc goals.

On the other hand, the inability of even the most economically advanced Third World state to exert significant influence on the international economic agenda contributes to group cohesion. The more industrially advanced countries in the developing world, to date, have resisted Western attempts to construct a graduation scenario in which they will progressively lose access to preferential treatment for develop-ing countries.

International economic organisations have been used by the Third World to effect transfers of resources and to improve their access to international decision-making. The debates between the North and the South and the strategies of individual Southern countries are con-ditioned by changes in the global political economy and perceptions of the benefits and costs of participation therein.

Notes

1. Stephen D. Krasner, *Structural Conflict: The Third World Against Global Liberalism* (Berkeley: University of California Press 1985) p. 97.
2. World Bank, *World Development Report 1991* (Oxford: Oxford University Press 1991) p. 186.
3. *Ibid.* p. 13.
4. World Bank, *World Development Report 1992* (Oxford: Oxford University Press 1992) p. 196.
5. Nigel Grimwade, *International Trade* (London: Routledge 1989) pp. 53–55.
6. This analysis does not pertain to oil which faces exceptional market conditions.
7. John Spraos, 'The Statistical Debate on the Net Barter Terms of Trade between Primary Commodities and Manufactures', *Economic Journal* vol. 90. (1980) p. 216.
9. *Ibid.* p. 13.
10. Peter Dicken, *Global Shift: The Internationalization of Economic Activity* 2nd ed. (London: Paul Chapman Publishing 1992) p. 33.

11. *World Development Report 1990* p. 12.
12. *World Development Report 1992* p. 249.
13. *World Development Report 1990* p. 121.
14. For critiques of ISI see, for example, I. M. D. Little, T. Scitovsky and M. F. G. Scott, *Industry and Trade in Some Developing Countries* (Oxford: Oxford University Press 1970); Anne Krueger, *Liberalization Attempts and Consequences* (Cambridge, Mass.: Ballinger 1978).
15. See, for example, Bela Balassa, *The Newly Industrializing Countries in the World Economy* (New York: Pergamon 1981); James Riedel, 'Trade as the Engine of Growth in Developing Countries', *Economic Journal* (March 1984) pp. 56–73.
16. See, for example, Robert Wade, *Governing the Market: Economic Theory and the Role of Government in East Asian Industrialization* (Princeton, NJ: Princeton University Press 1990); Stephan Haggard, *Pathways from the Periphery: The Politics of Growth in the Newly Industrializing Countries* (Ithaca: Cornell University Press 1990) and Alice H. Amsden, *Asia's Next Giant: South Korea and Late Industrialization* (New York: Oxford University Press 1989).
17. See Thomas Biersteker, *Distortion of Development* (Cambridge, Mass.: MIT Press 1978) ch. 1 for a discussion of this debate.
18. See Susan Strange, 'Big Business and the State', *Millennium* (Summer 1991) pp. 245–250, and Sanjaya Lall, 'Multinational Enterprises and Developing Countries: Some Issues for Research in the 1990s', *Millennium* (Summer 1991) pp. 251–255 for competing explanations of this phenomenon.
19. See John Stopford and Susan Strange, *Rival States, Rival Firms* (Cambridge: Cambridge University Press 1991).
20. The countries in declining order of importance are Singapore, Brazil, Mexico, China, Hong Kong, Malaysia, Egypt, Argentina, Thailand and Colombia. See United Nations Center on Transnational Corporations (UNTC), *World Investment Report 1991* (New York: United Nations 1991) p. 10.
21. *Ibid.* p. 6.
22. OECD, *Twenty-five Years of Development Co-operation: A Review* (Paris: OECD 1985) pp. 92–105.
23. *World Development Report 1992* p. 254.
24. Denmark, the Netherlands and Sweden. France also meets the target but French ODA is distorted by the inclusion of the DOM/TOM countries. Saudi Arabia and the United Arab Emirates gave 3.90 and 2.65 per cent of GNP respectively.
25. See Robert Cassen and Associates, *Does Aid Work?* (Oxford: Clarendon Press 1986); and Uma Lele and Ijaz Nabi (eds), *Transitions in Development* (San Francisco: International Center for Economic Growth 1991) for attempts to probe these issues.
26. See, for example, Peter Nunnenkamp, *The International Debt Crisis of the Third World: Causes and Consequences for the World Economy* (Hemel Hempstead: Harvester Wheatsheaf 1986); Susan George, *A Fate Worse Than Debt* (London: Penguin 1988); and Trevor W. Parfitt & Stephen P. Riley, *The African Debt Crisis* (London: Routledge 1989) for analyses of the causes and consequences of the Third World debt crisis.
27. See Stephany Griffith-Jones (ed.), *Managing World Debt* (Hemel Hempstead: Harvester Wheatsheaf 1988).

3

Regimes, international organisations and development diplomacy

This study of the relationship between international economic organisations and the Third World is centrally concerned with one aspect of contemporary international cooperation. North–South relations are frequently approached from the perspective of international conflict. But although conflictual patterns are discernible in North–South economic relations, these interactions cannot be reduced to a conflictual framework. Conflict and cooperation may be the ideal ends of a spectrum but in the real world issues often have both conflictual and cooperative aspects. Any study of international organisations will encompass analysis of cooperative behaviour. Explanation of the relationship between the Third World and international economic organisations requires understanding of the reasons why Third World states find it in their interest to seek membership of such organisations and the ways in which the organisational processes structure the level and scope of their participation in the global political economy.

This chapter will examine the dominant approach, in the study of international relations, to the problem of international cooperation and the analysis of international organisations (IOs). Regime theory is currently the most widely used approach to the study of international organisation. But, as this chapter will argue, although regime theory has provided important insights into international regulation and international cooperation it has been deficient in providing explanations for the outcomes of international organisations. The conceptual vocabulary and research agenda of regime theory has focused increased attention on international organisational processes but has failed to develop theoretical propositions concerning the roles of formal international organisations.[1] In order to understand the outcomes of internal bargaining in IOs, it is necessary to develop a conceptual framework which links the internal dynamic of the organisation with the external environment. A task central to a wider study of the role of international organisations is that of establishing a connection between the interactions internal to the organisation and the environmental context in which organisations are embedded. Consequently, after discussing regime theory the chapter will focus on the organisational structure and process of intergovernmental organisations. Focus on the institutional aspects of regime formation and maintenance provides a way of maintaining the insights of regime analysis, and expanding the application of the concept.[2]

Regimes provide a useful starting point to the study of international organisations because regimes can be conceived as contextual factors which enhance, limit and proscribe state action. The specification of a particular regime does not provide us with a description of a set of 'norms, rules, principles and decision-making procedures' that will be adhered to by all parties covered by the regime. Nevertheless, the concept of regime allows us to posit the existence of conformity-supporting injunctions, which exist over time, and which cannot be reduced to the present capabilities of major actors.[3] A regime analysis helps us to see that conformity in international relations need not arise, solely, through coercion or fear of sanctions. Conformity may arise through agreement with, or attachment to, an internationally agreed set of values.

Regimes and regime theory

Regime theory has provided the most widely accepted answer to the problem of international cooperation. Despite widespread usage and numerous applications the concept of regime is nevertheless, vague, woolly and imprecise.[4] Regime theory is an attempt to harmonise the separate disciplines of economics and political science and to provide a starting point for international political economy.

Defining the concept

The concept of international regime was first coined by John Gerard Ruggie. He defined a regime as 'a set of mutual expectations, rules and regulations, plans, organizational energies and financial commitments, which have been accepted by a group of states'.[5] In his subsequent development of the concept of international regime, Ruggie argues that regimes comprise not just what actors say and do but also what they understand and find acceptable within an intersubjective frame of meaning.[6] Such a framework of meaning cannot be deduced from the distribution of economic capabilities but must be sought in the configuration of state–society relations that is characteristic of the regime-making states. In other words, regimes cannot be understood as external objects which impose order on states. Given that in international relations external authoritative interpretations of meaning are infrequent, the interpretation of acts by the actors becomes a necessary component of participation in the global system.[7] Regimes are hence composed of a series of interconnected, intersubjective meanings which modify the basic power distributions of states. This hermeneutic approach, however, fails to address the key question of the origin of regimes. The establishment of the international state–society relation is imprecisely grounded and therefore the concept of regime deployed fails to show how the normative content of a new regime is established.

In their influential study of interdependence, Robert Keohane and Joseph Nye introduced the concept to a wider audience and defined it somewhat differently from Ruggie. For Keohane and Nye, regimes consisted of 'networks of rules, norms and procedures that regularise behaviour and control its effects'.[8] In other words, regimes are the governing arrangements which affect the relationships of interdependence. International regimes are intermediate factors between the power structure of an international system and the political and economic bargaining that takes place within it. The relationship between the regime and the system is a reciprocal one. The structure of the system profoundly affects the nature of the regime and the regime in turn affects and to some extent governs the political bargaining and decision-making that occurs in the system. This formulation is exceedingly loose and imprecise. Regimes are given as an intervening variable but in fact explain nothing. What at first glance appear to be levels of causality and multi-causality in fact disappear into thin air. Regimes are supposedly affected by power resources but do not in themselves affect power resources. But regimes are said to affect bargaining and decision-making and yet bargaining and decision-making are not held to affect power resources. Hence, although there is implicitly an interrelationship between the power structure and the outcome, when developed in this manner that connection all but disappears. It appears evident that all three levels must be interconnected and yet Keohane and Nye keep them separate. Moreover, for the theory to have causal significance we need to know more than the fact that these three levels are related. We need to know *how* they fit together.

In 1983, Stephen Krasner and a group of 'regime theorists' proffered what has become the standard definition. International regimes were defined as

> sets of implicit or explicit principles, norms, rules and decision-making procedures around which actors' expectations converge in a given area of international relations. Principles are beliefs of fact, causation and rectitude. Norms are standards of behaviour defined in terms of rights and obligations. Rules are specific prescriptions or proscriptions for action. Decision-making procedures are prevailing practices for making and implementing collective choice.[9]

According to these definitions an international regime is an intervening variable between actors and outcomes. Krasner argues that regime is 'an intervening variable standing between basic causal factors on the one hand and outcomes and behaviour on the other'.[10] Regimes are thus social institutions defined in terms of four components – principles, norms, rules and decision-making procedures. This formulation, however, leaves us with the problem of distinguishing among the four components. The concept of norms is not unambiguously distinct from those of rules and principles.

The main interest in regime analysis has focused on two key questions: first, those pertaining to why regimes 'form, endure and change', and secondly, those concerned with the ways in which regimes affect behaviour in given issue areas.[11] The answer to the question concerning the formation, maintenance and transformation of regimes has been answered in various ways but these answers can conveniently be divided into two major categories, which can be labelled hegemony and reciprocity. Although hegemony as an explanatory variable and hegemonic stability theory can be used *contra* regimes and regime theory it is, nevertheless, possible to consider hegemony and hegemonic stability theory as a variant of regime theory; that is, it provides one explanation for the creation, maintenance and eventual dissolution of regimes.

Hegemonic stability theory

Hegemonic stability theory is firmly rooted in the tradition of political realism and therefore shares the key assumptions of that perspective. Realists have long been transfixed by power. It is a widely held realist view that power in international relations is synonymous with political and military power vested in one or more hegemonic states. These states, in ensuring a balance of power provide international order as a side effect. Hegemonic stability theory is based on the premise that the presence of a single dominant actor in the international system leads to collectively desirable outcomes for all states. On the other hand, it is argued that the absence of a hegemon will lead to disorder in the global system and harmful consequences for individual states.[12] Hegemonic stability theory is based on the assumption that a concentration of power is more likely to promote international cooperation. Conversely, a diffusion of power in raising transaction costs will inhibit the search for joint agreement.

International economic order is conceived as a public or collective good.[13] It is argued that the provision of collective goods in specific issue areas are unlikely to be made, other things being equal, unless a dominant state has both the interest and ability to provide the necessary leadership to ensure that a regime is brought into existence. The hegemon creates the regime out of self-interest but the provision of the collective good benefits all states. It follows from this argument that the weaker states gain more than the hegemon because they enjoy fully the benefits produced by the regime but do not share any of the costs of providing or maintaining it.[14] This is an unconvincing argument since it fails to acknowledge, first, the possibility that the regime may well not be in the interests of some weaker states and, secondly, that over time the weaker states may well be asked to pay some of the costs of providing the public good.

The empirical support for hegemonic stability theory has been provided by the experience of Britain in the nineteenth century and the United States in the post-1945 international system. Hegemonic stability theorists argue that Britain as the nineteenth-century hegemon could impose a regime of free trade suiting its basic interest and also ensuring that political market failure did not occur. Similarly, the United States was able to impose a liberal trading order after World War II because of its hegemonic position. Conversely, the failure of international economic cooperation in the interwar period is explained by the absence of a hegemon.

Hegemonic stability theory has come under attack both in relation to its theoretical adequacy and its empirical accuracy.[15] Snidal suggests that in order to test the strength of hegemonic stability theory we need to test two propositions: (i) the presence of a dominant state leads to greater stability in the international system and (ii) this greater stability benefits all states in the international system and benefits smaller states more than large states.[16] It is relatively simple to test the first proposition but the problem involved in specifying size creates enormous difficulties in the attempt to test the second proposition. Snidal concludes that the evidence in respect of the first proposition only establishes that hegemons are associated with stable regimes. The evidence is not strong enough to support the claim that stable regimes possess the distributive properties entailed in the second proposition.[17] Hegemonic stability theory has also been challenged in relation to the evidence on the development and maintenance of international regimes. In a study of British trade in the nineteenth century, Lipson concluded that hegemony could not explain the continuity of a regime when the original hegemon is no longer as powerful as before.[18]

The assumption that collective action in the international system is impossible in the absence of a hegemon is challenged by a number of other examples. Oran Young provides evidence from the issue area of natural resources and the environment to dispute this contention, e.g. he shows how the 1911 regime for northern fur seals involved a mutually beneficial deal between the four major powers – the United States, Japan, Russia and the United Kingdom. Moreover, he challenges the state-centric assumptions of hegemonic stability theory through showing the importance of intergovernmental organisations and international non-governmental organisations in promoting the establishment of regimes.[19] Young further argues that hegemony is an extreme case in international society because of the difficulty of transferring power over resources into power over outcomes and because a number of states have an effective veto against the creation of institutional arrangements they dislike.[20]

Two further criticisms can be levelled against hegemonic stability theory. First, hegemonic stability theory requires the issue to fulfil the conditions of a public good but the public good hypothesis has limited applicability to most issues in international relations.[21] Secondly, leadership should be seen in entrepreneurial terms and not as the result of benevolent behaviour. As Young argues, 'it involves a combination of imagination in inventing institutional options and skill in brokering the interests of numerous actors to line up support for such options'.[22]

Reciprocity

The reciprocity approach to regime formation and regime maintenance assumes rational actors, i.e. utility maximisers who will create arrangements in their own self-interest.[23] This utilitarian conception of regimes relies on a functional argument combined with an assumption of rational egoistic behaviour. Regimes are the result of purposive rational responses by states to the increased complexity of the international system. Complex interdependence produces increased issue-linkage and the process of interaction creates distinct contract zones in which actors can seek agreement. Regimes are thus a process whereby particular and converging actor orientations become generalised into norms, rules and decision-making procedures. Reciprocity refers to behaviour that is dependent on like behaviour and equivalence and therefore in this perspective a concentration of power will inhibit rather than promote regime creation.[24]

Keohane argues that the generalised norms, rules and decision-making procedures have to be attached to the ego-rational interests of a group of actors. He claims first, that generalisations reduce the trans-action costs of bargains when interests converge and secondly, that generalisation reduces uncertainty.[25] The concentration of power leads to a misallocation of resources and reduces social welfare.

Four main objections have been levelled against reciprocity approaches.[26] First, reciprocity approaches fail to take sufficient account of the damaging behaviour of actors who resort to strategic behaviour or committal tactics in order to ensure that the agreement reflects their interests. Secondly, insufficient attention is paid to the impact of domestic politics on national bargaining positions. Domestic opposition could inhibit the attempt to reach international consensus. Thirdly, in looking at bargaining solely within specific issue-areas, not enough attention is paid to the possibility of linkage strategies which sometimes inhibit parties from reaching agreement on one issue for fear of what the consequences might be for another issue. Fourthly, in so far as negotiators suffer from an absence of trust of other negotiators, agreement will be stymied. These four deficiencies of reciprocal approaches highlight the limitation of the assumption that rational utility maximisers will be able to realise feasible joint gains. In other words, rational actors in pursuit of egoistic goals may well fail to realise optimal gains.

Regime change

The difficulties in specifying both the nature and origin of regimes is also present in any consideration of regime change. Various attempts have been made to explain the reasons why regimes change. Keohane and Nye delineated four models of regime change – economic process, overall power structure, issue structure and international organisa-tional.[27]

The economic process model is based on two premises. The first pertains to the impact of technological change on existing regimes and the second to the influence of domestic interest groups and domestic political concerns on foreign policy-making. According to this view, increasing interdependence brought about as the result of changing technology will render existing regimes obsolete. But governments will be forced to create new regimes and adapt existing ones in order to maintain the high standard of living demanded by the electorates. In other words, cooperation will result from the rational calculation of interest since failure to establish new international regimes which reflect the transnational nature of economic processes will lead to suboptimal results for all state actors. This explanation, however, is not particularly convincing since the classical rational assumptions it postulates cannot be accepted without some reservations. It seems to assume that states will be neutral towards the content of regimes as long as they are efficient. This presupposes that there will be no value conflicts over the economic policies to be followed. This is an assumption which is quite clearly incorrect in the context of North–South negotiations. Secondly, the economic process model of regime change in separating the military/security dimension from the economic one presents a distorted view of reality. In short, it might tell us why regimes form in issue-areas characterised by converging interests in a stable international environment but it would prove an unreliable guide if these assumptions were relaxed.

The overall power structure explanation views international regime change from the standpoint of state power and the international structure. Hegemonic stability theory uses this explanation of change. In this perspective the international structure is reduced to the relation between the power capabilities of states. As these Waltzian structures[28] change, so the content of international regimes will change. In other words, the stability of regimes will reflect the fortunes of the hegemonic leader. Regimes in this version will decline when the hegemon loses its power. The criticisms levelled against hegemonic stability theory above are relevant here and need not be repeated. In this context, however, we can make two further critical comments. First, as an explanation of change this structural argument suffers from a problem common to many attempts to operationalise the concept of power in international relations. The concept of resources used is too general since it remains unclear exactly which resources establish hegemonic power. It also assumes a fungibility of resources which may well not be applicable. It is far from clear that resources can be shifted from one area to another and retain precisely the same effect.

This leads us to the second objection to the overall power structure approach, namely, that an explanation of overall structure is not sufficient to explain change. The difficulty involved in deriving explanations of regime change from shifts in the overall power structure underlies the arguments concerning the decline of American hegemony.[29] It is no wonder that the debate is an essentially sterile one and that the various protagonists are unlikely to convince each other. In so far as the concept of power is essentially problematic then it will prove impossible to discover satisfactorily which resources are most important in establishing hegemony. Moreover, attachment to the idea that shifts in hegemonic power explain regime change will lead to a tendency to emphasise the continuation of a particular state's hegemonic power as long as the regimes identified with that state remain in operation. I am not arguing that regimes may not outlast the hegemon which created them but rather that the positivist methodology underlying these arguments is incapable of providing satisfactory answers to the questions under investigation. Radical theories of the international political economy wedded to a structuralist explanation which assumes that Third World states are incapable of influencing international regimes because of the dominance of Western, industrial states, suffer from similar shortcomings.

The issue structure model is similar to the overall power structure model and shares its main assumptions concerning the role of hegemonic states in implementing change. The major difference between the two models arises from the issue-specific approach taken by the issue structure model. Rejecting the crude approach to power of the overall power structure explanation it posits an alternative view. Where the power structure explanation sees power as power over resources, this perspective sees power as power over actors. It accepts that the most powerful states do not always get their way and furthermore that it is not always possible to transform resources into influence over other actors. Change in this perspective occurs from shifts of power and relevant bargaining strategies in particular issue areas. In any given issue area states will calculate the costs and benefits of adhering to particular regimes in the face of economic and political change. It is this difference between the utility of existing regimes and the hopes, fears and beliefs of dissatisfied states about the new rules which accounts for regime change.[30]

Although an improvement in some respects on the overall power structure model, the issue structure model still possesses an inadequate conception of power. Control over actors does not ensure control over outcomes and this state-centric approach cannot adequately explain international outcomes. Its inadequacy arises not solely because it ignores actors other than state actors, e.g. transnational actors, but because it conceives of power solely in instrumental terms. In other words, the conception of structure posited in this approach is too restricted. Structure is seen solely in terms of the distribution of capabilities among states. Moreover, this approach fails to establish a sufficiently clear linkage between the dominant states and the dissatisfied (Third World) states, or to account for the political process which will bring about change.

The international organisational model sees international organisations as an intervening variable which is capable of modifying regimes once they are created. The creation of regimes will reflect the power resources of states, but once established, change will not be reducible to the capabilities of state actors. The international organisational network is characterised as a set of networks, rules, norms and institutions. And it is the relevant networks, rules, norms and institutions which determine the ability of actors to transform existing regimes. In other words, change results from the capacity of state actors to mobilise the relevant institutional resources. The international organisational network becomes both an obstacle to change, in so far as these rules, norms and institutions once established become resistant to change. And it also becomes a source of power to be used by states in their attempts to change existing regimes since specific organisational resources, e.g. voting power and the ability to form coalitions, become important variables in the attempt to exert influence. The ability to implement regime change is no longer a direct function of the traditional capabilities of states. The existence of international organisational networks transforms the underlying distribution of power.

The importance of organisational variables in specifying the outcomes of international economic organisations will be developed below. It should be noted here that care has to be exercised so that explanation does not become tautologous. In the Keohane and Nye approach the definition of the international organisational model is strikingly similar to that of a regime. We thus seem to be explaining change in 'networks of rules, norms and decision-making procedures' through the impact of rules, norms and institutions on state power. The dependent variable and the independent variable appear indistinguishable.

The four models of international regime change discussed so far serve to confirm the difficulties attendant on the usage of the concept highlighted in the explication of the concept. An alternative approach by Oran Young[31] to the question of regime change does not resolve the key problems involved in trying to understand how international actors succeed in forming regimes, why some regimes persist and why others fail. Young's approach is to look at the types of pressure that account for regime change. He suggests that there are three major types of pressure for regime change. These are internal contradictions, shifts in underlying power structures and exogeneous forces. The types of pressure in themselves do not account for regime change, and the success or failure of any particular form of pressure has to be related to the three different ways in which regimes are formed.

International regimes can be the result of spontaneous order, a negotiated order or an imposed order. Although this approach provides some important qualifications to standard regime analysis, it does not suggest a radically different approach. First, it is helpful in moving attention away from a single type explanation for regime creation and regime change. It suggests instead that different types of regime exist and that different causal mechanisms will be at work in both the establishment and maintenance of regimes. Nevertheless, it fails to establish the basis on which we can tell if a regime has changed.

One of the main problems facing regime analysis has been the difficulty of specifying when a change in regime occurs. In other words, the distinction between changes of regime and changes in regime has not been established with any certainty. An interesting intervention in this debate was made by Kratochwil, who argues that we cannot delineate regime change without recourse to the interpretation of the relevant actors.[32] We cannot know if a regime has changed or not unless we have a consensus on what we are supposed to be measuring. Given the absence of agreement in regime analysis on the concept of regime such a consensus cannot be effectively established. An interpretive framework, he suggests, enables us to distinguish between changes in the regime and changes of the regime. For example, in the case of an agreed departure from agreed norms then, technically, the norms have not been violated. In the more complicated case where other participants accept that a violation has taken place even though they refuse to attach negative consequences to the failure to comply by the agreed principles, 'change remains norm-governed provided that the basic set of social purposes served by the regime remains more or less intact, and provided that most of the actors agree that this is so.'[33] In this perspective we can specify changes of regime when the underlying purpose of the regime is no longer served and the majority of the international actors recognise this to be the case. Essentially, the analyst needs to investigate the tolerance of the actors for the rules, norms, institutions and decision-making procedures created. It is obvious, however, that more than mere numerical majorities against prevailing practices are necessary in order to establish the demise of an international regime. If this were the case the Third World states would have been successful in their quest to establish a New International Economic Order. Moreover, abstracting from the bases on which communication is established enshrines a conservative bias towards change. The original social purpose is taken as a given and any attempt to change original purpose in the context of a specific issue-area will be seen as destabilising. It also allows dominant actors effectively to change the regime whilst pretending that they are maintaining social purpose and merely instituting changes within the regime. The use and abuse of the Multi-Fibre Arrangement is an example of this tendency.

Regimes and international cooperation

This section has discussed competing perspectives on international regimes, which are designed to explain how regimes are established, why they endure and the nature of change. The two major approaches to regime analysis that have been identified are (i) reciprocity theory; and (ii) hegemonic stability theory. In discussing the applications of regime theory to international cooperation we have looked at some of the weaknesses of the various approaches without rejecting outright the entire enterprise. Regime theory, as currently conceived suffers from two major deficiencies.

First, there is a tendency to assume that international cooperation is the result of rational behaviour on the part of self-interested states.[34] In this rational-choice approach, insufficient attention is paid to the motives, meanings and aspirations of actors. This is a limiting assumption since a rational choice calculus, although a convenient starting point for analysis, may be blind to the complex of motives – some non-rational – behind individual or group behaviour. Cooperation in this perspective arises from the goal-seeking activity of independent, rational decision-makers. In other words, it is an instrumental relation. Regime theory is predicated in terms of the goal-seeking behaviour of states in an interdependent international system. Regimes can be seen to form as the result of system adaptation to increased complexity. Increased complexity results in greater uncertainty, increases the cost of individual solutions to global problems and pushes actors towards joint solutions to common problems. The development of norms, rules and decision-making procedures in providing for stable expectations reduces the cost of uncertainty to the strategic-rational state.[35] This argument seems to suggest that states are neutral to the content of norms but that content does matter. For most of the post-war period, the Third World has expressed dissatisfaction with the prevailing international regimes in trade and payments.

Secondly, there has been a tendency in the regime literature towards reification. In other words, regimes have been treated as separate and autonomous entities with an independent existence.[36] Furthermore, the dynamic and changing nature of regimes has been subsumed in a static and ahistorical analysis.

In summary, regime theory has failed to provide a satisfactory theory of international cooperation. Regimes have both analytical and prescriptive contents but these often seem to be confused. As an analytical tool regimes are supposed to explain both why cooperation arises and why it is maintained. As a prescriptive tool regimes are lauded as an effective solution to the problem of international anarchy. From a prescriptive standpoint, then, the problem becomes one of how do we institute international regimes so that self-interested behaviour ceases to be that of rational egoists, conducive to instability and disorder and replace it with shared values and expectations which lead to stability and order in the international system.

Despite these deficiencies the concept of regime can be useful in analysing world politics. Even an ardent adherent of realpolitik would admit that state behaviour is constrained by norms, rules, principles and decision-making procedures. And in so far as it is possible to identify common and consistent 'ideological' features in a given issue-area, the term regime may well be an appropriate description for the set of norms and procedures which condition behaviour. In the light of the arguments above it is possible to conclude that regimes are important in influencing state behaviour and fostering international cooperation. As Beverly Crawford has argued, there are three related reasons why regimes matter.

> First, state actors desire certainty in their future relationships with others; regimes enhance stable expectations about the future. Second, regimes provide information which affects the actors' incentives to coordinate their policies or refrain from policy coordination. Third, regimes attenuate the destabilising effects of unequal power relationships among states by institutionalising the principle of reciprocity.[37]

Both functionalist and hegemonic approaches to regime theory fail to give an adequate account of international negotiations. They take a static approach to negotiations and by extension regime formation. Contrary to such assumptions, negotiation is a fluid process in which the participants change, bargaining strategies are altered, knowledge is limited and value preferences over outcomes are unfixed. Regime theory, however, assumes that the identity of the parties is known at the outset and remains unchanged throughout the negotiations; that bargaining strategies are clearly demarcated at the outset; that the parties possess perfect knowledge concerning the choices to be made; and that the orderings of individual preferences is fixed at the outset.[38]

The following section concentrates on the institutional structures of international organisations in order provide a more convincing explanation of the outcomes of international economic organisations.

International organisations as international institutions

It is mistaken to assume that international organisations simply reflect international regimes. The failure of the literature on international regimes adequately to theorise the roles of IOs has resulted in confusion concerning the relation between IOs and regimes. Because regime refers to the governing arrrangements in a given issue-area, IOs are frequently confused and conflated with the regime. IOs are not regimes but they often play key roles in the creation and maintenance of regimes. In this context, IOs can be important in structuring regime outcomes.[39]

In order to analyse the outcomes of IOs it is necessary to identify both continuities and discontinuities of behaviour. Furthermore, analysis should assess the relationship between organisational identity on the one hand, and the roles played by members of the organisation on the other. An IO is not simply reducible to its membership. On the contrary, IOs have impacts on world politics which show that IOs are in some sense independent of state actors. The members of an international organisation, from the initial moment of cooperation, are enmeshed within a precise organisational framework which conditions the outcomes of their decisions.

State behaviour in an international organisation is a product of factors internal to the organisation, and also of factors originating in the wider international environment. Although analysts are agreed that the external environment is of importance in affecting the outcomes of international organisations, the precise nature of the international environment and the specification of the relevant environmental variables for any given international organisation or case study is, however, open to debate.[40]

As noted above, regime theory contains an inadequate specification of the process of institutionalisation. The following sections will discuss some of the key features of IOs relevant to considerations of the role of IEOs in world politics. The concept of organisational politics employed here is deliberately broad in order to subsume the wide range of factors which influence the outcomes of IEOs and to provide a linkage between the internal processes of IEOs and the external environment.

Organisational politics

The concept of organisational politics provides a starting point for an investigation of how interests are produced and why certain outcomes are reached in international economic organisations. Organisational politics refers to the interactive process of influence between states and international organisations. The two most important aspects of organisational politics can be termed institutional venue and negotiating processes. Institutional venue refers to the organisational structure and political process of an international organisation. The institutional venue will affect the manner in which negotiations are conducted. Negotiations in this perspective are viewed as a social process, and not in the ahistorical and asocial manner of the rational-choice approach. Organisational politics is seen to be a key factor in the explanation of organisational outcomes. In other words, consideration of institutional venue and the negotiation process is constitutive of the very practices actors engage in when they embark on cooperation. Institutional venue and the negotiation process are important institutional features which order and give meaning to the behaviour of the actors.

Institutional venue

The organisational structure of an international organisation refers primarily to the formal, institutional framework which can be found in the constitutional document which outlines its main functions and organs. This relates to a number of organisational features including the following:

1. The explicit function of the organisation, i.e. whether it is a forum or a service organisation, and the extent to which it combines both roles.
2. The conduct of proceedings, i.e. the agenda of the organisation and its rules of procedure.
3. The formal decision-making apparatus, e.g. voting provisions, the types of decisions permitted, the time available to take decisions.
4. Membership, i.e. the criteria for membership and the number and type of actors permitted membership.
5. Budgetary provisions, i.e. the source of finance and the size of financial requirements.
6. The structure of authority, e.g. formal division of responsibility between various organs in the organisation, and the number and scope of subsidiary organs.
7. The role of the secretariat, i.e. the formal role of the secretariat and the responsibilities assigned to the executive head.

The legal, institutional framework is of importance but cannot in itself explain the processes of change in international organisations. Legal institutional analysis is biased towards the static and unchanging aspects of organisations and cannot explain why or how actors redefine tasks and change priorities.[41] It does not enable us to analyse changes in the scope and level of organisational behaviour, conflictual behaviour or the changing impact of the environment.

Political process, the second aspect of institutional venue consists of a set of variables which attempt to account for the structure of influence in organisations. If the organisational structure can be conceived as a skeletal framework, then the political process provides the remaining parts in order to transform the organisation into a dynamic body. The political process is composed of a number of key characteristics as follows:

1. The standard operating procedures. Organisations frequently develop rules of thumb, and sets of practices which cannot always be inferred from the formal, constitutional provisions.
2. The development of groups and the institutionalisation of group behaviour. States seldom exist outside the framework of some reference group in the context of an international organisation. In North–South diplomacy the lines are usually clearly drawn between the G77 and the OECD.
3. Decision-making procedures, i.e. the provisions for the taking of decisions and the informal methods arrived at will affect the behaviour of participants. Different skills can be called for and different resources brought to bear depending on whether decision is reached by consensus, majority vote (simple or complex) or the existence of a veto provision.
4. The nature and sources of conflict, between groups and within groups, is an important variable. The major sources of conflict can be either endogenous or exogenous to the organisation. The origin and nature of the conflictual process provides a key link between the internal and external environments of the organisation. In the substantive chapters which follow we will be investigating a range of conflicts and conflict behaviour.
5. Conflict resolution refers, in this case, to the different 'levels' at which conflict can be resolved. To a large extent this depends on the view that is taken of conflict. If one takes a behavioural view, then the absence of visible conflict behaviour will be taken as a sign of conflict resolution in the circumstance where the parties had previously been in dispute. A non-behavioural focus alerts us to the existence of latent conflict and to the importance of structural conflict as an explanatory variable.[42] In the context of North–South

negotiations a solely behavioural focus is too restrictive, since the Third World is attempting a structural transformation of the international economic order. The origin of many of their complaints and the limited impact of 'procedural' solutions can only be properly understood if the broader definition of conflict is adopted.

6. The stratification of power in the organisation is another variable which clearly links the internal and external environments. Power in this sense will be understood as the ability to affect outcomes. This ability in an international organisation is partly determined by capabilities possessed outside the organisation. In the context of international economic organisations it can refer, for example, to control over certain raw materials or other aspects of market power. The stratification of power is also influenced by control over internal resources, e.g. the distribution of posts or bargaining skills.

7. An often-neglected dimension of international organisations is the importance of organisational ideology. Organisational ideology is defined by Ansari as a tool which enables the leadership to engage in task expansion and systemic transformation. He asserts that it is formulated by the leadership of an organisation and based upon the values and aspirations of its constituents.[43] Cox and Jacobson adopt the standard social science definitions of ideology and outline the three essential features of organisational ideology. First, it provides an interpretation of the environment as it relates to action by the organisation. Secondly, it provides a specification of goals to be attained in the environment. Thirdly, it provides a strategy of action for attaining these goals.[44] Both approaches capture some of the essential features of the concept as it will be used here but do not exhaust the possibilities of the term. Organisational ideology will be used to refer to the conception of the role of the organisation and the intellectual rationale for its economic programmes articulated by the secretariat and also adhered to by the dominant groups in the organisation. This definition is intended to link knowledge and interests. In other words, knowledge does not stand distinct from the interests it serves. Organisational ideologies are social constructs whose role is to provide legitimation for certain specific courses of action. In so far as the secretariat and major members espouse the same framework of economic reasoning, the challenge to the prevailing orthodoxy may be vociferous or numerically strong but it will tend to be marginalised as an important part of the decisional process. On the other hand, if the major powers and the secretariat do not share the same set of assumptions, then it is likely that conflicts over economic analysis will play a large part in the negotiating process. The IMF and UNCTAD provide illustrative

examples. In the IMF where the organisational ideology is shared by the dominant members and the secretariat there is little overt challenge by these members to IMF policies, whereas in UNCTAD, economic reasoning has been the subject of fierce debate because the major states view the organisational ideology as hostile to their interests.

8. Organisational leadership refers to the role played by the secretariat and the executive head in the distribution and structure of influence. The secretariat of an international economic organisation is able to exert influence through two roles it plays. First, it has a logistic role to inform all members, e.g. through note-taking and the collection, duplication and dissemination of documents, of matters arising and requiring discussion. Secondly, the secretariat performs a research function: it is the duty of the secretariat to educate the members of the organisation about the issues under discussion. To this end it conducts primary research on matters pertaining to its jurisdiction. In performing these tasks the secretariat is necessarily engaged in a selective process, thus giving it a degree of influence. This influence can be used to support task expansion of the organisation. The ability of the executive head to exercise influence is dependent upon personal qualities, experience, the control s/he can exert over the resources of the organisation and the relative financial autonomy of the organisation.

Negotiation

Negotiation is a process which includes a range of behaviours and goals, leading to a variety of outcomes. To define negotiation as a process implies a recognition of two important elements often omitted from most analyses of bargaining and negotiation, i.e. time and social context. Approaches to negotiations which exclude considerations of time assume that the parties are fixed and that the environment is unchanging. A dynamic rather than a static conception provides a more realistic approach. Most international negotiations take place over a considerable period of time and both the environment and the actors are liable to change. In other words, the defining situation rarely remains the same at the close of the negotiating process, as it had been at the outset. For example, a change of government may take place in one or more of the states involved in the negotiations and this can lead to a shift in foreign policy. Moreover, the negotiations might decrease or increase in importance to (some of) the participants as a result of changed market conditions. This happens frequently during negotiations on international commodity agreements.

The organisational politics model stresses the social character of the negotiating process. Negotiations are located in time and place and space, and cannot be separated from an historical context. Thus perceptions, values, beliefs and political culture play an important role in determining the structure and outcome of negotiations.

The relationship between bargaining and negotiations is not clearly defined in the international relations literature. Some writers treat bargaining and negotiation as synonymous processes. Other writers argue that bargaining is distinct from negotiation. Michael Nicholson argues that, 'the activity whereby two contending parties decide between themselves what actions to take, when some are better for one than the other, is called bargaining. When it is done by explicit verbal communication, we refer to it as negotiation.'[45] If we follow Nicholson we would regard negotiation as a type of bargaining. However, this definition seems to exclude considerations of tacit bargaining in the conduct of negotiations. Rangarajan takes a different view and asserts that there is no difference between negotiation and bargaining. To him they are both processes involving an element of give and take and communication between the participants. The object of negotiation is to arrive at mutual agreement and to resolve perceived conflict between the parties.[46]

The approach taken here identifies bargaining as a type of activity which takes place within the context of negotiations. If negotiation refers to the 'process of combining divergent viewpoints to produce a common agreement',[47] then bargaining refers to the techniques employed in order to secure the common agreement. This distinction between bargaining and negotiation suggests that bargaining can be subject to distinct analytical techniques. The most developed and widespread attempt to do so is through the use of game theory.[48] However, the game theory approach contains a number of clear difficulties. First, quantitative utilities cannot be assigned to all alternative positions or outcomes; that is, the whole process of choice cannot be matrically expressed or determined. This would only be possible if we could create an absolute scale of utility valid for all those involved in the bargaining process. Secondly, the assumption of non-communication between the two parties, prevalent in game theory, is obviously an unreal one in the context of international bargaining. Moreover, even when game theorists hold communication to be important, they tend to conceptualise it in terms of trust. But, in international negotiations, it is arguable that interpretation is as important as trust. Thirdly, the key assumption of rationality is a limiting one.

Rationality in this model is characterised by logical, informed and purposeful decision-making. Bargaining in international relations is not always logical, the parties do not always possess either equal or relevant information and purposes may vary or be combined. In this sense, game theory is prescriptive rather than descriptive. It prescribes ideal conditions, rather than describing the real world of international negotiations, which is more complex and messy than the theory indicates. Bargaining includes both rational and irrational aspects. Finally, game theory has no place for memory. All games start afresh with a new set of payoffs. To some extent iterative games do contain some element of memory since the parties can use the previous games as part of a learning experience. Nevertheless, the overall thrust of game theory is to play down the role of memory.

In the manner described above, the negotiation process is made up of a bargaining process and the social context of action. It is the task of the analyst to identify the specific bargaining mode. The literature elaborates three analytical modes of bargaining.[49] These are *distributive* (all parties cannot gain because the 'pool' is fixed and therefore they attempt to increase their individual shares); *integrative* (the parties attempt to increase the share of the joint gain in a situation where all can gain); and *mixed* (this refers to the process in which the parties attempt to increase joint gain and also decide how to distribute the shares from the 'pool'). Most bargaining situations are mixed and hence involve both cooperative and conflictual behaviour. The social context of the negotiations refers to the actors involved, the type and range of issues under discussion, the time element involved and the institutional venue in which the negotiations are conducted.

In the organisational politics model, international organisations are not viewed as closed systems, sealed off from their environment. On the contrary, international organisations must be situated in the wider international environment. Students of international organisation do not agree on the specification of the relationship between an international organisation and the external environment.[50] Regimes, as social structures, provide a link between the internal dynamic of the organisation and the international system. In relation to IEOs we can specify two dimensions of the external environment. The general environment refers to the key systemic features of the international political economy. It therefore includes the changing configuration of economic, political and military power, patterns of conflict and alignment in the world system and the economic and political characteristics of states.[51] The task environment refers to the specific issues and areas of concern with which the particular organisation is concerned. For example, the IMF's task environment will be located in international monetary relations and GATT's will be found in relation to developments in international trade.

Development diplomacy

Development diplomacy is the term I give to the process whereby Third World countries attempt to negotiate improvements in their position in the international political economy. These negotiations largely take the form of bargaining with Western industrialised countries. This term is still relevant even if one does not assume that the Northern countries enter North–South negotiations with the intention of improving the developmental prospects of the South.

North–South negotiations cannot properly be understood without some consideration of the role of norms in structuring expectations, needs and demands in the bargaining process. Indeed, the attempt by the Third World to restructure the international economic order is in large measure an attempt to change various international norms. The positions taken by the developing countries on the efficiency and justice of the prevailing world order reflect a set of ethical presuppositions. Development diplomacy, understood as the dialogue between the industrialised states and the developing countries over the management of the global economy, is centrally concerned with the importance of norms.

North–South negotiations are characterised by three key features. First, a marked asymmetry of power exists between the two sides. In broad terms, whether overt, covert or structural forms of power are being considered, Northern countries are dominant. The patterns of dependence and interdependence and the roles of transnational corporations and other interest groups in structuring interests and perceptions are of crucial importance in analysing development diplomacy. This does not, of course, mean that under particular market conditions Third World producers and economic agents cannot affect outcomes. The unequal interdependence between the North and the South in the global economy is reflected in IEOs. Moreover the limitations of IEOs in affecting regime change and the difficulties of enforcing agreements on the major trading states exacerbates this issue. The AICs can, and often do, shift negotiations away from IEOs to other fora.

Secondly, the two parties possess different visions of the past, present and future. These different orientations generate different interpretations of how much needs to be or can be changed. This leads to different tactical emphases on the priority to be given to negotiating (or re-negotiating) principles or concrete agreements. The Third World has tended to insist on the negotiation of principles, whereas the industrialised states have given priority to the conclusion of practical agreements. This reflects the Third World's desire for a change of the *status quo* and the satisfaction felt by the developed states with existing arrangements.

Thirdly, for most of the period under review, the fact that both groups have the desire to maintain unity within each coalition creates structural and institutional impediments to change. Although the necessity for coalition maintenance is often seen to be only a Southern requirement, it has not been completely absent from Northern behaviour in the context of North–South negotiations.

Conclusion

The four case studies that follow focus on four broad issue areas: money (IMF), finance (World Bank), trade (GATT) and development (UNCTAD). These issue areas are not hermetically sealed and, as will be seen, there are varying degrees of overlap between the functional areas of competence of the four organisations. We will examine Third World participation in these four organisations to determine the extent to which such participation has modified their structure and functioning and to assess their influence on the Third World. IEOs are conceived as sites of power and struggle and not as technical instruments to achieve functional cooperation.

Each of the case studies discusses the origins of the IEO, seeking to show how the organisation is embedded within a particular regime. IEOs are not neutral, apolitical organisations. They are created to fulfil specific social purposes and their constitutions and decision-making processes reflect the outcome of a struggle between competing interests. An examination of the organisational ideology of each IEO demonstrates the close connections between knowledge and interests. Organisational ideologies define objectives, pose questions and provide research frameworks for the actors. Each of the case studies examines the changing relationship between the Third World and IEOs through analysis of the characteristics of the IEO and key features of the external environment. The external environment is not taken as a given but is reconstructed historically for each IEO.

The case study chapters have been constructed to answer similar questions but the idiosyncratic features of each issue area and IEO determine the structure of individual chapters. The case studies are linked through the central concerns of the book and the approach to regimes and IEOs outlined in this chapter. IEOs are seen as important multilateral instruments through which regimes are created and maintained. International cooperation is centrally concerned with conflict over values and preferences. Regimes, therefore, express certain values and interests and the content of regimes is important. In other words, regimes are not conceived, in this study, as external objects which impose order on states. They may provide solutions to the problem of cooperation in an anarchical international society, but in so doing they structure expectations and outcomes in particular directions and embody specific value preferences.

Notes

1. Duncan Snidal, 'IGOs, Regimes, and Cooperation: Challenges for International Relations Theory' in Margaret P. Karns & Karen A. Mingst (eds), *The United States and Multilateral Institutions: Patterns of Changing Instrumentality and Influence* (Boston: Unwin Hyman 1990) p. 322.
2. For different attempts to amend regime theory through a focus on institutional aspects see Roger K. Smith, 'Institutionalisation as a Measure of Regime Stability: Insights for International Regime Analysis from the Study of Domestic Politics', *Millennium* (Summer 1989) pp. 227–244 and Oran Young, 'The Politics of Regime Formation: Managing Global Resources and the Environment' *International Organization* (Summer 1989) pp. 349–377.
3. Regime theory is not the only approach to the study of international relations which focuses on the importance of normative phenomena. For a comparative analysis of regime theory and one such approach see Tony Evans & Peter Wilson, 'Regime Theory and the English School of International Relations: a Comparision', *Millennium* (Winter 1992) pp. 329–351.
4. See Susan Strange, 'Cave! Hic dragones: a Critique of Regime Analysis', *International Organization* (Spring 1982) pp. 479–496, for a rejection of regime analysis.
5. John Gerard Ruggie, 'International Responses to Technology: Concepts and Trends', *International Organization* (Summer 1975) p. 570.
6. John Gerard Ruggie, 'International Regimes, Transactions, and Change: Embedded Liberalism in the Postwar Economic Order', *International Organization* (Spring 1982) pp. 379–415.
7. Friedrich Kratochwil, 'Regimes, Interpretation and the "Science" of Politics: a Reappraisal', *Millennium* (Summer 1988) p. 277.
8. R. O. Keohane & J. S. Nye, *Power and Interdependence* (Boston: Little, Brown 1977) p. 19.
9. Stephen D. Krasner, 'Structural Causes and Regime Consequences: Regimes as Intervening Variables', *International Organization* (Spring 1982) p. 186.
10. *Ibid.* p. 185.
11. Charles Lipson, 'The Transformation of Trade: The Sources and Effects of Regime Change', *International Organization* (Spring 1982) p. 417.
12. Duncan Snidal, 'The Limits of Hegemonic Stability Theory', *International Organization* (Autumn 1985) p. 579.

13. A public good has the defining characteristics of jointness and non-exclusiveness. In other words, the consumption of such a good cannot be limited to those who bear the costs of production and the consumption of such goods by 'free riders' does not diminish the supply available to others.
14. Snidal, 'Limits of Hegemonic Stability Theory' *op. cit.* p. 580.
15. See Stephan Haggard & Beth A. Simmons, 'Theories of International Regimes', *International Organization* (Summer 1987) pp. 491–517.
16. Snidal, 'Limits of Hegemonic Stability Theory' *op. cit.* p. 581.
17. *Ibid.* p. 583.
18. Lipson, *op. cit.* pp. 437–441.
19. Young, *op. cit.* pp. 353–354.
20. *Ibid.* p. 354.
21. Snidal, 'Limits of Hegemonic Stability Theory' *op. cit.* pp. 593–594.
22. Young, *op. cit.* p. 355.
23. The main exponent of this approach is Robert Keohane. For an extended treatment of his neo–liberal institutionalist approach see Robert O. Keohane, *International Institutions and State Power: Essays in International Relations Theory* (Boulder: Westview 1989).
24. See Robert O. Keohane, 'Reciprocity in International Relations', *International Organization* (Winter 1986) pp. 1–27.
25. Robert O. Keohane, *After Hegemony* (Princeton, NJ: Princeton University Press 1984) p. 115.
26. Young, *op. cit.* pp. 356–359.
27. Keohane & Nye, *op. cit.* pp. 38–60.
28. See Kenneth Waltz, *Theory of International Politics* (Reading, Mass.: Addison-Wesley 1979).
29. See, for example, Bruce Russett, 'The Mysterious Case of Vanishing Hegemony: Or is Mark Twain Really Dead?', *International Organization* (Spring 1985) pp. 208–231 and Susan Strange, 'The Persistent Myth of Lost Hegemony', *International Organization* (Spring 1985) pp. 234–59.
30. Keohane & Nye, *op. cit.* pp. 52–53.
31. Oran Young, 'International Regimes: Toward a New Theory of Institutions', *World Politics* (October 1986) pp. 104–122.
32. Kratochwil, *op. cit.* pp. 277–278.
33. *Ibid.* p. 288.
34. See K. Oye (ed.), *Cooperation Under Anarchy* (Princeton, NJ: Princeton University Press 1986).
35. See Robert Axelrod & Robert O. Keohane, 'Achieving Cooperation under Anarchy: Strategies and Institutions', *World Politics* (October 1985) pp. 226–254.
36. Beverly Crawford, 'How Regimes Matter: Western Control of East–West Trade Finance' *Millennium* (Winter 1987) p. 432.
37. See James N. Rosenau, 'Before Cooperation: Hegemons, Regimes, and Habit-driven Actors in World Politics', *International Organization* (Autumn 1986) pp. 849–894.
38. Young (1989), *op. cit.* p. 358.
39. See Margaret P. Karns & Karen A. Mingst, 'The United States and Multilateral Institutions' in Karns and Mingst (eds.), *op. cit.* pp. 1–24.
40. See R. W. Cox & H. K. Jacobson, 'The Framework of Enquiry' in R. W. Cox & H. K. Jacobson (eds), *The Anatomy of Influence* (New Haven: Yale University Press 1974) pp. 25–28.

41. L. T. Farley, *Change Processes in International Organizations* (Cambridge, Mass.: Schenkman 1981) p. 41.
42. See C. R. Mitchell, *The Structure of International Conflict* (London: Macmillan 1981) pp. 15–46 for a discussion of different approaches to conflict.
43. Javed A. Ansari, *The Political Economy of International Economic Organization* (Hemel Hempstead: Harvester Wheatsheaf 1986) p. 80.
44. Cox & Jacobson, *op. cit.* p. 22.
45. Michael Nicholson, *Conflict Analysis* (London: English Universities Press 1968) p. 4.
46. L. N. Rangarajan, *The Limitation of Conflict* (London: Croom Helm 1985) p. 23.
47. I. W. Zartman, *The Politics of Trade Negotiations between Africa and the European Economic Community* (Princeton, NJ: Princeton University Press 1971) p. 202.
48. See, for example, the essays in Oye, *op. cit.*
49. See R. E. Walton & R. B. McKersie, *A Behavioral Theory of Labor Negotiations* (New York: McGraw-Hill 1965) p. 13 and Peter Warr, *Psychology and Collective Bargaining* (London: Hutchinson 1973) pp. 118–121.
50. See, for example, Georges Abi-Saab (ed.), *The Concept of International Organization* (Paris: UNESCO 1981); and J. Pfeffer & G. R. Salancik, *The External Control of Organizations* (New York: Harper and Row 1975).
51. See Cox & Jacobson, *op. cit.* pp. 37–58 for a similar formulation.

4

The IMF and the Third World

In recent years the relationship between the International Monetary Fund (hereafter referred to as the IMF or the Fund) and the developing countries has been shrouded in controversy. Intense debate has focused on the political and economic consequences of the Fund's stabilisation and adjustment policies and programmes. It is not the intention of this chapter to concentrate exclusively on recent events, or to confine discussion to the debate on conditionality. It will examine, instead, the changing relationship between the Fund and its Third World constituency. It will evaluate the ways in which the Fund has responded to the demands of its Third World members as articulated by Third World spokespersons in the IMF. Secondly, it will examine the evidence concerning the social and economic impact of the Fund's stabilisation and adjustment policies on the Third World.

Assessment of the IMF's role in the international monetary system and the impact of its policies on the Third World is not an easy task. Critics and supporters of the IMF are unable to agree on the relevant variables to be taken into account and hence arrive at different conclusions. Cheryl Payer asserts that 'The IMF has been the chosen instrument for imposing imperialist financial discipline upon poor countries under a facade of multilateralism and technical competence.'[1] The view that 'IMF policies tend to be counterproductive, especially for the Third World's poor' is a widely held one.[2] On the other hand, sympathetic observers claim that 'IMF policies it may be argued are more likely to generate economic success and avoid the political instability associated with economic chaos.'[3] The most extensively quoted defence of Fund policies was provided by Bahram Nowzad who in a trenchant essay defended the Fund against a range of criticisms.[4]

The absence of agreed criteria by which to assess the impact of Fund policies is compounded by the failure to establish the relevant conditions surrounding IMF intervention. In other words, as Haggard argues, the success or failure of Fund policies can be judged 'against what went before, what would have happened in the absence of policy change, or some normative standard'.[5] Furthermore, no agreement exists on the power of the IMF, or other international financial institutions, to impose policy changes on Third World governments. One perspective argues that external actors and structures play a crucial role in determining economic policy in Third World countries. This perspective emphasises market conditions, linkages between domestic elites in the Third World and international actors, and the leverage exercised by international financial institutions and other actors.[6] An alternative perspective places greater stress on the role of domestic variables in determining economic policy change in the Third World. Miles Kahler reviewed IMF and World Bank conditionality and concluded that 'external agencies have had limited influence on decisions for and successful implementation of stabilization and adjustment programs.'[7]

An assessment of the problematic relationship between the IMF and the developing countries cannot be confined to an analysis of the interaction of the units or to a single issue. Moreover, the current relationship between the IMF and the Third World is the outcome of an historical process, and a clear understanding of the Third World's attitudes to the IMF has to be placed in an historical context. The following account will therefore begin with a discussion of the creation of the IMF in order to highlight the intended purposes of the Fund and its designated role within the international monetary system. This will be followed by a short historical overview of the development of the IMF since its inception including a survey of the evolution of Fund policies in relation to the Third World. This historical overview should facilitate a clearer understanding of the objectives of the Fund and its ability to respond to change. This will be followed by a focus on the organisational politics of the IMF. A commonly agreed indicator of a measure of influence within an international organisation is the decision-making mechanism. In order to assess the Third World's ability to transform the IMF's policies it is necessary to examine the voting procedures and the formal and informal methods of decision-making and conflict resolution in the organisation. Formal voting procedures do not exhaust the structure of influence and therefore an attempt will be made to explicate the organisational ideology of the Fund since this is a crucial element in the determination of outcomes by international economic organisations. The second part of the chapter analyses Third

World demands and IMF responses in three issue-areas: participation, financial resources and conditionality. As Chapter 3 demonstrated, international organisations are embedded in an international system which provides an environmental context within which they function. This chapter will position the IMF in the wider context of the international political economy of money and finance.

The IMF can be characterised as a multilateral institution with three functional areas of operation, that is, consultative, regulatory and financial.[8] The three strategic issues chosen for analysis correspond to the three functional areas of operation, viz. participation (consultative), financial resources (financial) and conditionality (regulatory) and to the major issues of contention between the IMF and the Third World. Finally, it should be noted that Third World interaction with the IMF is shaped by domestic politics in Third World societies. The reactions to IMF policies, especially the imposition of conditionality, reflect deep divisions within and the impact of social and economic crises on these countries. This chapter cannot detail the widely differing social and political contexts surrounding policy formulation in the Third World.[9] But in seeking to assess the consequences of IMF policies for Third World economies and societies, attention will be given to the interaction between the domestic and external environments.

The origins of the IMF

The IMF and the World Bank were the fruits of wartime collaboration between the United States and the United Kingdom on the future of the international economic system in the post-war world. As World War II drew to a close an International Monetary and Financial Conference of the United and Associated Nations was convened at Bretton Woods, New Hampshire on 1 July 1944. Attended by 44 nations the Bretton Woods Conference established the liberal international economic regime of the post-war era. The Fund was a concrete response to the perceived international monetary problems of the 1930s and the imperatives of post-war economic reconstruction. It was argued at the time that the rise of economic nationalism, competitive devaluations and the absence of international economic cooperation had contributed to economic crisis and chaos, domestic political instability and the resultant world war.[10]

The main goal of the architects of the Bretton Woods system was to establish an international economic order that would prevent another political and economic collapse. In the issue-area of international monetary relations two interests remained uppermost: first, the provision of adequate liquidity so that countries experiencing short-term balance of payments problems would not resort to nationalistic measures (it was feared that countries temporarily in payments crisis might curtail imports or impose restrictions on trade); secondly, the creation of an adequate mechanism for international adjustment. Underlying the monetary arrangements lay a commitment to free trade and an open international economy. This new order under the leadership of the United States aimed to prevent a return to economic nationalism by fostering free trade and a high level of international interaction. The prime goal of the IMF agreed at Bretton Woods was to assist its members in resolving short-term balance of payments problems under a regime of fixed exchange rates,[11] thus permitting the orderly expansion of international trade. The Fund was created as an international institution to supervise and promote an open and stable international monetary system. Exchange rate supervision and balance of payments surveillance presaged a movement away from sole national control of economic policy and the acceptance of a degree of international interference in domestic economies. The purposes of the International Monetary Fund are stated in Article I of the IMF's constitutive document. These are:

(i)   To promote international monetary cooperation through a permanent institution which provides the machinery for consultation and collaboration on international monetary problems.

(ii)   To facilitate the expansion and balanced growth of international trade, and to contribute thereby to the promotion and maintenance of high levels of employment and real income and to the development of the productive resources of all members as primary objectives of economic policy.

(iii)   To promote exchange stability, to maintain orderly exchange arrangements among members, and to avoid competitive exchange depreciation.

(iv)   To assist in the establishment of a multilateral system of payments in respect of current transactions between members and in the elimination of foreign exchange restrictions which hamper the growth of trade.

(v)   To give confidence to members by making the general resources of the Fund temporarily available to them under adequate safeguards, thus providing them with opportunity to correct maladjustments in their balance of payments without resorting to measures destructive of national or international prosperity.

(vi)   In accordance with the above, to shorten the duration and lessen the degree of disequilibrium in the international balance of payments of members.[12]

From the above it is possible to extract the key functions of the IMF.

The Fund is designed to perform three important roles in the international monetary system. First, to regulate the financial relations of its members. This regulatory function includes an element of rule supervision and law enforcement with respect to exchange rates and balance of payments restrictions. Secondly, to provide financial assistance to members experiencing balance of payments difficulties. The Fund has acted as a lender of the last resort to countries with chronic payments problems. The regulatory and financial roles are closely entwined with access to the Fund's resources being made dependent on following the code of conduct devised by the Fund. Thirdly, to act as a consultative organ. The IMF's role is to create a climate in which governments are persuaded to dismantle exchange controls and to permit free trade and the free movement of capital.

Although 28 of the 44 nations represented at the Bretton Woods Conference can be classified as underdeveloped, these countries exerted minimal influence on the negotiations and the final outcome. The negotiations at Bretton Woods reflected the prevailing distribution of political and economic power in the international system. The deliberations were based around the plans developed by John Maynard Keynes (UK)[13] and Harry Dexter White (US).[14] American hegemony ensured that the final agreement bore a greater resemblance to the White Plan than the Keynes Plan. The developing countries were in a subordinate position and closely linked through imperial ties to the leading European states. Nevertheless, some developing countries, notably India, attempted to influence the final outcome of the conference. India called on the IMF to 'assist in the fuller utilization of the resources of the underdeveloped countries' and was supported in this request by Ecuador.[15] An amended version of this request which called for 'the development of the resources and productive power of all member countries with due regard to the needs of the economically backward countries'[16] also failed. The developed countries insisted that development was within the terms of reference of the World Bank and not the IMF. Thus from the outset the concern of the Fund was with short-term balance of payments financing and not development.

This has led to charges that the IMF is anti-development and sacrifices development for stability. The Fund's retort is that a stable economic environment is a necessary prerequisite for the achievement of economic development. It has been argued, however, that since the Articles of Agreement of the IMF acknowledged the 'development of the productive resources of all members' as a salient objective, this is an indication that some importance was given to the special problem of development.[17] However, this rather cursory reference to development, when taken in the context of the Fund's overall approach at its inception, which was to treat countries in an undifferentiated manner, did not suggest that the Fund would be sensitive to the special needs of the developing countries.

This review of the origins of the IMF shows that the main purposes of the Fund at its inception were to foster international cooperation and promote stability. Economic development was not a prime goal of the international regime established at Bretton Woods. The efforts of the Third World states to increase their participation in the international monetary system led them to demand changes in the IMF. The concerted campaign by the developing countries for a recognition of their particular interests has, to date, achieved limited success. The next section will examine the evolution of the IMF and its responsiveness to the specific demands and needs of the developing countries.

The IMF in the international monetary system

The IMF's history has been divided into four periods for closer examination. The first period covers events from the creation of the Fund until the return to full convertibility by the European economies at the end of the 1950s. The second period extends from the beginning of the 1960s until the collapse of the Bretton Woods exchange rate regime at the beginning of the 1970s. The third period stretches from the acceptance of floating rates in 1973 until the early 1980s. The final period begins with the onset of the debt crisis in 1982.

On tracing the history of the IMF it becomes evident that the Fund's importance to its members and its ability to affect the course of international monetary relations has varied over time. It has rarely been able to exercise any effective degree of control over the AICs but has increasingly done so over a Third World dependent on the financial resources it can provide. The organisation has exhibited a remarkable resilience and adaptability to changed circumstances, a result both of effective management strategies of task expansion and its usefulness to leading actors in the international monetary system. Although marginalised as a key forum for the discussion of important monetary issues it has become the AICs' principal instrument for the imposition of economic reform in the developing world and in the countries of the former Soviet bloc. The current role of the IMF is very different from the one envisaged by its founders.

The early years: 1946–60

For approximately the first decade and a half of its existence the IMF stood on the sidelines of international monetary cooperation. Inadequately equipped to cope with the tasks of post-war reconstruction and lacking the resources to contribute effectively to the liquidity needs of its members the Fund nevertheless provided a forum for cooperation and consultation in monetary and financial matters. The Fund had been established to supervise a system of convertible exchange rates but with most major currencies remaining inconvertible until the end of the 1950s new institutions arose for the purpose of conducting multilateral settlement.[18] The IMF presided over a system under which the member states pledged to work towards the full implementation of its codes. In other words, a weak international monetary regime was established. The commitment to the future application of the principles of Bretton Woods underpinned the negotiations and discussions on international monetary relations.

The hegemony of the United States in the global political economy enabled it to exercise a dominant role in the IMF during this early phase. Frank Southard, a former American executive director and former deputy managing director of the IMF recollected that

> in the 1950s the US voice in the Fund was decisive – indeed a task of the US Executive Director was to keep that voice muted so as not to frustrate Board and Management/staff activity. The practical question in those years, in any prospective large use of Fund resources, was whether the United States would agree – and the answer was usually obtained by direct enquiry.[19]

During this period the United States never lost an open policy conflict, successfully initiated policy changes and controlled access to the Fund's resources.[20] Although the US continues to exert considerable influence in the IMF it never regained the hegemonic position of the early years once the reconstruction of the European economies and Japan was completed.

At the outset of this period the IMF, in common with other multilateral agencies, exhibited minimal interest in the problems of the developing countries. The absence of an effective coalition of developing countries contributed to the marginalisation of their interests in international monetary relations. Nevertheless, a number of developments in IMF lending policy during this period were to affect relations between the Fund and the developing countries. The low level of drawings in the late 1940s and early 1950s[21] worried both Fund officials and member countries. Discussions on the provision of improved access to credit coincided with American fears concerning the length of repayment periods. The negotiations in the Executive Board culminated with the adoption of the 'Rooth Plan' in February 1952.[22] Drawings in the gold tranche were made automatic and access to the first credit tranche became more easily available. However, conditionality was imposed on any drawings beyond 25 per cent of a member's quota. It was further decided that borrowings should be repaid within a period of three to five years. The decision to institute the Stand-by Arrangement in October 1952[23] produced a significant relaxation of access to Fund credit since it allowed countries not in immediate balance of payments difficulties future access to IMF funds. Some analysts[24] argue that these developments were beneficial to the Third World. A further series of measures taken in this period have also been viewed as helpful to Third World development.[25] These included the provision educational courses and the dispatch of technical and advisory missions to the Third World. Critics of IMF thinking would no doubt consider these activities in a less positive light.[26]

The Bretton Woods years: 1961–71

The Bretton Woods exchange rate regime functioned at best for little more than a decade, i.e. between 1959 and 1971.[27] It was plagued by a series of monetary crises for leading industrial states, a severe liquidity problem and challenges to American leadership. The IMF suffered a loss of influence and became increasingly marginalised as a centre for the coordination of international monetary cooperation.

The 1960s witnessed unprecedented economic growth for the major capitalist economies. The foundations of economic progress laid in the first decade after the end of World War II came to fruition as national economies expanded and international trade grew at phenomenal rates. The long boom of post-war economic growth, however, created two major problems for the management of international monetary affairs. As trade increased, a severe liquidity problem became apparent. World trade was increasing faster than world reserves and in the absence of increased reserves it was feared that world trade would diminish, thus harming economic prosperity. The United States had provided liquidity for European economies during the 1950s but now it became increasingly apparent as the US ran into serious balance of payments problems that it could not continue indefinitely providing resources for the rest of the world. This was a consequence of the inherent contradictions of the Bretton Woods system and US misuse of the dollar's hegemonic position. This state of affairs could not be sustained because sooner or later confidence in the value of dollar assets would lead to investors refusing to hold dollars and converting their dollar holdings into gold.[28] Indeed, the US official reserve recorded an annual outflow of gold every year between 1958–68.[29] The liquidity problem was compounded by difficulties with the adjustment mechanism. As the 1960s progressed it became clear that changing international competitiveness was creating a problem of balance of payments adjustment. Declining American competitiveness was matched by increasing European and Japanese efficiency. Exchange rates became the main preoccupation of the leading AICs in the latter half of the 1960s, and it was the adjustment problem rather than the liquidity issue which led to the demise of the Bretton Woods system.

Increasing European influence in the international monetary system was not immediately translatable into increased influence in the IMF since revision of quotas only took place periodically. The European states began to shift discussion of international monetary issues away from the IMF and towards the Group of Ten (G10), a grouping of the 10 most industrialised Western nations.[30] It was under the auspices of the G10 that the General Arrangements to Borrow (GAB) were instituted. The GAB was a pool of currency resources created by the 10 countries to be borrowed by any of their number should IMF funds not be sufficient to meet their needs. Initially created outside the IMF, it was placed under IMF supervision at the insistence of the Fund's Managing Director, Per Jacobsson. However, the Fund could not lend the money at its own discretion.

The proposed solution to the problems of the overvalued dollar and liquidity crisis was the creation of a new reserve asset. The negotiations leading to the creation of the Special Drawing Rights (SDR) was the outcome of an initiative from the G10 and the group continued to play an active role in the subsequent discussions. Pierre Paul Schweitzer, Jacobsson's successor as managing director was determined that the creation of a new reserve asset should not be left to an exclusivist club and he actively campaigned for a role for the Fund. He was supported by the United States, which was worried about European pre-eminence in the G10 and the developing countries. Agreement was reached on the SDR facility in September 1967 after a series of meetings between the Fund and the G10.

In this period the developing countries began to emerge as a distinct group within the IMF. A number of developments in world politics and the response of the IMF to the new constituency of developing countries marked a change from the 1950s. Reports on the special problems facing the exporters of primary commodities, the convening of the first United Nations Conference on Trade and Development (UNCTAD) and the creation of the G77 brought awareness of the special needs of the developing world and mechanisms through which the developing countries could aggregate and articulate their interests.

In the context of the international monetary system the Third World demanded increased financial resources, lending activities tailored to their economies and increased participation in decision-making. The United States and Fund officials, as previously mentioned, were willing to include Third World countries in international monetary negotiations, the former as a political counterweight to Europe and the latter in order to preserve a role for the Fund. The Fund responded to the call for increased resources through increasing the size of quotas and shifting funding away from the AICs towards the Third World. The creation of the Compensatory Financing Facility (CFF) in 1963 and the Buffer Stock Financing Facility (BSFF) in 1969 were responses to the pleas for special financial resources. Thus at the beginning of the 1970s the IMF had to some extent responded positively to the demands of the Third World. This response was largely dictated by the IMF's desire to preserve its central role in the international monetary regime and as will be shown below did not involve any major change in Fund thinking and approach to economic analysis.

The post-Bretton Woods decade: 1972–81

In this third period monetary relations were thrown into crisis and renewed conflict in response to severe shocks in the international political economy. President Nixon's decision on 15 August 1971 to suspend dollar–gold convertibility is often seen as the end of the Bretton Woods system of fixed exchange rates. Attempts to create a new system of fixed parities, e.g. the Smithsonian Agreement of December 1971, ended in failure and by April 1973 all the major currencies were floating. The quadrupling of the price of oil in 1973 and the second oil price rise in 1979 created adjustment problems and recycling difficulties. For the non-oil exporting developing countries the oil shocks increased their import bills and worsened their payments positions. The IMF responded to the collapse of the Bretton Woods exchange rate regime by creating the Committee on Reform of the International Monetary System and Related Issues (commonly referred to as the Committee of Twenty or C-20). From the outset the developing countries were given representation on the C-20. Their allocation of nine seats equalled their representation on the Executive Board.

This decade marked the high point of developing countries' ability to exert influence in IMF decision-making circles and to affect IMF policies. In this period the gains made in the previous decade were consolidated, the level of participation in Fund decision-making improved and new flows of financial resources targeted to the special needs of the Third World instituted. Participation in the C-20 resulted in the establishment of two technical groups to investigate issues of special concern to the developing countries. A technical group to 'examine arguments for and against, and analyse the technical aspects of proposals for the establishment of a link between the allocation of SDRs and development finance'[31] was created with representation similar to that in the C-20. A joint IMF/IBRD (International Bank for Reconstruction and Development) Ministerial Committee on the Transfer of Real Resources to Developing Countries (the Development Committee) was set up in October 1974.[32]

Four major changes to Fund financing were made in this period. The deliberations of the C-20 resulted in the creation of an Oil Facility (OF) in 1974 for a two-year period to assist countries with payments difficulties arising from the oil price hike. The Extended Fund Facility (EFF) also established in 1974 provides assistance for longer periods than under Stand-by Arrangements for economies suffering 'serious payments imbalances relating to structural maladjustments in production and trade . . . and characterised by slow growth and an inherently weak balance of payments position'.[33] A Trust Fund (1976–82) extending concessional loans to the poorest developing countries was created on the recommendation of the Development Committee.[34] Furthermore, a Supplementary Financing Facility (SFF) was initiated in 1979 with the aim of providing balance of payments assistance to countries whose imbalances were large relative to their quotas. With the demise of the SFF in 1982 it was replaced by the Enlarged Access Policy (EAP) In addition to these new measures the CFF was liberalised in 1975 and again in 1979. In 1981 a cereal import facility to assist importers of cereals facing balance of payments problems because of increased cereal prices was integrated into the CFF.

This was a turbulent period in the Fund's history. It had been powerless to prevent the collapse of the system of fixed exchange rates it had been established to supervise. Increasingly marginalised by the G10 countries on significant issues the IMF appeared to be heading for extinction. Attempts to reform the international monetary system met with abject failure as the pace of events outstripped the bumbling efforts of the negotiators.[35] The Fund could do little more than bow to market pressure.

At the end of the 1970s and the beginning of the 1980s it is possible to argue that the Third World had achieved a measure of success in its quest for effective participation in the IMF. Increased access to decision-making had resulted in a larger share of Fund resources. The recycling of petrodollars and the provision of credit for countries most seriously affected by the oil crisis presented the Fund with new challenges. The second oil shock of 1979, and the recession of 1981–82 created large payments deficits in many developing countries. The IMF responded to the increasing external indebtedness of the developing countries by making provision for increased borrowing. Repayment periods were extended and countries were permitted to borrow a larger percentage of their quota than previously. In responding to the payments crisis of the Third World the IMF began to recover the influence it had earlier lost with the collapse of the adjustable peg exchange rate system.

The debt crisis and the end of the Cold War: 1982–90s

The transition from an organisation concerned solely with short-term stabilisation measures to one with an interest in growth and development started at the end of the 1970s and intensified in the 1980s. The IMF developed an extended role in the provision of finance to developing countries and spearheaded a change in international development policy. In return for its loans it urged debtor states to follow market-oriented policies. The economic liberalisation policies so resisted at the beginning of the 1980s have now become the new orthodoxy in the developing world.

Another major innovation in this period has been the closer collaboration between the IMF and the World Bank. The increased cooperation between them has affected the orientation and performance of both institutions. The Bank began to place greater emphasis on market-oriented reforms and the Fund has taken more interest in development.[36]

The Fund, which in the early 1970s appeared moribund, is now an important actor in the international monetary system. The Fund's new-found importance arose from the debt crisis and the role assigned to it by the United States and the leading industrial countries in the management of that crisis. Its role in the management of international financial relations was further enhanced following the collapse of communism in Eastern and Central Europe. The IMF has been given a central role in assisting the former communist states in the transition to capitalism.

The moratorium on debt servicing by Mexico in August 1982 heralded what has come to be called the Third World debt crisis. As a financial crisis the debt crisis threatened the stability of the international banking system. The fear of widespread Third World debt default and the potentially devastating consequences of such actions on Western economies led the United States and other Western nations actively to intervene in the debt rescheduling process. The IMF was viewed as the appropriate institutional mechanism through which debt rescheduling would take place. The Fund has played a threefold role in this process.

The IMF's 'seal of approval' acts as a catalyst for other sources of finance.[37] Commercial banks are reluctant to lend to developing countries in debt arrears unless the country first agrees a package of measures with the IMF. The agreement with the IMF signifies for commercial lenders an ability and a willingness to repay loans.[38] Developing countries have thus been forced into seeking IMF legitimation of their economic policies by concluding stabilisation agreements with the Fund. Secondly, the IMF has developed an interventionist role between borrowers and commercial lenders. The IMF plays a pivotal role in securing finance for major debtors. The IMF's 'seal of approval' serves to secure additional finance through so-called involuntary lending by its refusal to endorse an economic package until it feels that the level of financing from government creditors and commercial banks is adequate. Thirdly, and most controversially, the IMF has imposed rigid financial discipline on borrowing countries. It is the increased scope and incidence of IMF austerity measures which has sparked the debate on conditionality. As the number of Third World countries seeking assistance from the Fund grew in the 1980s the debate on conditionality became more intense.

This period witnessed increasing Third World disenchantment with the Fund as the gains of the 1970s were eroded with increased emphasis on high conditionality and short-term lending. The Reagan administration played a crucial role in reshaping the lending policies of the IMF.[39] In the context of shrinking credit and ballooning debt the major Western countries – especially the United States, Britain and Germany – began to use the IMF as an instrument of financial discipline. The IMF has been transformed into a quasi-central bank with the power of surveillance over national economies. It is unlikely that increased Fund surveillance and regulation of domestic economic policy will be used against AICs. The IMF is only able to influence those countries in receipt of its loans. Developing countries are the major borrowers from the Fund and the price of access to resources is the application of IMF stabilisation policies.

This is evident in two new facilities created in the latter half of the 1980s. In 1986 the Fund created a Structural Adjustment Facility (SAF) and in 1987 an Enhanced Structural Adjustment Facility (ESAF). These special concessional facilities enable the low-income countries to borrow up to 250 per cent of their quota at an interest rate of only 0.5 per cent. The governments of developing countries have welcomed these facilities and the provision of extra finance at low interest rates but have criticised the high conditionality attached to the loans. With the advent of structural adjustment lending in 1986 and close collaboration with the World Bank the IMF has properly entered the realm of development financing. Its loans are no longer solely targeted to stabilisation but have the added goal of achieving structural change, i.e. helping deficit economies to adapt to world market conditions.

The IMF's role as a regulator of the international monetary system was further enhanced by the collapse of communism in the Soviet bloc between 1989 and 1990. The end of the Cold War changed the political circumstances under which the IMF operated and produced new members and fresh challenges. The leading Western nations are using the Fund in the former Soviet bloc in much the same manner that they used it in the Third World, i.e. to impose a particular free market economic philosophy and practice. The IMF is in the forefront of efforts to reform the economies of the ex-communist states.

The threat to the world economy posed by the economic chaos in the former Soviet Union is small and the scale of hardship likely to be endured by populations is no greater than that faced by African peoples over the last decade. The involvement of the IMF in the reconstruction of Russia, the former Soviet territories and the countries of Central Europe arises from the political imperatives of the post-Cold War world. Western governments, led by the United States are worried over the twin dangers of the Soviet nuclear arsenal and the environmental hazards posed by dangerous nuclear power plants. The Western fear is that political instability and economic chaos following the disintegration of the Soviet state might unleash forces hostile to accommodation with the West. The Western nations under the aegis of the Group of Seven (G7) have undertaken to provide economic assistance during the transition to market economies. Unable to arrive at agreement on how best to support economic change, and heedful of the supposed impartiality and objectivity of the IMF, the G7 is using the IMF (and the World Bank) as the tool to effect the transition to capitalist democracy.[40] The Fund's bureaucracy, eager for task expansion, has welcomed these developments, Michel Camdessus, the Managing Director of the Fund stated in October 1991 that helping the (then) Soviet Union would be a 'thrilling challenge' for the IMF.[41]

The developing countries have expressed concern that the preoccupation of the G7 with the problems of Eastern Europe and Central Europe will be detrimental to their interests.[42] The entry of the former Soviet republics to the IMF in April 1992 gives them access to Fund resources. The developing countries argue that IMF resources should not be diverted to the ex-communist states at the expense of provision of financing for their needs. The debt crisis is still a consideration for many

Third World countries and access to longer-term financing still a priority.

In the 1980s, the asymmetrical power relations in the Fund were starkly exposed. The Fund continues to impose high conditionality on deficit countries whilst ignoring the problems caused for the world economy by surplus countries and the US deficit. The Third World has, therefore, campaigned for the Fund to be more interventionist against the industrialised nations.

The IMF: organisational structure and political process

Membership and resources

As at 15 January 1993 IMF membership stood at 175 countries. The Fund's membership reflects a number of economic and political systems. Initially a largely Western, capitalist organisation, decolonisation brought an influx of developing countries and these countries make up the largest constituency of Fund membership. During the Cold War a number of communist states were members of the organisation.[43] The membership has been swollen in the last year by the collapse of communism in Europe and the decision of the successor states to the Soviet Union to join.

The Fund raises finance in two ways. The chief source of financing for the Fund comes from members' subscriptions, which are identical to their quotas. Quotas are calculated on the basis of a state's GNP, its reserves of convertible currencies, current account transactions, its export dependence and the size and composition of its foreign trade. Secondly, the Fund can borrow directly from some of its members to lend to others. Extra resources have been provided through the GAB, the Bank for International Settlements, a credit arrangement with the Saudi Arabian Monetary Agency, and Japan.

The primary resources of the Fund are increased through quota reviews. To date nine quota reviews have taken place. Agreement on the Ninth General Review of Quotas was reached in 1990 but, so far, it has not been implemented. When implemented it will increase subscriptions by 50 per cent from approximately SDR 90.1 billion to SDR 135 billion, i.e. from $120 billion to $180 billion. This increase is inadequate to meet the demands for finance. Between the 1983 quota increase and 1989, the size of the world economy grew by 58 per cent. The planned increase in IMF subscriptions continues the erosion in the value of quotas as a percentage of world trade. The size of quotas relative to world trade has progressively declined since the Fund began operations in 1946. The quota increase cannot be implemented until the Third Amendment to the Articles of Agreement takes effect.[44] This amendment authorises the Fund to suspend the voting and related rights of members who fail to fulfil their obligations under the Articles of Agreement. This is an attempt to penalise countries in arrears to the Fund. It requires the consent of three-fifths of the membership possessing 85 per cent of the total voting power in order to be adopted. The main obstacle to the implementation of these changes is the US government, which wanted to limit the quota increase. It is likely that the Clinton administration will break the deadlock.

Decision-making in the IMF

The decision-making process of any international organisation is the result of the interaction of two different structures: the formal decision-making structure and an informal set of practices developed by the members of the organisation over time. In the IMF the formal structure is set out in the Articles of Agreement.[45] Although the Articles of Agreement have been amended, the structure of decision-making and the rules governing voting have remained unchanged.

The highest decision-making body in the IMF is the Board of Governors on which all member countries are represented. The Board of Governors meets annually (in conjunction with the World Bank) and is made up largely of ministers of finance and governors of central banks. However, in practice the Board of Governors has delegated most of its authority to the Executive Board. The Executive Board originally had a total of 12 members but now comprises 24 executive directors. Five directors are appointed by the five members having the largest quotas (the United States, Germany, Japan, France and the United Kingdom); 15 directors are elected from the other members; and provision is made for the appointment of a further 4 directors. Apart from the five largest subscribers, executive directors from three countries – Saudi Arabia, China and Russia – represent single-member constituencies. Four of the 15 elected constituencies comprise a membership of both developed and developing countries. It is the Executive Board which executes the substantive work of the Fund, e.g. responding to requests for loans from the membership.

The Interim Committee established in October 1974 is a departure from the original Articles of Agreement.[46] It was created to serve as a high-level advisory body after the C-20 ceased to exist. The Interim Committee meets at ministerial level two or three times a year and advises the Board of Governors on the role of the Fund in the context of a changing world economy.

To oversee the day-to-day operations of the Fund the executive directors select a managing director. The managing director is the chairman of the Executive Board and also participates in meetings of the Board of Governors. S/he is the head of the Fund's staff and is responsible for the organisation of the staff's duties. Since the creation of the organisation the managing director of the IMF has always been a European. The present office-holder is Michel Camdessus from France who has held the post since 1987.

The distribution of power within the organisation starkly outlined in its voting procedures reflects the economic and political distribution of power in the global political economy. A country's voting strength depends on its quota. A state's quota determines how many votes it possesses, its payment obligations to the Fund and its access to Fund lending. Political and economic factors are important in determining the size of quotas and the periodic realignment and increase in quotas. In effect this weighted voting system ensures that states with the largest quotas, i.e. those who contribute most to Fund finances have the largest amount of influence in the organisation. The structure of influence is thus biased in favour of creditor countries and against debtor countries. Influence in the IMF is determined by a state's political and economic power. Those in greatest need of the IMF's resources are therefore permanently in a subordinate position.

Critics of the IMF argue that the weighted voting system discriminates against the developing countries, since although these countries comprise the majority of the Fund's membership their share of the vote is less than 50 per cent.[47] But, as Killick has pointed out, it is the currencies of the leading industrialised states which are overwhelmingly used by the Fund. Moreover, the share of quotas held by the AICs is less than their share of world trade.[48] It would appear that any attempt to alter the voting structure so that the link between financial contribution and voting power was weakened would result in the major industrial countries boycotting the IMF.

Decision-making in the Fund is based on the principles of weighted voting and majority voting. Most decisions are taken by simple majority vote but for certain important decisions majorities of 70 and 85 per cent are necessary. The provision for special majorities effectively grants veto power to the United States, the European Community (EC) and the developing countries acting as a group. Since, however, the developing countries are not a monolithic bloc and are far less coordinated than the

OECD countries it is more difficult for a Third World alliance to exert effective veto power. Moreover, in the Executive Board some developing countries are represented by directors from developed countries.

Decision-making in the Fund has moved away from a reliance on the formal apparatus of majority voting and weighted voting towards the practice of consensus.[49] In the IMF consensus has become both a procedure for the taking of decisions and the final outcome of the decision-making process.[50] The search for consensus in international organisations is conducted within the context of the overall distribution of power in the organisation. Consensus in the IMF arose mainly from the efforts of the G10 to exercise collective management. The Bretton Woods regime ushered in an era of collective management but for approximately the first 15 years after the end of World War II the United States enjoyed unprecedented hegemony. The resurgence of Europe and Japan and the growth of interdependence created the conditions whereby international economic cooperation among the leading industrial countries for the provision of international public goods began to resemble a bargaining model instead of a dominance model. In other words, the relative decline of the United States resulted in greater attempts at collective decision-making by the OECD countries. The US could no longer simply impose its policy preferences and needed to seek accommodation with other leading capitalist states. The breakdown of the Bretton Woods system in 1971 and the subsequent failed attempt to return to a system of adjustable peg exchange rates clearly demonstrated the limits of American power. Consensus was an institutional response to these new circumstances and reflected the countervailing power of the EC and Japan. But it should be noted that the US still occupies the leading position in the world economy and the likelihood of a US veto is an important factor in the shaping of consensus.

The development of a group system in the IMF has made an important contribution to the decisional process. The leading capitalist states were the first to constitute themselves into a group for the purposes of policy coordination. The size of the group deemed necessary for collective leadership has varied over time, e.g. three, five, seven and ten countries. The G10 instituted in 1962 was an attempt by the major AICs to enhance policy coordination in the Fund. In so doing they sought to pre-empt discussion at the Executive Board and the Board of Governors and to move effective decision-making away from the institutional framework of the IMF.[51] Composed of the finance ministers and central bank governors of the 10 leading industrial countries the G10 was influential in setting the agenda of international monetary reform in the 1960s. In the 1980s, attempts at collective leadership moved from the G10 to the Group of 5 and latterly to the G7.[52]

The Group of 24 (G24) is one of the many groups created by the developing countries in international organisations. The Third World, which enjoys numerical superiority in most international organisations but little effective decision-making power, has tried to increase its influence through the aggregation of its membership. The main Third World group on international economic issues is the G77, initially created in the framework of UNCTAD. The G24 was set up by the G77 in January 1972 in response to the activities of the G10 and the discussions on the reform of the international monetary system in the wake of the collapse of the Bretton Woods system. The G77 argued that it was 'unacceptable that vital decisions about the future of the international monetary system which are of concern to the entire world community are sought to be taken by a limited group of countries outside the framework of the International Monetary Fund'.[53] The G24 was therefore created to review international monetary developments, evaluate events in the international monetary system and coordinate the positions of the developing countries. The group consists of eight members from each of the three regional groups – Africa, Asia and Latin America – of the G77. Originally created to act as a pressure group during the negotiations of the C-20 the G24 was constituted as a permanent group after the C-20 was disbanded.[54]

The structure of decision-making in the Fund reflects the realities of economic and financial power in the global system, in that states with the largest economies are given the most control over the decisions made. From the point of view of the developing countries this structure of influence discriminates against them on two counts. As the major borrowers from the Fund they have the least influence over the Fund's lending policies. Furthermore, the control of the Fund by the AICs, principally the United States, effectively prevents it from taking action against policies favoured by the rich nations. These policies may be detrimental both to the world economy in general and the developing countries in particular. Three key aspects of Fund decision-making to some extent dilute the influence of the leading AICs, but does not and cannot overturn their control since influence in the Fund derives from status and control over resources in the international monetary system. First, the development of consensus decision-making provides the Third World with a measure of greater equality. A system based solely on voting procedures would place them in a position of permanent inferiority since they could never muster sufficient votes to defeat the large quota holders and, moreover, would not be consulted on proposals. Secondly, the provision for special majorities on important decisions combined with weighted voting effectively gives the developing countries veto power. Thirdly, the development of group politics in the IMF strengthened the Third World bargaining position. The G24 gives a sense of purpose and direction to Third World diplomacy in the Fund. This enables the Third World to achieve greater unity in the bargaining process and provides technical support to the least developed members of the coalition. But it is, nevertheless, difficult to coordinate the diverse Third World membership.

Organisational ideology

The previous chapter argued that all IEOs possessed an organisational ideology. The aim of this section is to outline the organisational ideology of the IMF and to assess the manner in which this ideology functions. This is not an uncontroversial task since much of the argument over the IMF's role in the Third World arises from contention over the existence of and content of the IMF's ideology. It is vital that the IMF's economic philosophy and underlying political assumptions are subject to scrutiny since a common illusion persists that the IMF is a non-political organisation, concerned solely with economic issues.[55] In this view, economics can be reduced to a technical discourse and the political and ideological content are held to be irrelevant. This widespread view is propagated even by analysts who otherwise show cognizance of the political content of international economic relations. For example, Miles Kahler labelled the IMF 'quintessentially technocratic and apolitical' in an essay devoted to measuring the impact of US influence on the Fund![56] The success of neoclassical economics in separating economics from politics underpins the ability of the IMF to project an aura of economic neutrality when in reality it performs an economic and a political function.

The original organisational ideology of the Fund consisted of three elements. First, the Fund is based on the uniformity of treatment of its members. For most of its history it refused to accept that different levels of development require different policy measures. Even when it initially created facilities directed to the problems faced by the developing countries as exporters of primary commodities, e.g. the CFF, drawings were made open to all members. This core belief, although still of some relevance, is less central today. The move to structural adjustment lending in the 1980s was an admission by the Fund of economic difference.

Secondly, Fund policies are designed and applied with monetary and fiscal stability as the main goal.[57] The opinion expressed by Ivar Rooth, the second managing director, in 1955 that 'the proper objective of economic policy [in developing countries] is development with stability. Without stability the objective of development will not be achieved'[58] has guided IMF policy until the present. In the 1980s the IMF changed from an organisation concerned solely with balance of payments financing into one with an interest in development finance but with a strong commitment to stabilisation policies.

Thirdly, the underlying premise of IMF economic philosophy is rooted in the liberal economic paradigm.[59] Although the Fund does not possess a written theoretical framework on which policy advice is framed, the analytical basis of the programmes are articulated in a series of papers by Fund staff. This liberal approach can be characterised as monetarist in outlook and is based on a number of assumptions. It is committed to the market economy and the belief that the principles of the market economy as expressed through the free and unobstructed operation of market forces provides the best remedy for economic recovery and growth. It is the market rather than governments according to this view which ensures the efficient allocation of resources. In designing programmes to solve balance of payments problems the Fund attaches crucial importance to the role that money and monetary policy can play. The Fund argues that balance of payments disequilibria reflect the mismatch between the demand for real money balances and the real value of money supply. The major problem confronting economic policy is to reduce the current account to fit a sustainable net flow of capital, or in other words, to bring aggregate demand into equilibrium with aggregate supply. The IMF approach to cutting excessive demand is through public sector cuts since it is an unnecessary increase in the money supply which is held to be responsible for the problem in the first place. Moreover, IMF policies are based on the assumption that the free and unrestricted movement of goods and services across national boundaries increases the welfare of individual nations and the world economy as a whole. Perfect competition and the operation of the laws of comparative advantage according to this approach ensure gains from trade for all countries. Liberalisation of foreign exchange facilities is concomitant on trade liberalisation and guarantees the flow of scarce foreign exchange to the most efficient sectors of the economy. These underlying assumptions provide the rationale on which the economic programmes of the Fund are constructed. Criticism of the Fund's economic policies will be discussed later but it should be pointed out here that some critics of the Fund accept its underlying premises about the nature of political and economic activity but differ on the application of specific economic tools.

The neo-liberal approach of the IMF is only one of a number of available strategies. It is based on a particular conception of the market and market forces. In this vision the market and economic activity is delinked from the political and social conditions of its existence. It assumes that if countries behaved rationally and observed the rules of the game the market would automatically adjust balance of payments problems. All countries irrespective of their levels of development would benefit from such a liberal system. Hence an impartial bureaucracy like the IMF can devise lending policies to overcome temporary disequilibria in balance of payments without the need for countries to revert to disruptive behaviour.

The beliefs inherent in the IMF's approach are deeply ideological. The assumptions and prescriptions of neo-liberal economic thought are not value-free. They are essentially normative and political and hence open to dispute. The doctrine of the free world market is contested by those who argue that market forces benefit those who stand to gain most, e.g. transnational corporations and international banks, from successfully competing in an open world market.[60] Others point out that unregulated market forces give rise to periodic booms and slumps. Government intervention is necessary to manage both capitalist crisis and to promote economic development.[61] In addition, IMF stabilisation policies imply a particular conception of the relationship between the state and the economy. These policies favour a minimal role for state intervention. Thomas Biersteker in a telling critique argues that,

In the abstract, the programmes are directed principally against the more extensive forms of state intervention associated with state capitalism and wider Keynesianism. As such they have important political implications both for domestic relations of production (between capital and labour, as well as between foreign, local and state sectors) and ultimately upon the position of countries in the international division of labour (generally moving away from forms of state-led, socially reformist, import substitution industrialisation toward private sector-led, export oriented growth). What initially began as a series of short-term measures for stabilisation and economic adjustment turns out to have significant long-term applications for the choice of development strategy.[62]

And Thomas Scheetz argues that the IMF's value bias 'undercuts its claims to present an objective, scientific approach to a country's financial problems that does not violate its sovereignty and political institutions'.[63]

The Third World's demands and the IMF's response

Participation

From the perspective of the Third World the decision-making structure in the IMF discriminates against them. The weighted voting system condemns developing countries to an inferior position in the organisation. But if the importance of special majorities is taken into account it becomes apparent that the Third World has a greater say in decision-making than is suggested by a focus solely on the weighted voting provisions. But despite the influence that the Third World can exert as a collective voice, few individual nations command the resources necessary to affect decisions taken in the organisation. It is concern for individual as well as collective power which lies behind the demands of the Third World on this issue.

The demand for greater and more effective participation in IMF decision-making springs from two different strands of Third World thinking. On the one hand, it arises from the political imperative to make full and effective use of their sovereignty; on the other, the recognition that monetary instability is harmful to development and the desire to extract increased development financing from the rich countries produces a substantive interest in the organisation of the international monetary system. The Third World challenge to the liberal international economic order, most clearly expressed in the demand for a NIEO, attempted to (i) change the intellectual climate and to gain acceptance for certain ideas considered by the South to be conducive to economic development; (ii) negotiate specific international economic agreements; and (iii) create new international economic organisations or to restructure existing ones in order to increase Third World influence over decision-making. The demand for increased access to the centre of power in existing institutions highlights the political nature of the confrontation between the North and South. In foregrounding the power of the North over international economic organisations, especially the Bretton Woods organisations, the Third World exposed the fallacy of separating the economic from the political. The demand for increased influence in IMF decision-making is therefore part of a wider campaign for reform of international organisations.

Ferguson divides the Third World's challenge to IMF decision-making into two phases.[64] The first phase was concerned with countering the marginalisation of the Fund in decision-making on monetary issues and lasted until the end of the 1960s. In the second period the developing countries have been concerned with restructuring Fund decision-making in order to improve their level of participation.

The developing countries first adopted a critical attitude to decision-making on international monetary issues in the 1960s.[65] The immediate cause of their disquiet was the creation of the G10 and that group's attempt to make international monetary policy outside the framework of the IMF. The decision, in 1962, to inaugurate the GAB and the initiative the following year to set up a study group to 'undertake a thorough examination of the outlook for the functioning of the international monetary system and of its probable future needs for liquidity'[66] threatened to remove consideration of major monetary problems from the IMF. The developing countries objected to this trend and found support from a Fund unwilling to accept a diminution of its role. The power of the G10 rested not only on the international trading position of its members but also in their control of IMF decision-making since at this stage they accounted more than two-thirds of the total votes.

The major reform negotiations in the 1960s concerned the creation of a new international reserve asset. Although the G10 was in the forefront of the negotiating process, the IMF under Pierre Paul Schweitzer, nevertheless contributed to the process through policy studies and the four joint meetings between the IMF Executive Board and the G10 deputies held in 1966–67. The decision in principle to create a new reserve asset was taken at the ministerial meeting of the G10 in The Hague in July 1966. It was after the series of meetings between the Fund and the G10 that final agreement was reached on the nature of the new reserve asset. The 'Outline of a facility based on special drawing rights in the Fund' was approved by the Board of Governors in Rio in 1967.[67] Without IMF involvement in the reform negotiations the interests of the developing countries would have been excluded from consideration. It is not therefore surprising that they 'became vociferous advocates of the centrality and institutional authority of the IMF in the international monetary system'.[68]

The unilateral decision by the United States to suspend dollar–gold convertibility clearly revealed the impotence of the IMF when faced by its dominant member and the vulnerability of the developing countries to actions taken elsewhere in the international monetary system. The Smithsonian Agreement among the G10 members once again revealed the marginalisation of the Third World and the Fund. The failure of the Smithsonian Agreement and the unsuccessful attempts to return to a system of fixed exchange rates led to new pressures for reform of the international monetary system. The developing countries, through the newly created G24, argued that debate on the reform of the international monetary system should be conducted under the auspices of the IMF. The United States supported the call for a wider forum since it had become increasingly isolated in the G10 since August 1971.[69] The inclusion of the developing countries in the negotiations to reform the international monetary system was a political necessity since any agreement required amendment of the IMF's Articles of Agreement and the developing countries now possessed sufficient votes to veto any change they disliked.[70]

In the 1960s the developing countries insisted on recognition of the authority of the IMF in international monetary negotiations. They argued that decisions affecting the entire international monetary system should be taken with the full participation of developing countries. From the beginning of the 1970s the argument on participation was developed to include two further aspects relevant to decision-making. It was argued that full participation in decision-making would not be attained unless the membership of restrictive-membership bodies in the Fund ensured adequate representation for developing countries. Furthermore, developing countries demanded that their voting power should be strengthened through an increase in quotas allocated to these countries.[71]

The creation of the C-20 marked a turning point in Third World participation in international monetary negotiations. For the first time these countries were involved from the outset of the discussions, and the decision to use representation on the Executive Board as the basis for membership on the new committee guaranteed the developing countries a sizeable number of seats. The acceptance of the principle that *ad hoc* limited-membership committees should be constituted along the lines of the Executive Board represented a victory for the Third World position. This policy is advantageous to the Third World since the representation of developing countries on the Executive Board is greater than their corresponding share of world trade. The continuation of the C-20 in the form of the Interim Committee gives the developing countries an avenue through which to exert influence on Fund decision-making. Thus on one level, the Fund has responded positively to the Third World's demand for increased participation.

Proposals to change the voting structure in the Fund have met with less success. A variety of approaches can be taken in order to adjust voting power. First, a readjustment in quotas can take place. Under its Articles of Agreement the IMF is committed to periodic reviews of quotas. Among Third World countries the oil-exporting states most notably have benefited from changes in quota allocations. Secondly, the ratio between quotas and votes can be changed by changing the amount of basic votes granted to each member. This could only be achieved through an amendment of the Articles of Agreement. Apart from the inherent difficulties of constitutional change[72] it is unlikely that the rich countries would be prepared to see a significant increase in the power of the developing countries through such a method. The third approach involves changing the criteria used in the determination of quotas, e.g. the inclusion of population size. The developing countries have failed in their campaign to change the voting structure of the Fund through changing quotas.

Raw power in the Fund is exercised through the votes allocated by quota. The developing countries have not been able to shift the structural imbalance in power but have at various times in the Fund's history been able to exercise some degree of influence on Fund policies. Since the beginning of the 1970s the ability of the developing countries acting collectively to exercise negative power through the use of the veto on questions requiring special majorities has increased their influence potential. Moreover, membership in Fund committees enables them to put the case for special consideration forward. From the end of the 1960s, the interests of the developing countries on international monetary issues have been articulated inside the IMF and in other fora. The opportunity to express political grievances and outline divergent policy preferences should not be dismissed too lightly. On the other hand, mere participation is not sufficient. If the opportunity to participate in discussions amounts to no more than an exercise in letting off steam, the gains will be negligible.

The extent to which increased Third World involvement in IMF decision-making translates into effective participation on international monetary issues is determined not by the Fund but by the distribution of power in the international economic system. Many issues are still discussed by the leading industrial states outside the Fund. The G7 countries appear to have little optimism that the IMF can effectively manage monetary interdependence. The Fund is unable to play a more effective role in coordinating national monetary policies because it cannot impose accountability on the United States, the leading member of the G7. The developing countries are thus caught in a dilemma. On one hand the G7 countries can evade the IMF unless the changes sought require specific rule changes. Decisions affecting the international monetary system, if taken solely by the G7, perpetuate unrepresentative decision-making. The Third World is therefore forced to support the IMF as the central institution in the management of the international monetary system. On the other hand the developing countries cannot exercise effective control in the IMF, and it is unlikely that the structural change favoured by most developing countries will be implemented given the distribution of power in the organisation.

Financial resources

The Fund's role in the provision of financial resources to member states has evolved over time in response to pressures from the developing countries and changes in the international monetary system. The Fund provides members with financial resources to cover balance of payments deficits. The provision of foreign exchange reserves is designed to prevent deficit countries from resorting to restrictive measures when faced with balance of payments difficulties. The Articles of Agreement make it clear that the aim of the Fund in providing financial assistance is the maintenance of an open world economy, and the provision of full employment and the development of productive resources in the domestic economy. National economic prosperity in this view is inextricably linked with a free trade and free enterprise international economic system.

The Fund operates a number of lending facilities through which it provides balance of payments finance. Members are permitted to borrow (draw) from the Fund depending on the size of their quota. The Fund's regular lending facilities comprise drawings under the credit tranches, the extended arrangements and the enlarged access policy. Under its special lending facilities the Fund provides finance for the Compensatory and Contingency Financing Facility (CCFF), the BSFF and emergency assistance. The special lending facilities for low-income countries are made up of the SAF and ESAF.

The most basic form of lending open to all members is that under the credit tranches. Members can draw from the reserve tranche or one of the four credit tranches. The reserve tranche corresponds to that part of a member's quota which the Fund holds in SDRs or other reserve assets. In other words, a member has a reserve tranche position if the Fund's holdings of its currency are less than 100 per cent of its quota. Reserve tranche holdings belong to a member and hence access to them is automatic and unconditional. The four credit tranches, each corresponding to 25 per cent of a member's quota, represent the next source of credit. Drawings on the first credit tranche is subject to minimal conditionality. A government requesting credit under this facility has to demonstrate that it is making reasonable efforts to overcome its payments problems. In practice, the definition of 'reasonable efforts' is left to the borrower's discretion since policy conflicts with the Fund tend to be resolved in the borrower's favour. Requests for drawings from the higher credit tranches are subject to increasing conditionality. These drawings are normally granted under a stand-by arrangement. Members seeking recourse to the upper credit tranches must agree a stabilisation programme with the Fund. Drawings are issued in instalments subject to the satisfactory completion of agreed performance criteria.

The developing countries have achieved some success for the demand that the IMF should recognise the specific problems of development. A number of special lending facilities have been created at their insistence. It is therefore incorrect to claim that the Fund consistently ignores the demands of the Third World. The Fund has adapted to enable it to meet some of the development needs of the Third World, as articulated by official representatives in the organisation.

The first special facility to cater directly to the development needs of the Third World was the Compensatory Financing Facility created in 1963 to provide finance to primary producers experiencing shortfalls in their export earnings. A contingency financing element was addded to the CFF in August 1988, transforming it into the Compensatory and Contingency Financing Facility. In 1990 coverage of the CCFF was widened to include all services with the exception of investment income. At the same time in an attempt to increase the speed of disbursement the rules were changed to allow members to use estimates rather than actual data in submitting details of the shortfall in earnings, and in 1990 coverage was wide. The BSFF had been established in 1969 in order to assist members to meet their contributions to international buffer stock agreements. Both the CFF and the BSFF represented an acceptance of the argument that the unpredictable and volatile nature of commodity markets hampered development prospects. A Trust Fund financed by the sales of a sixth of the Fund's gold stock was established in 1976, and until its final loans were disbursed in March 1981 it made concessional loans to low-income countries. The oil price rise in 1973 seriously worsened the balance of payments positions of the non-oil-exporting developing countries. Two Oil Facilities (1974 and 1975) were created to assist countries most seriously affected by the oil price increases and provided finance to cover part of the deficit attributable to higher oil prices.

During the early 1970s the Fund responded to the need for longer-term balance of payments support to correct structural imbalances by creating the Extended Facility. The problem of members with large imbalances relative to their quotas was first addressed through the establishment in 1979 of the SFF. Funds under this scheme were fully committed by 1981 and it was replaced by the Enlarged Access Policy. The Fund moved more fully into structural adjustment lending with the creation in 1986 of the SAF. This facility provides long-term concessional finance in support of balance of payments adjustment in low-income countries. The ESAF was established in 1987 to refinance low-income countries' obligations to the Fund.

The SAF and ESAF share similar objectives, eligibility and programme features. Sixty-two of the Fund's poorest members are eligible for SAF/ESAF loans. Both facilities provide concessional finance to support three-year adjustment programmes on the same financial terms, but the financial assistance available under ESAF lending is much greater. The SAF was created with approximately SDR 2.5 billion and the ESAF was established with SDR 6 billion. Under the SAF the Fund commits up to 63.5 per cent of a member's quota under a three-year arrangement. The member accepting an adjustment loan has to develop a medium-term policy framework to cover the period of the loan. SAF loans are disbursed annually and linked to success in meeting the macroeconomic targets agreed between the Fund and the member. The interest rate on adjustment loans is 0.5 per cent and the principal is repayable over five and a half to ten years, with a five-year grace period. Under ESAF members receive up to 250 per cent of quota over a three-year period; in exceptional circumstances the loan could be extended to 350 per cent of quota. ESAF funds are disbursed half-yearly. Performance criteria and monitoring procedures are more stringent than under the SAF. The performance objectives of a SAF/ESAF programme are set out in a policy framework paper (PFP) prepared in conjunction with the Fund and the World Bank. The PFP establishes the macroeconomic and structural policy objectives of the borrowing member over the period of the loan. It identifies the economic strategy to be pursued and the financing needs. PFPs contain an analysis of the social and distributional impact of the structural adjustment programme and indicate the approach of the domestic authorities to the adverse short-term impact of these measures on the most vulnerable groups in society.

Apart from these facilities the Fund provides additional finance for developing countries through the SDR Account. The SDR Account was created by the Fund in 1970 and SDRs are allocated periodically to members in proportion to the value of their quotas. The SDR Account provides an unconditional access to international reserves and may be used by members to settle payments deficits.

The pattern and geographical distribution of Fund lending are presented in Tables 4.1 and 4.2. The Fund classifies 24 of its 175 members as industrial countries; all others are classed as developing countries. Table 4.1 shows that most Fund lending is for stabilisation rather than adjustment purposes. It is the more intrusive nature of adjustment lending which is responsible for the greater attention this type of lending receives. Table 4.2 confirms that the Fund's resources are targeted exclusively to the non-industrial countries. The enlarged membership of the Fund following the collapse of communist regimes in

Table 4.1 Fund credit outstanding from principal facilities, 31 December 1992

Facility	Amount (millions of SDRs)	Number countries
Stand-by Arrangements	5,789.52	22
Extended Arrangements	12,631.58	7
Structural Adjustment Arrangements	105.35	4
Enhanced Structural Adjustment Arrangements	2,290.31	18

Source: International Monetary Fund, *International Financial Statistics* February 1993.

Table 4.2 Total fund credits and loans outstanding

Region	1989	1990	1991	1992
World	24,644.9	23,290.2	16,668.3	17,746.0
Industrial countries	–	–	–	–
Developing countries	24,644.9	23,290.2	16,668.3	17,746.0
Africa	6,172.9	5,749.3	5,882.7	5,722.7
Asia	5,378.8	3,609.0	5,030.8	5,958.2
Europe	905.5	917.1	3,464.6	4,644.9
Middle East	196.8	154.1	155.2	407.0
Western Hemisphere	11,909.9	12,860.8	12,134.9	11,013.2

Source: International Monetary Fund, *International Financial Statistics* February 1993.

Eastern and Central Europe and the financial needs of these countries accounts for the increase in lending to Europe.

The existence of the range of special facilities demonstrates the adaptability and flexibility of the Fund to the demands of its Third World members and to a changing international political economy. The provision of extra resources does not guarantee a satisfactory solution to the balance of payments problems of indebted members. The extent to which these policies achieved their declared goals will be discussed later. However, the creation of new facilities does not in itself contribute effectively to the solution of the problems of the developing countries. Nor can the existence of new lines of credit be taken as providing a satisfactory response to the demands of the developing countries. An analysis of the adequacy of the Fund's response needs to consider three further questions. First, did these facilities meet the demands of the developing countries for the creation of new forms of IMF support? Secondly, to what extent do these facilities meet the financial needs of the developing countries? And finally, under what terms and conditions is financing provided? This final question will be discussed at greater length in the section on conditionality. We will for the moment, focus on the first two issues.

The major political initiative in the IMF for additional resources came in the form of a proposal to link reserve creation with development assistance. The developing countries first voiced the link proposal in the IMF in 1965[73] and this issue became one of their key demands on international monetary reform until the end of the deliberations of the C-20, by which time it had become apparent that agreement could not be reached with the developed countries on the link.[74] The concept of a link between reserve assets and development finance was not new. Keynes' plan for an International Clearing Union contained the idea of a link and a number of schemes were proposed in the 1950s and 1960s.[75] The link favoured by the developing countries had the following features. First, a fraction of SDRs destined for developed countries on the basis of quota share would instead be given to the poorer members of the IMF. Second, the link would be direct, i.e. it would not be disbursed through an intermediary agency. Third, distribution among developing countries would be according to existing IMF quotas, except for the least developed who would receive a disproportionately larger share. Fourth, SDR emissions would be based on the need for liquidity rather than the need for development finance. In the ensuing debate proponents of the link stressed its role as an instrument to increase development assistance and opponents countered by arguing that it would undermine confidence in the SDR as a monetary asset by confusing the provision of liquidity with the demand for aid.[76] The link proposal was defeated by the unity of the developed countries, the absence of support from the IMF staff[77] and the failure to resolve the technical arguments.[78]

IMF financing of balance of payments deficits rests on the Fund maintaining a constantly revolving pool of member currencies. This implies that lending should be short-term with a stress on the obligation to repay. Once developing countries became the principal creditors of the Fund, a process which occurred in 1980,[79] it became apparent that a conflict exists between the needs of these countries and Fund provision. Short-term balance of payments financing although alleviating a temporary problem was unable to cure the real cause of payments difficulties in developing countries. For developing countries the major problems arose from long-term structural imbalance in their economies. A move to longer-term lending with greater emphasis on the structure of the economy was therefore imperative. The Fund responded to the needs of low-income countries in the 1970s with the EFF and the Trust

Fund and in the 1980s with the SAF and ESAF. But the lending activities of the Fund depend on its capital assets and the Fund has been underfinanced in recent years. Because increases in quota are political as much as technical, the economic requirements of the Fund cannot guarantee a quota increase sufficient to support the scale of lending envisaged. As already stated, the Ninth General Review of Quotas scheduled to be completed by March 1988 was only agreed in June 1990. It was argued by the managing director and others that a doubling of quotas was necessary to meet the financial needs of the organisation.[80] In the end a 50 per cent increase was agreed but has still not been implemented over two years later. The second method of raising capital depends on the willingness of the surplus countries to lend to the Fund. In recent years Japan and Saudi Arabia have lent large sums to the Fund[81] and the GAB can now be lent to non-GAB contributors under certain circumstances.

There are therefore financial limits to the ability of the Fund to provide direct assistance to the developing countries. It is necessary, however, to make two qualifications to the above analysis. Fund contribution to the financing needs of its members is not restricted to its own financial resources. The Fund plays a catalytic role in the provision of financial resources to the developing world. Agreement with the Fund opens the door to loans from commercial banks, governments and international organisations. Over the last decade the Fund has played a pivotal role in debt rescheduling and refinancing, largely through the Paris Club of creditors, thus increasing the flow of resources to developing countries. Fund pressure on commercial banks and participation in the Baker Plan (1985) and Brady Plan (1989)[82] increased the amount of 'involuntary lending' to the heavily indebted countries.

Moreover, in discussing the adequacy of the Fund as a source of finance it is necessary to be aware of the divergencies among developing countries. For example, in the 1970s a clear distinction emerged between those countries able to raise capital on the international financial markets and those with a low credit rating. For the former, access to Fund resources was not crucial and they preferred to use the Fund only as a last resort or to provide a 'seal of approval' to enhance borrowing from private banks. For the latter group of countries the Fund often represented the only source of funding open.[83]

The onset of the debt crisis increased the importance of the Fund for the heavily indebted middle-income countries but the distinction between middle-income and low-income countries is still pertinent. The 'lost decade' of the 1980s witnessed the fall in living standards in many low-income countries, particularly in Africa, and the need for balance of payments assistance became urgent. One response to this by the Fund was the creation, first, in 1975 and later in 1980 of subsidy accounts to assist low-income countries to meet higher charges on amounts lent to them from resources borrowed by the Fund at market interest rates. The attractiveness of Fund finance to developing countries depends on the level of conditionality attached to the facility. One way of measuring the benefits accruing from the various special facilities is through an examination of the degree of conditionality attached to these forms of lending. The Trust Fund with no conditionality attached stands at one extreme and the high-conditionality facilities like the EFF, SFF, EAP, SAF and ESAF at the other. The CFF, initially a low-conditionality facility, was liberalised in 1975 and 1979 but toughened in 1983, before being liberalised again and transformed in 1988 and 1990.[84] The majority of Fund financing as is evident from the above falls under the category of high conditionality. The trend since 1979 has been for a larger proportion of Fund lending to require high conditionality.[85] The high political profile of the IMF, especially in the developing world, revolves around the policies attached to its high-conditionality lending. It is to that heated and bitter debate that we now turn.

Conditionality

The IMF would be unable to place a revolving pool of currency at its members' disposal if members were unwilling or unable to repay loans. The policy of conditionality, although not clearly articulated at Bretton Woods, is implied in the structure of the Fund. The basic principle of conditionality, i.e. that some conditions should be attached to loans, is no longer questioned.[86] Nevertheless, some left-wing writers castigate conditionality as an unwarranted intervention in the affairs of a sovereign state.[87] And Third World governments faced with difficult economic negotiations with the IMF often resort to the sovereignty argument.[88] But without debating the contemporary meaning and relevance of sovereignty the objection to the IMF on these grounds is somewhat disingenuous. The acceptance of this point does not carry an entailment that one accepts the economic policies of the IMF but a recognition that it is futile to wish for a world in which bankers did not attach conditions to their loans. Failure to exercise caution in lending policies is likely to end in disaster for both lender and borrower. The debt crisis is a salutary reminder of the effects of profligate and irresponsible lending. Unfortunately, because of the structural power of capital, penalties have fallen mainly on the debtors, although the blame for the debt crisis lies as much with Western banks and Western governments[89] as it does with Third World governments. Indeed, the often disenfranchised Third World populace, hardest hit by the draconian austerity measures imposed in order that the commercial banks and official agencies are repaid, bear no reponsibility for the economic disaster, and yet the workings of global capital determine that their sacrifices should form an important part of the solution.

The real debate on conditionality concerns the impact of Fund policies and not the existence of conditionality.[90] The same strictures applied above to the sovereignty argument also apply to Fund staff and defenders of the Fund who dismiss the impact of Fund policies on vulnerable sectors of society. The claim that the Fund merely proffers advice but does not determine policy and therefore it is absolved from responsibility for the distributional impacts of its programmes does not stand up to scrutiny. First, contrary to the claims of the Fund, numerous examples exist of the intimate connection between Fund staff and the policies implemented by recipient governments.[91] Moreover, many recipient countries are in a poor bargaining position when they seek Fund assistance and are unlikely to resist Fund demands.[92] But even if the above assertion of Fund direct influence is unproven, Fund conditionality constitutes an intervention in the domestic economy. IMF policy reforms have significant consequences for the domestic relations of production, between capital, labour and the state, and between national and international capital. It affects income distribution both directly and indirectly, supporting certain types of change and inhibiting others. This section will examine the controversy surrounding the impact of Fund stabilisation and adjustment programmes. But first we will present a brief overview of the central aspects of IMF stabilisation and adjustment programmes.

The secrecy surrounding Fund programmes makes it difficult to generalise about the conditions attached to Fund lending and to assess the impact of Fund policies. Nevertheless, enough evidence exists on the preconditions, performance criteria and other policy recommendations attached to conditionality to enable analysis of Fund policies. The available evidence suggests that while the IMF does not apply identical remedies irrespective of a country's circumstances, it possesses an approach or paradigm which determines the parameters of the programmes it supports.

Although Fund-supported programmes encompass a wide variety of policy measures and no two programmes are identical, they nevertheless exhibit certain similarities. The IMF adopts a monetary approach to the balance of payments.[93] The monetarist approach places emphasis on demand management since serious balance of payments difficulties are in this view caused by excessive government spending, high inflation and unrealistic and overvalued exchange rates. The chief goals of IMF macroeconomic policies are a rectification of the payments imbalance and reduction in inflation. Subsidiary goals include the promotion of growth and the continued maintenance of debt service payments. Among the measures most commonly found in the IMF 'package' are the following:

1. A decrease in budget deficits by, for example, cutting government expenditure, reducing subsidies and raising taxes.
2. A devaluation of the national currency.
3. A reduction in government borrowing by placing limits on government borrowing from the central bank and ceilings on external borrowing.
4. Liberalisation of foreign trade through the reduction of tariff and non-tariff barriers.
5. Demand management policies concentrating on reducing real wages particularly in the public sector.
6. Price liberalisation and deregulation.
7. Changes in interest rates so that they reflect the real interest rate.

Stabilisation policies aim to correct financial imbalance whether caused by domestic economic mismanagement or external shocks. Payments imbalances can be classified into three types.[94] The first are temporary deficits caused by temporary loss of market or cyclical variations in the terms of trade; and the second, temporary deficits caused by excess demand, i.e. disequilibrium between aggregate demand and supply. A third form of imbalance arises from fundamental disequilibria in the structure of the economy. Before the mid-1970s the Fund focused on the short-term imbalances rather than the longer-term deficit. Increasingly since then the Fund has given more attention to the structural causes of balance of payments deficits. The move to what has come to be called structural adjustment lending retained the monetarist approach but added a set of related policy measures. Structural adjustment measures allow for more gradual changes in both aggregate demand and supply. Moreover, increased emphasis is given to supply-side measures with emphasis on initiating sectoral change. Such measures include policies concerned with the pricing of goods and services, reducing the role of the public sector and encouraging the expansion of the private sector, the pattern of public expenditure, the creation of financial intermediaries and the mobilisation of domestic savings.[95]

Criticism of Fund conditionality comes from a variety of theoretical and ideological viewpoints. Pastor[96] identifies two major schools of criticism, the structuralist and dependency and, Bird[97] distinguishes at least three separate groups of critics. Instead of rehearsing the range of criticism levelled at Fund conditionality I will present a mix of criticisms with special emphasis on the broad structuralist critique since that has been the most influential. The structuralist approach starts from the premise that demand restraint and short-term adjustment policies are inadequate[98] because the balance of payments problems experienced by developing countries arise from the development process and external conditions.[99] To the structuralists, inflation is not a transient phenomenon resulting from short-term disequilibria but is embedded in internal and external structural imbalances basic to developing economies. The most important of these imbalances include the fluctuation and slow growth of earnings from the export of primary commodities, the dependent enclave character of import-substituting industrialisation, the stagnation of domestic food agriculture and excessive dependence on food imports.[100]

Structuralists argue that Fund measures are inappropriate and misguided and harm the growth prospects of developing countries. In relation to Africa, Loxley argued that restraining domestic demand was unlikely to reduce imports or to release local goods for expanded export earnings. The substitutability of traded for non-traded goods is low in Africa, imports do not compete with exports and exports are not consumed locally.[101] Structuralists contend that devaluation fails to meet its stated goals of achieving a realistic and sustainable exchange rate, transferring resources to the export sector and restraining aggregate demand.[102] Instead they argue that devaluation has fuelled inflation, since if imports constitute a significant proportion of aggregate demand price increases are unlikely to have a significant effect on demand. On the export side, devaluation will fail to restore competitiveness to the export sector since supply elasticities might be low and non-price factors might be more important in restraining demand. Furthermore, in export industries with a high import content devaluation, in forcing costs up, defeats the ostensible objective of export expansion.[103] Moreover, the harsh external environment militates against the export-oriented and trade liberalisation approach. The drive for export-led growth according to the critics is based on the fallacy of composition, since all Third World countries cannot simultaneously increase market share. Further, competitive devaluations result in increased exports but declining revenues, since productivity gains are passed on to consumers. And, in addition, increased protectionism in the industrial world discriminates against Third World exports.[104] Further criticisms relate to the role played by interest rate reform. Taylor takes the view that positive real interest rates could be stagflationary, i.e. produce both inflation and recession if interest costs are a significant part of total production costs.[105] And Giovannini finds no evidence to support the claim that increases in the rate of interest leads to increased savings in developing countries.[106]

A number of other criticisms are made of Fund conditionality by structuralists and other critics. Some analysts have pointed out the adverse distributional impact of Fund programmes.[107] They allege that low-income urban workers are particularly adversely affected by the cuts in real wages, increased unemployment, reduction in subsidies and increased inflation.[108] Other critics suggest that Fund programmes privilege foreign capital at the expense of domestic producers.[109] The political costs of Fund programmes have also come under attack, with some observers alleging that they lead to domestic instability and political disturbances.[110]

Since the late 1970s, Fund officials have responded to the accusations of the critics. They reject the argument that the Fund takes a demand-management approach to adjustment, stressing instead the eclectic nature of Fund programmes.[111] They accept that attention is given to monetary indicators but insist that the Fund's programmes are diverse and include supply-side policies.[112] On exchange rate policies, Fund officials have argued that in many cases devaluation is an important instrument in restoring external balance. They emphasise the inimical effects of overvalued exchange rates on producers and consumers.[113] Furthermore, studies by IMF staff have shown that exchange rate policies do not harm the export receipts of developing countries. Contrary to the structuralist assertion the IMF insists that the potential for downward movements in price arising from simultaneous devaluations depends on the ability of producers to influence supply. This, however, is unlikely to happen in most cases. In terms of the overall impact on the economy, IMF officials argue that primary commodity exports of Third World countries have been declining for the non-oil exporting countries and that it is unlikely that competing countries will be adjusting their exchange rates at the same time.[114]

The Fund refutes the charge that its policies impede economic growth. Whilst acknowledging that in some cases short-term output may fall, it nevertheless, asserts that in the medium term output will expand.[115] Moreover, Fund staff point to commitments in the Articles of Agreement to promote economic growth. In the Fund's retort to its critics, the SAF and ESAF are promoted as pro-growth facilities. The IMF argues that failure to correct balance of payments imbalances is the real impediment to sustainable growth.[116]

The criticism that Fund policies adversely affect income distribution, harming the poorest sections of society, is adamantly refuted. Fund officials argue that their policies, especially since 1980, have been targeted at the poorest and most vulnerable groups in society, i.e. the rural poor. The Fund admits that its programmes attempt to shift the internal terms of trade in favour of the rural sector but argues that the urban poor are not the poorest groups in society.[117] In contradistinction, the Fund argues that it is the unsustainable programmes followed prior to IMF intervention which have had a deleterious impact on the poor. A Fund study published in 1986 concluded that,

> while the types of policies undertaken in the context of Fund-supported adjustment programs do, in their role to restore the framework for sustained economic growth, have implications for the distribution of income, they have not in general been inimical to the goal of improving distribution of income. In particular Fund programs have not been directed against the poor.[118]

Another Fund study concluded that,

> without adequate means to quantify the effects of Fund adjustment programs it is not possible to specify conclusively their impact on internal income distribution, but the preceding discussion gives little reason to believe that the programs lead to any increase in income inequality. It is also unlikely that the programs lead to a significant decrease in the living standards of the poorest quartile. The only identifiable actions detrimental to the poor were those that increased the income of the wealthy.[119]

Studies emanating from the Fund also dismiss the charge that IMF policies do not work, i.e. they fail to remedy the balance of payments deficit. On the contrary, Fund staff assert that their programmes not only achieve balance of payments viability but also improve the efficient allocation of existing resources and increase the amount of resources available to countries.[120] A recent study by two Fund staffers of Korea's experience concluded that Fund policies were instrumental in stimulating export-led growth, reducing inflation and improving the external position.[121]

The IMF also refutes the accusation that Fund policies lead to so-called IMF riots. As A. Shakour Shalan argues, it is the delay in implementing adjustment rather than Fund measures which gives rise to social and political disturbances.[122]

The Fund has been robust in its defence and essentially its rejection of the critics of its conditionality is based on three assumptions. First, adjustment will have to take place, i.e. a country cannot indefinitely accumulate a deficit. Orderly adjustment designed by the Fund is better both for the country and the world economy. Secondly, governments often postpone adjustment too long, so that by the time the Fund is called in the measures taken will be tough and politically sensitive. As one Fund official bluntly explained, 'The longer the introduction of the program is delayed, the greater the effort needed to see it through, and the greater the chance of failure.'[123] The final assumption is that Fund policies do cater for the special circumstances of development and growth. Fund policies are eclectic and realistic and not the rigid and inflexible instrument portrayed by the critics.

As this survey of the dispute between the Fund and its critics has shown, it is not possible to settle this debate by an appeal to empirical evidence. The dispute between the IMF and its critics is an indication of competing approaches and different methodologies.

Limited agreement exists on the best method to estimate the macroeconomic effects of Fund programmes. The use of competing methodologies to evaluate Fund programmes means that care must be taken when attempting a comparision of the results of different tests. Mohsin Khan[124] distinguishes four different approaches which have been used to evaluate the effectiveness of Fund programmes:

1. The before-after approach – compares macroeconomic performance before and after under a Fund programme.
2. The control group approach – compares the difference in macroeconomic performance between countries with a Fund-supported programme and a group of similar countries without a Fund-supported programme.
3. The actual-versus-target approach – compares the actual results under the programme with the targets specified in the programme.
4. The comparison of simulations approach – uses simulation to compare hypothetical performance of Fund-type programmes and an alternative set of policies.

All four approaches are severely limited.[125] The first three have difficulty in overcoming the counterfactual, i.e. what would have happened in the absence of a programme. Although the simulation model avoids this pitfall, the parameters of the model will vary with the policy regime thus invalidating the results which treat policy as fixed.[126]

Even if these problems could be overcome, it is unlikely that agreement will be reached on the best way to evaluate Fund programmes. The difficulties inherent in assessing Fund policies are not reducible to competing methodologies. These neo-classical models are silent on the concept of class, and from a Marxist or radical perspective incapable of providing an adequate understanding of the impact of Fund policies.[127] They are economistic and fail to address the social and political context of policy-making. In abstracting economics from the social whole any measurements can only be partial and inadequate.

Conclusion

The relationship between the Third World and the IMF is neither reducible to a single, simple issue nor is it an unchanging one. This chapter has examined the Fund's response to the demands of the Third World and examined the evidence concerning the impact of Fund policies on the Third World. The results are mixed and unqualified support cannot be given either to the claims of the Fund or the arguments of its critics.

It is incorrect to claim that the IMF ignores Third World demands. The Fund is a dynamic organisation and the role it currently plays in the international monetary regime is different from that envisaged at Bretton Woods. An almost exclusive focus on balance of payments stabilisation has been supplemented with greater interest in development and concern about the distributional impact of its policies. The Fund's role in recycling petrodollars, managing the debt crisis and providing finance for structural adjustment were all responses to the financial needs of its poorest members. In debates on monetary reform, in the 1960s and 1970s, Fund staff were supportive of increased Third World participation in decision-making. This, of course, was in order to further the interests of the IMF's bureaucracy but this point shows that an uncritical identification of the Fund with the United States (and other industrial nations) gives a distorted picture of the operation of the organisation.

The weighted voting system of IMF decision-making is certainly biased in favour of the AICs, but it nevertheless, provides channels of access through which positions taken by Third World countries, individually and collectively, can be heard. The representation of Third World countries on the Executive Board and Interim Committee gives them some influence over Fund policy and they possess a blocking veto on decisions requiring a special majority. Criticism which focuses on the voting provisions misses the point. Influence on IMF policy is related to the size of a member's quota but the organisation rarely resorts to voting. The dominant members of the organisation would exercise a similar influence on decisions even if the voting system was changed. The demand for increased participation has been clearly met but this does not, in and of itself, guarantee effective participation. This chapter has argued that the IMF is limited in its impact on the international monetary system and it follows that increased Third World participation in the IMF does not necessarily translate into an ability to influence outcomes in the international monetary regime. In this case increased access to decision-making is insufficient to guarantee regime change.

Moreover, the debate on influence highlights a dilemma faced by

Third World countries in their attempt to make IEOs more responsive to their needs. The power of the AICs in the IMF arises from their economic and financial strength in the global economy. Furthermore, the leading industrial nations coordinate international monetary policy through the G7 rather than the IMF. They are not dependent on IMF financial resources and consequently can effectively evade IMF strictures. Since no AIC has sought a Fund (high) conditionality loan since 1978 this means in practice that there is an an asymmetry in the power the Fund exerts over its membership. The IMF's managing director has claimed that the Fund can influence the policies of the AICs through moral suasion and the annual discussions between members and the Fund.[128] These may well be conceivable channels of influence but they are very weak. And compared with the control the Fund exerts over the economies of Third World debtor nations they are less than insignificant. The Fund is used by the United States and the other industrial nations to impose financial discipline and liberal economic policies on the Third World, but no mechanism exists which forces the rich countries to play by the rules they set for others. In this respect the Fund reflects the unequal power structure of a stratified international society.

The lending policies of the Fund have changed in response to the needs of its poorer members. The one-year stand-by arrangement was first supplemented by the EFF and in the late 1980s the Fund developed two new facilities, the SAF and ESAF to provide longer-term lending to low-income countries. It is indeed ironic that in responding to the Third World's demand for structural adjustment lending the Fund has engendered the most intense controversy in its history. Moreover, the CCFF and BSFF recognise the special problems faced by developing countries as exporters of primary commodities. A debate can take place on the adequacy of Fund resources and the conditions attached to them but the Fund cannot be accused of an unwillingness to innovate.

Claims about the impact of Fund-supported programmes remain shrouded in controversy. The Fund's evidence concerning the success of its adjustment and stabilisation programmes does not convincingly demolish the arguments of its critics. A Fund review covering 21 countries and 44 annual programmes (stand-by arrangements and EFF lending) concluded that performance in the 1990s was superior to that in the 1980s. It argued that a strong link existed between a member undertaking planned fiscal and credit policies and achieving balance of payments, inflation and growth objectives.[129] On the other hand, detractors of stabilisation and structural adjustment have mounted evidence of the devastating impact of Fund programmes in a number of countries. In the light of these studies and given the competing methodologies and theoretical frameworks it is likely that the evidence will remain inconclusive and disputed. The evidence does, however, support the contention that a general conclusion about the impact of IMF policies on Third World countries is unsafe. Much will depend on the local circumstances: the severity of the economic crisis, the political context in which stabilisation or adjustment measures are implemented and the measures taken. In other words, the political economy of stabilisation is a fusion of domestic and external factors.

Both critics and Fund supporters fail to take sufficient account of the political economy of the borrowing state. Fund programmes are mediated through local state structures and the success or failure of Fund-supported programmes depends not on elegant abstract economic modelling but on the political conditions surrounding implementation.[130] The results of bargaining between the Fund and the borrower will determine the shape and content of IMF packages. A number of studies have shown that borrowing governments do have greater autonomy in bargaining with the Fund than is commonly supposed.[131] It is therefore incorrect to assume that the Fund imposes policy programmes on *all* Third World governments. Moreover, policies agreed are not always fully implemented and domestic variables appear to be more important in explaining the degree of implementation of Fund policies than the influence of external actors.[132]

If we accept that considerations of state and class are pertinent then examination of so-called IMF riots also requires greater theoretical sophistication. The most comprehensive examination of this accusation finds no correlation between Fund programmes and political instability.[133] Riots are a response not necessarily to an IMF programme *per se*, but to its implementation. It is also important to note that if the success of Fund programmes depends on local conditions then domestic elites cannot be absolved of their share of the blame for so-called IMF riots.

Arguments concerning the relationship between the Fund and the Third World will continue as long as the Fund plays a key role in financing the payments crises of Third World countries. Fund programmes affect income distribution both directly and indirectly and are therefore political rather than technical or functional. The insistence by the Fund that it cannot intervene domestically because that would constitute an infringement of sovereignty is disingenuous. A Fund programme is an intervention and it is unhelpful to pretend otherwise. The Fund's recent concern with regard to the distributional impact of its policies is unlikely to result in any significant change. Its basic economistic approach is still prevalent and this restricted vision limits the policies it proposes.

This chapter has argued that the IMF has not been completely unresponsive to the demands of its Third World members. But the form of the Fund's response is defined and conditioned by its decision-making process and its organisational ideology. The Fund's role is shaped by the structures of the international political economy and the actions of states over whom it has no control. Judgement as to whether the Fund's response to Third World demands meet the needs of Third World societies depends on the perspective of the analyst. I have suggested that for any specific case study attention should focus both on the structural constraints and the specific economic and political aspects of the particular case.

Notes

1. Cheryl Payer, *The Debt Trap: The IMF and the Third World* (London: Monthly Review Press 1974) pp. ix–x.
2. Patricia Adams, *Odious Debts: Loose Lending, Corruption and the Third World's Environmental Legacy* (London: Earthscan 1991) p. 79.
3. Henry S. Bienen & Mark Gersovits, 'Economic Stabilization, Conditionality and Political Stability' *International Organization* (Autumn 1985) p. 279.
4. Bahram Nowzad, 'The IMF and its Critics', *Princeton Essays in International Finance No. 146* (Princeton University December 1981).
5. Stephan Haggard, 'The Politics of Adjustment: Lessons from the IMF's Extended Fund Facility' *International Organization* (Summer 1985) p. 508.
6. See Barbara Stallings, 'International Influence on Economic Policy: Debt, Stabilization, and Structural Reform' in Stephan Haggard & Robert R. Kaufman (eds), *The Politics of Economic Adjustment: International Constraints, Distributive Conflicts, and the State* (Princeton, NJ: Princeton University Press 1992) pp. 41–88.
7. Miles Kahler, 'External Influence, Conditionality and the Politics of Adjustment' in Haggard and Kaufman, *op. cit.* p. 99.
8. See Benjamin Cohen, *Organizing the World's Money* (London: Macmillan 1977) for a similar definition.
9. A number of studies have examined the importance of the domestic political context for the success of stabilisation policies. See, for example, Joan M. Nelson (ed.), *Fragile Coalitions: The Politics of Economic Adjustment* [Overseas Development Council U.S. – Third World Policy Perspectives, No.12] (New Brunswick: Transaction Books 1989); Joan M. Nelson (ed.), *Economic Crisis and Policy Choice: The Politics of Adjustment in the Third World* (Princeton, NJ: Princeton University Press 1990); and Haggard & Kaufman, *op. cit.*. (Part II).
10. See David P. Calleo, *America and the World Economy* (Bloomington: Indiana University Press 1973) pp. 35–37.
11. In reality this was an adjustable peg system since exchange rates could move within 1 per cent of parity.
12. J. Keith Horsefield (ed.), *The International Monetary Fund 1945–1965 vol. III* (Washington DC: International Monetary Fund 1969) pp. 187–188.
13. See 'The Keynes Plan' in Horsefield, *op. cit.* pp. 3–36.

14. See 'The White Plan', in Horsefield, *op. cit.* pp. 37–96.
15. J. Keith Horsefield (ed.), *The International Monetary Fund 1945–1965 vol. I* (Washington DC: International Monetary Fund 1969) p. 93.
16. *Ibid.* p .94.
17. Graham Bird, *The International Monetary System and the Less Developed Countries* 2nd ed. (London: Macmillan 1982) pp. 15–16.
18. See Brian Tew, *The Evolution of the International Monetary System 1945–88* 4th ed. (London: Hutchinson 1988) pp. 15–43.
19. Frank Southard, 'The Evolution of the International Monetary Fund' *Princeton Essays in International Finance No. 135* (Princeton University December 1979) pp. 19–20.
20. Miles Kahler, 'The United States and the International Monetary Fund: Declining Influence or Declining Interest?' in Margaret P. Karns & Karen A. Mingst (eds.), *The United States and Multilateral Institutions* (Boston: Unwin Hyman 1990) p. 95.
21. In the calendar year 1950 there were no drawings on the Fund. See Horsefield vol. 1, *op. cit.* p. 276.
22. Executive Board Decision No. 102–(52/11), 13 February 1952. Horsefield vol. III, *op. cit.* pp. 228–230.
23. Executive Board Decision No. 155–(52/57), 1 October 1952. Horsefield vol. III, *op.cit.* pp. 230–31.
24. For example, A. I. MacBean & P. N. Snowden, *International Institutions in Trade and Finance* (London: George Allen & Unwin 1981) p. 41; Bird, *op. cit.* p. 16.
25. Bird, *op. cit.* pp. 16–17.
26. Dependency writers would view any further incorporation into the capitalist world system as detrimental to Third World interests.
27. See Susan Strange, *International Monetary Relations* vol. 2 of A. Shonfield (ed.), *International Economic Relations of the Western World 1959–1971* (London: Oxford University Press 1976) for a review of this period.
28. This was the so-called Triffin paradox.
29. Tew, *op. cit.* p. 104.
30. The members of the G10 are Belgium, Canada, France, Germany, Italy, Japan, the Netherlands, Sweden, the United States and the United Kingdom.
31. Committee on Reform of the International Monetary System and Related Issues (C–20), *International Monetary Reform: Documents of the Committee of Twenty* (Washington DC: International Monetary Fund 1974) p. 95.
32. *Ibid.* pp. 47–8.
33. Executive Board Decision No. 4377–(74/114) of 13 September 1974 paras I(ii) a&b. See Margaret Garritsen de Vries, *The International Monetary Fund 1972–1978 vol. III* (Washington DC: International Monetary Fund 1985) p. 504.
34. Executive Board Decision No. 5069–(76/72) of 5 May 1976, *ibid.* pp. 563–564.
35. See John Williamson, *The Failure of World Monetary Reform, 1971–74* (London: Nelson 1977) for an analysis of these negotiations.
36. On the changing relationship between the Fund and the Bank see Richard E. Feinberg, 'The Changing Relationship between the World Bank and the International Monetary Fund', *International Organization* (Summer

1988) pp. 545–560; Azizali F. Mohammed, 'The Role of the Fund and the World Bank in Adjustment and Development' in Said El-Naggar (ed.), *Adjustment Policies and Development Strategies in the Arab World* (Washington DC: IMF 1987) pp. 73–87; and Hiroyuki Hino, 'IMF–World Bank Collaboration', *Finance and Development* (September 1986) pp. 10–14.

37. M. Guitián, 'Fund Conditionality and the International Adjustment Process: A Look into the 1980s', *Finance and Development* (February 1981) pp. 14–17; Derek Gorman, 'The IMF: Its Financial Role', *Barclays Review* (February 1984) p. 8; and Louis Goreaux, 'The Fund and the Low-Income Countries', in Catherine Gwin, Richard E. Feinberg and contributors, *The International Monetary Fund in Multipolar World: Pulling Together* [Overseas Development Council U.S. – Third World Policy Perspectives, No. 13] (New Brunswick: Transaction Books 1989) pp. 152–156.

38. See H.O. Ruding, 'Lenders ought to consult the IMF', *Euromoney* (February 1980) pp. 34–38 for a discussion of the benefits to commercial banks flowing from closer coordination between private lenders and investors and the Fund.

39. Kahler, 'The United States and the International Monetary Fund', *op. cit.* pp. 103–107.

40. Peter Norman, 'G7 passes the future of Russia to the IMF', *Financial Times* 13 July 1992 p. 13.

41. Quoted in Peter Norman, 'A poor guest at the party', *Financial Times* 8 October 1991 p. 16.

42. *The Guardian* 29 April 1991 p. 7; and George Graham, 'Third World stresses aid need' *Financial Times* 27 April 1992 p. 4.

43. See Valerie J. Assetto, *The Soviet Bloc in the IMF and IBRD* (Boulder: Westview Press 1988).

44. The new provisions will be placed in Article XXVI, section 2, and a new Schedule L; also in Article XII, section 3(i), para 5 of Schedule D.

45. See Horsefield, *op. cit.* vol. III pp. 187–214 for the original. Articles of Agreement and de Vries, *op. cit.* vol. III pp. 379–427 for the amended Articles of Agreement (30 April 1976) which entered into force on 1 April 1978.

46. For the text of the resolution establishing the Interim Committee see de Vries, *op. cit.* vol. III pp. 213–215.

47. P. Korner, G. Mass, S. Thomas & R. Tetzlaff, *The IMF and the Debt Crisis* (London: Zed Books 1986) p. 46.

48. Tony Killick, 'An Introduction to the IMF' in Tony Killick (ed.), *The Quest for Economic Stabilisation* (London: Heinemann 1984) pp. 130–131.

49. See Tyrone Ferguson, *The Third World and Decision Making in the International Monetary Fund* (London: Pinter 1988) pp. 65–66.

50. See Joseph Gold, *Voting and Decisions in the International Monetary Fund* (Washington DC: International Monetary Fund 1972) pp. 195–201.

51. Tew, *op.cit.* pp. 128–129.

52. See Robert D. Putnam & Nicholas Bayne, *Hanging Together: Cooperation and Conflict in the 7 Power Summits* (London: Sage 1987) for a history of the G7.

53. See Second Ministerial Meeting of the G77, 'The Declaration and Principles of the Action Programme of Lima' in Karl P. Sauvant (ed.), *The*

Collected Documents of the Group of 77 vol. II (New York: Oceana Publications 1981) p. 199–232.

54. Third Ministerial Meeting of the G77, 'Report of the Chairperson of the G24' in Sauvant (ed.), *op. cit.* vol. V. pp. 285–289.
55. Kendall W. Stiles, *Negotiating Debt: The IMF Lending Process* (Boulder: Westview Press 1991) pp. 4–6 outlines a functionalist model of IMF decision-making which views the Fund as a technocratic, non-political organisation.
56. Kahler, 'US and the IMF' *op. cit.* p. 92.
57. Joseph Gold, *Conditionality* (Washington, DC: International Monetary Fund Pamphlet Series No. 31 1979) p. 59.
58. Quoted in Bird, *op. cit.* fn. 4 p. 304.
59. See Wilfred L. David, *The IMF Policy Paradigm: The Macroeconomics of Stabilization, Structural Adjustment, and Economic Development* (New York: Praeger 1985) pp. 7–11.
60. See Payer, *op. cit.*
61. M. Honeywell, 'The World Debt Crisis' in M. Honeywell (ed.), *The Poverty Brokers: The IMF and Latin America* (London: Latin American Bureau 1983) p. 3.
62. Thomas J. Biersteker, 'Reducing the Role of the State in the Economy: A Conceptual Exploration of IMF and World Bank Prescriptions', *International Studies Quarterly* (December 1990) p. 488.
63. Thomas Scheetz, *Peru and the International Monetary Fund* (Pittsburgh: Pittsburgh University Press 1986) p. 151.
64. Ferguson, *op. cit.* p. 107.
65. *Ibid.* p. 84.
66. Group of Ten Communique 2 October 1963; reprinted in Robert Solomon, *The International Monetary System 1945–1976* (New York: Harper & Row 1977) p. 65.
67. See Stephen D. Cohen, *International Monetary Reform 1964–69. The Political Dimension* (New York: Praeger 1970) for an account of the birth of the SDR.
68. Ferguson, *op. cit.* p. 87.
69. Williamson *op. cit.* p. 61.
70. *Ibid.* p. 61.
71. Ferguson, *op. cit.* p. 90.
72. *Ibid.* p. 99.
73. *Ibid.* p. 125.
74. See William R. Cline, *International Monetary Reform and the Developing Countries* (Washington, DC: The Brookings Institution 1976). p. 49; Williamson, *op. cit.* pp. 143–147; Solomon, *op. cit.* p. 265.
75. On the history of the link concept see Y. S. Park, 'The Link between Special Drawing Rights and Development Finance' *Princeton Essays in International Finance No. 100* (Princeton University 1973); John Williamson, 'International Liquidity: A Survey', *Economic Journal* (September 1973) pp. 685–746; and Cline, *op. cit.* pp. 50–57.
76. For an extended discussion of these arguments see H. G. Johnson, 'The Link that Chains', *Foreign Policy* (Fall 1972) pp. 113–120; Graham Bird, *International Financial Policy and Economic Development* (London: Macmillan 1987) ch. 10; John Williamson, 'SDRs: The Link' in Jagdish N.

Bhagwati (ed.), *The New International Economic Order* (Cambridge, Mass: MIT Press 1977) pp. 81–100; and Cline, *op. cit.* pp. 212–229.

77. Ferguson, *op. cit.* p.133.

78. Williamson, 'Failure' *op. cit.* p. 147.

79. The last loan to a developed country was made in 1978.

80. See 'Statement by Michel Camdessus, Managing-Director', *Summary Proceedings of the Annual Meeting of the Board of Governors of the International Monetary Fund 1989* (Washington, DC 1989) p. 19.

81. Saudi Arabia began recycling a portion of its petrodollar surplus in 1974 through the Fund. Saudi Arabia was prepared to lend to the Fund largely for political reasons. It increased its status and prestige among the developing countries, defused the anger of non-oil exporting countries towards OPEC and gained Saudi Arabia more influence in the Fund, through an increase in quota and a guaranteed seat on the Executive Board. Japan and the Fund agreed in December 1986 on an arrangement whereby Japan made SDR 3 billion available to finance adjustment programmes. Borrowing on these funds was fully committed by the end of March 1991. Sensitive to criticisms about its balance of payments surplus this loan represented a move to deflect criticism.

82. Named after the US Secretaries of State, the Brady and Baker Plans sought to increase the flow of resources to developing countries during the debt crisis.

83. John Williamson, *The Lending Policies of the International Monetary Fund* (Washington DC: Institute for International Economics August 1982) pp. 12–14.

84. For analysis of the evolution of the CFF see Stephany Griffith-Jones, 'Compensatory Financing Facility: A Review of its Operation and Proposals for Improvement' in Sidney Dell (ed.), *The International Monetary System and its Reform. Part II* (Amsterdam: North-Holland 1987) pp. 691–712; and Louis M. Goreaux, *Compensatory Financing Facility* (Washington DC: International Monetary Fund Pamphlet Series No. 34 1980).

85. See I. S. Gulati, 'IMF Conditionality and the Low-Income Countries', *Economic Bulletin for Asia and the Pacific* (June 1982) pp. 5–7.

86. See Sidney Dell, 'On Being Grandmotherly: the Evolution of IMF Conditionality', *Princeton Essays in International Finance No. 144* (Princeton University 1981). On the legal aspects see Gold, 'Conditionality' *op. cit.*

87. See Payer, *op. cit.;* Honeywell, *op. cit.;* and Korner *et. al.*, *op. cit.* for examples of this approach.

88. The number of negotiations in which this factor surfaces are too many to note. But see Michael Manley, *Jamaica: Struggle in the Periphery* (London: Third World Media Ltd. n.d.) pp. 183–192 for an account of domestic opposition to IMF intrusion and its impact on the government's negotiating stance.

89. See Harold Lever & Christopher Huhne, *Debt and Danger: The World Financial Crisis* (London: Penguin 1987) pp. 51–63.

90. Frances Stewart, 'Alternative Conditionality' *Development: Seeds of Change* 1984:1 pp. 64–75 argues that Third World Countries should present alternative conditionality, i.e. a policy package in keeping with their own 'objectives, philosophies and circumstances' to the Fund.

91. See, for example, the case studies in Kjell J. Havnevik (ed.), *The IMF and*

the World Bank in Africa (Uppsala: Scandinavian Institute of African Studies 1987); and those in Bade Onimode (ed.), *The IMF, The World Bank and The African Debt vol. 2 The Social and Political Impact* (London: Zed Books 1989).

92. See the case studies in Havnevik (ed.), *op. cit.;* Onimode (ed.), *op.cit.*
93. See Scheetz, *op. cit.* pp. 9–19 for a formal presentation of the IMF's model. See also, E. Walter Robichek, 'The IMF's Conditionality Re-examined' in Joaquin Muns (ed.), *Adjustment, Conditionality and International Financing* (Washington: DC: IMF 1984) pp. 67–75. Robichek, an IMF staff member argues in favour of the monetary approach.
94. Williamson, *Lending Policies op. cit.* p. 12.
95. See Alejandro Foxley, 'Stabilization Policies and Their Effects on Employment and Income Distribution: A Latin American perspective' in William R. Cline & Sidney Weintraub (eds), *Economic Stabilization in Developing Countries* (Washington DC: The Brookings Institution 1981) p. 197; and Mohammed, *op. cit.* p. 74.
96. Manuel Pastor Jr, *The International Monetary Fund and Latin America* (Boulder & London: Westview 1987) p. 20.
97. Bird, *International Financial op. cit.* pp. 64–69.
98. John Loxley, 'Alternative Approaches to Stabilization in Africa' in Gerald K. Helleiner (ed.), *Africa and the International Monetary Fund* (Washington DC: IMF 1986) p. 121.
99. Pastor, *op. cit.* p. 21.
100. E. Hutchful *The IMF and Ghana: The Confidential Record* (London: Zed Books 1987) p. 13.
101. Loxley, *op. cit.* p. 121.
102. Samba Mawakani, 'Fund Conditionality and the Socio-economic Situation in Africa' in Helleiner (ed.), *op.cit.* p. 110.
103. See Daniel M. Schydlowsky, 'Alternative Approaches to Short-term Economic Management in Developing Countries' in Tony Killick (ed.), *Adjustment and Financing in the Developing World: the Role of the IMF* (Washington DC: IMF 1981) pp. 105–135; and Sidney Dell, 'Stabilization: the Political Economy of Overkill' *World Development* (August 1982) pp. 597–612.
104. E. I. M. Mtei, 'Comments' pp. 96–99 and David Phiri 'Comments' pp. 93–96 in Helleiner (ed.), *op. cit.*
105. Lance Taylor, 'IS/LM in the Tropics: Diagrammatics of the New Structuralist Macro Critique' in Cline & Weintraub (eds.), *op. cit.* pp. 465–502.
106. Alberto Giovannini, 'The Interest Elasticity of Savings in Developing Countries: The Evidence' *World Development* (July 1983) pp. 601–607.
107. See Loxley, *op. cit.* pp. 124–125. See Joan Nelson, 'Poverty, Equity and the Politics of Adjustment' in Haggard & Kaufman (eds), *op. cit.* pp. 221–270 for a detailed consideration of this issue.
108. See Manuel Pastor Jr, 'The Effects of IMF Programs in the Third World: Debate and Evidence From Latin America' *World Development* (February 1987) pp. 254, 258; Yusuf Bangura & Bjorn Beckman, 'African Workers and Structural Adjustment: The Nigerian Case' in Dharam Ghai (ed.), *The IMF and the South: The Social Impact of Crisis and Adjustment* (London: Zed Books 1991) pp. 156–158.
109. This is a recurrent theme in the case studies in Bade Onimode (ed.), *The*

IMF, The World Bank and The African Debt vol. 1 The Economic Impact (London: Zed Books 1989).

110. See, for example, Dharam Ghai & Cynthia Hewitt de Alacantara, 'The Crisis of the 1980s in Africa, Latin America and the Caribbean: An Overview' in Ghai (ed.), *op. cit* p. 38; and Walden Bello & David Kinley, 'The IMF', *Multinational Monitor* (July 1983) p. 12.

111. See Manuel Guitián, 'Economic Management and International Monetary Fund Conditionality' in Killick, *Adjustment op. cit.* pp. 73–104; Alassane D. Ouattara, 'Design, Implementation and Adequacy of Fund Programmes in Africa' in Helleiner (ed.), *op. cit.* pp. 68–92.

112. Robichek, *op. cit.* p. 73 argues that it is the eye of the beholder whether any policy is supply-oriented or demand-management.

113. Ouattara, *op. cit.* p. 91.

114. See Morris Goldstein, *The Global Effects of Fund-Supported Adjustment Programs* (Washington DC: International Monetary Fund Occasional Paper No. 42 1986) pp. 45–46; and Morris Goldstein, 'Global effects of Fund-supported programs', *Finance and Development* (March 1986) pp. 24–27.

115. Mohsin S. Khan & Malcolm D. Knight, *Fund-Supported Adjustment Programs and Economic Growth* (Washington DC: International Monetary Fund Occasional Paper No. 41, 1985) p. 24; and Mohsin S. Khan & Malcolm D. Knight, 'Do Fund-supported adjustment programs retard growth? *Finance and Development* (March 1986) pp. 30–32.

116. 'Ten Misconceptions about the IMF' (Washington DC: International Monetary Fund n.d.) pp. 4–5.

117. *Ibid.* p. 7.

118. Charles A. Sisson, 'Fund-supported programs and income distribution in LDCs', *Finance and Development* (March 1986) p. 36.

119. The Fiscal Affairs Department of the International Monetary Fund, *Fund-Supported Programs, Fiscal Policy and Income Distribution* (Washington DC: IMF Occasional Paper No. 46 1986). p. 37.

120. See *Annual Report of the Executive Directors for the Fiscal Year ended April 30 1992* (Washington DC 1992) p. 49 where it is reported that a major study of 21 countries undertaking 44 programmes demonstrated a strong link between successfully implementing fiscal and credit policies and achieving balance of payments, growth and inflation objectives.

121. Bijan Aghevli & Jorge Màrquez-Ruarte, *A Case of Successful Adjustment: Korea's Experience During 1980–84* (Washington DC: International Monetary Fund Occasional Paper No. 39 1985); and Bijan Aghevli & Jorge Màrquez-Ruarte, 'A Case of Successful Adjustment in a Developing Country: Korea's Experience During 1980–84' in Sir Frank Holmes (ed.), *Economic Adjustment: Policies and Problems* (Washington DC: IMF 1987). pp. 91–113.

122. A. Shakour Shalan, 'Adjustment Challenges and Strategies Facing Arab Countries in Light of Recent Experience and New Initiatives' in El-Naggar (ed.), *op. cit.* pp. 24–43.

123. John Odling-Smee, 'Adjustment with Financial Assistance from the Fund', *Finance and Development* (December 1982) p. 30.

124. Mohsin Khan, 'Evaluating the Effects of IMF-Supported Adjustment Programmes: A Survey' in Kate Phylaktis & Mahmood Pradhan (eds),

International Finance and the Less Developed Countries (London: Macmillan 1990) pp. 17–21.

125. See Guitián in Killick (ed.) *Adjustment op. cit.* pp. 99–101 for a broadly similar treatment. He suggests an additional approach – the conceptual/judgemental. This measures actual programme performance and tests it against what would have happened in the absence of a Fund programme.

126. See Khan, *op. cit.* pp. 18–24 for an extended critique of the models.

127. See Pastor, *The International Monetary Fund op. cit.* passim; and Scheetz, *op. cit.* passim for extended critiques.

128. See 'Statement by Michel Camdessus, Managing-Director', *Summary Proceedings of the Annual Meeting of the Board of Governors of the International Monetary Fund 1989* (Washington DC: 1989) p. 19.

129. International Monetary Fund, *Annual Report 1992* (IMF: Washington DC: 1992) p. 49.

130. See Joan M. Nelson, 'The Political Economy of Stabilization: Commitment, Capacity, and Public Response', *World Development* (October 1984) for a brief account of the politics of stabilisation.

131. See, for example, Stiles, *op. cit.* pp. 197–198.

132. See, for example, Kahler in Haggard & Kaufman (eds), *op. cit.* pp. 89–136.

133. Scott Sidell, *The IMF and Third World Political Instability* (London: Macmillan 1988).

5

The World Bank and the Third World

The International Bank for Reconstruction and Development (IBRD), commonly known as the World Bank, is the leading international agency currently financing economic development. The World Bank Group comprises four agencies. The IBRD, established at Bretton Woods, makes loans linked to commercial rates of interest largely to middle-income developing countries. The International Development Association (IDA), created in 1960, is the soft loan affiliate of the IBRD and provides loans to the poorest developing countries on very favourable terms. The International Finance Corporation (IFC) was established in 1956 to assist economic development in poor countries through investing in private projects, supporting the growth of private capital markets and encouraging flows of domestic and foreign capital. The Multilateral Investment Guarantee Agency (MIGA), established in 1988, aims to encourage the flow of direct investment to developing countries through the lessening of non-commercial investment barriers.

Like its twin institution, the IMF, the World Bank is dogged by controversy and is the subject of bitter criticism. Until recently, however, criticism of the Bank was more muted, not because foreign aid is a non-controversial subject, but mainly because the Bank had successfully established a profile as a constantly adaptable institution. Critics of Bank policy existed, of course, but the Bank's high profile as the world's foremost development agency tended to shield it somewhat from its most outspoken critics. Two sets of events in the past decade have eroded the aura surrounding the institution. First, the shift to policy-based lending in the 1980s combined with increased collaboration with the IMF in the wake of the debt crisis and global recession focused greater attention on the Bank. Secondly, the eruption of environmental issues onto the global agenda brought increasing concern about the ecological impact of Bank policies.

In examining the relationship between the World Bank and the Third World this chapter will concentrate on the activities of the IBRD and the IDA. It will discuss the role of the Bank in the foreign aid regime[1] and the response of the Bank to the expressed demands of Third World countries. The chapter will begin with a discussion of the origins of the World Bank. This will be followed by an analysis of the World Bank as an international organisation. The next section will chart the evolution of the World Bank and in so doing will investigate the financial resources provided by the Bank in the context of the development needs of the Third World. The chapter will then explore two key issues relating to the World Bank's role in promoting economic development. First, it will discuss the controversy surrounding the Bank's structural adjustment programmes and secondly, it will examine the Bank's environmental policy.

The impact of the World Bank on world economic welfare and particularly the welfare of the poorer members of international society is a disputed issue. Critics of the Bank come from both the left and right of the political spectrum. The conservative critique of the Bank accuses it of promoting state planning, deterring private enterprise and fostering income redistribution in favour of the poor.[2] This critique is part of a wider critique of foreign aid. In this perspective economic development is best promoted through the unfettered operation of market forces. Official government-to-government transfers inhibit economic development by replacing the market with state planning which retards economic growth.[3]

Radical critics of the Bank, on the contrary argue that the Bank, in promoting private enterprise in the developing world suppresses revolutionary transformation and maintains the development of underdevelopment. Cheryl Payer, a leading critic of multilateral development organisations, argues that the Bank has 'deliberately and consciously used its financial power to promote the interests of private, international capital and its expansion to every corner of the "underdeveloped" world'.[4] These activities have transformed the Bank into

> perhaps the most important instrument of the developed capitalist countries for prying state control of its Third World member countries out of the hands of nationalists and socialists who would regulate international capital's inroads, and turning that power to the service of international capital.[5]

The 'aid as imperialism' argument first formulated in the context of

World Bank operations by Teresa Hayter[6] is rebutted by liberal critics of the Bank. Edward Mason and Robert Asher, in their magisterial and monumental history of the Bank's first 25 years, came to the conclusion that 'the Bank has had a significant and on the whole beneficial impact on the areas in which it has concentrated its lending.'[7] And Robert Ayres, surveying the McNamara years, argues that the Bank 'functions in an effective manner in the face of severe national and international constraints under which it must operate'.[8]

This chapter examines whether the World Bank has been effective in promoting economic development and to what extent any failures are attributable to the organisation of the Bank and its methods and objectives, or whether failure lies largely in constraints outside the control of the Bank.

The origins of the World Bank

Like the IMF, the World Bank was created at Bretton Woods in July 1944, the culmination of wartime discussions between the United States and the United Kingdom on the shape of the post-World War II international economic order. The Bank that emerged was essentially an American creation.[9] The IMF was established to provide funds for short-term balance of payments relief and the role of the International Bank for Reconstruction and Development was the provision of longer-term finance for the development of productive resources. The initial priority of the IBRD, which opened for business on 25 June 1946, was reconstruction.

The Bank that emerged from the Bretton Woods conference was mainly conceived in terms of the economic problems of the immediate post-war period. It was the tasks of reconstruction rather than the challenge of development which ranked uppermost in the minds of its major proponents. The developing countries attending the conference were concerned that if too high a priority was placed on reconstruction limited resources would be available for development. The Latin American countries therefore proposed that in the Articles of Agreement equal emphasis should be given to reconstruction and development. The United States conceded the inclusion of development functions in the Articles of Agreement so that Latin American countries would agree to join the IMF, access to the Bank's lending being tied to membership of the Fund.[10] It was decided that, 'The resources and facilities of the Bank shall be used exclusively for the benefit of members with equitable consideration to projects for development and projects for reconstruction alike.'[11] Nevertheless, the provision of capital for reconstruction of the war-damaged economies dominated the concerns of the organisation. It was envisaged that the Bank would fulfil its role in reconstruction largely by channelling US private investment to Europe through its guarantee of these loans. In the absence of private investment on reasonable terms the Bank was mandated to provide finance for investment purposes out of its own financial resources.

The founders of the Bank, i.e. the United States, the United Kingdom and other delegations at Bretton Woods were strongly influenced by the experience of international lending in the 1920s and 1930s. During the interwar period capital raised through the sale of securities in foreign capital markets had frequently been put to unproductive purposes and had made little or no contribution to the productive capacity of the borrowers. Many loans had been made at high interest rates without reference to the ability of borrowers to service new or even existing foreign debt.[12] In the light of these considerations certain safeguards were built into Bank lending. First, loans are made only for productive purposes and except in special circumstances only for specific projects. Secondly, the Bank only lends to governments or enterprises guaranteed by a member government, central bank or comparable agency. Thirdly, the Bank's loans are not tied, i.e. no conditions are attached to where they can be spent. Fourthly, the Bank is a lender of the last resort. The Bank only lends if it is satisfied that the borrower is unable to obtain finance from private sources under reasonable conditions.

The World Bank: organisational structure and political process

This section will outline the relationship between the four different agencies comprising the World Bank group. It will concentrate on the IBRD. Issues relating to decision-making and the structure of influence will be explored in the context of the IBRD.

The IBRD

Membership and financial resources

The IBRD established at Bretton Woods stands at the centre of the World Bank Group. Its membership has grown from 38 countries in 1946 to 160 in 1992. Membership of the IBRD is a prerequisite for membership of the IDA and IFC. It is owned by its shareholders, i.e. the 160 member countries, and makes loans on near-commercial terms to developing countries at more advanced stages of economic and social growth. Its loans have a grace period of 5 years and are repayable over 15–20 years. Unique among international organisations the IBRD finances most of its operations from its own borrowings in the world capital markets. The Bank's capital structure is made up of authorised capital, callable capital and its own borrowings. Each member pays in one-tenth of their share capital creating a common liquidity pool of paid-in capital which finances the operations of the IBRD. The remaining 90 per cent of share capital is held by governments as callable capital and is subject to call if and when required to meet obligations of the IBRD arising out of borrowings or guarantees. This guarantee fund or reinsurance capital cannot be used for administrative purposes, it has never been called upon and is unlikely ever to be used. The capital structure is designed to provide the IBRD with substantial resources of its own and a large guarantee fund enabling it to mobilise private capital. The reserve of callable capital underwriting Bank borrowing gives Bank bonds first class status (a Triple A rating in the United States) in the countries where it borrows. Initially borrowing was restricted to the United States but now the Bank borrows in European and Japanese markets in addition to the US.

Lending policy

The lending policy of the Bank is governed by the Articles of Agreement which placed a ceiling on lending. The Bank is forbidden to lend over and above its subscribed capital, plus surplus and retained earnings. The Bank has a very conservative ratio of loans to capital and reserves of 1:1, and a similar high liquidity level with a debt equity ratio of 1:24 compared with a 20:1 ratio for commercial banks. The Bank was founded on sound financial principles and one reason for its high standing in the international financial community is the continuation of this careful and prudent approach. Thus the Bank is constrained not by its capacity to borrow but by the size of its subscribed capital and the resrticted ratio of loans to capital. Bank loans are made below the prevailing commercial rates of interest.

Initially, apart from exceptional circumstances, the Bank lent almost entirely for specific projects but from the onset of the 1980s it has been heavily engaged in programme lending. Bank lending is shaped by a number of factors and considerations pertaining to the importance of the project and the creditworthiness of the borrower. It is vital that the project has a high priority in the development programme of the borrower and can show a financial and economic return. At the outset, the identification of projects was the sole responsibility of governments, but early in its history this became a collaborative venture between the Bank and the borrower.[13] Loans are made available only when other sources of finance on reasonable terms are not available. The role of the Bank is to assist in restoring and accelerating the time when the borrower will be able to raise funds in the international capital market. But as van de Laar points out, the application of the market-eligibility test leaves room for judgement particularly in respect of determining the 'sufficient volume to meet a country's needs'.[14] Moreover, as a lender of the last resort, the leverage the Bank can exert is thus greater than if the Bank was competing to finance projects with other agencies.

The Bank lends only to countries it regards as creditworthy. Assessment of creditworthiness is not based on any clearly defined criteria and is a mixture of economic analysis of the borrower's ability to repay and a psychological estimation of the borrower's willingness to repay debts. This makes it an inherently political process. The economic criteria used to determine a borrower's credit status include debt service ratio, the total share of medium-term and long-term debt held by the Bank, increases in annual per capita GNP, savings and investment rates, balance of payments position and the openness of the economy. Assessment of a country's willingness to repay is based on a subjective evaluation of the past repayment record and current resolution of a borrower to give priority to the interests of foreign creditors. The Bank takes the 'willingness to repay' criterion further and refuses to lend to countries in dispute with foreign private investors or official foreign governmental agencies. Disputes can arise from the nationalisation of the assets of a foreign corporation without adequate and effective compensation, failure to honour agreements, e.g. over taxation with foreign private investors or default on debt repayments without agreement on refinancing. The Bank is not concerned with disputes involving domestic creditors. Bank lending is largely for the financing of the foreign exchange costs of projects and Bank projects are subject to international competitive bidding. The Bank projects the image of an apolitical organisation and its loans are supposedly lent on solely economic criteria without political considerations. However, a number of researchers, not all from the radical left, have documented many instances when political pressure from donor countries forced the Bank either into providing or suspending a loan.[15]

Decision-making

The highest decision-making organ in the IBRD is the Board of Governors. All members are represented on the Board of Governors which meets annually. Apart from certain important functions such as amending the Articles of Agreement or admitting new members the Board has delegated its powers to the Executive Board. The Executive Board consists of 22 appointed and elected executive directors. The five largest shareholders appoint one director each and the others are elected every two years. Elected executive directors represent groupings of countries with some directors representing a constituency comprising both developed and developing states. The Executive Board operates on the basis of a weighted voting system with votes based on subscriptions to the IBRD. As at 30 June 1992 the five largest shareholders and their voting shares were the United States (17.59), Japan (8.01), Germany (6.19), France (5.93) and the United Kingdom (5.93). The smallest constituency consisting of 22 African states totalled 1.86 per cent of voting shares. Decisions are based on simple majority and this gives the major donor states, especially the United States, significant influence over Bank decisions. Recourse to formal voting, however, is rare, with most decisions based on consensus. But consensus should not be taken to imply either the absence of conflict or power in the decisional process. Influence is exercised in a more subtle fashion with the largest shareholder able to send signals of disapproval and so prevent issues from reaching the Executive Board. In other words, the US has frequently exercised non-decisional power[16] in agenda setting. Further, US influence arises from the unwritten understanding that the president of the Bank is a US citizen chosen by the President of the United States. To date all eight Bank presidents have been US citizens and with three exceptions they have been selected from the banking community.

The president of the Bank is the chairman of the Executive Board and exercises his/her vote only in the event of a tied vote. S/he is chief of the operating staff of the Bank and subject to the direction of the executive directors on questions of policy. S/he is responsible for the conduct of the ordinary business of the Bank, the organisation of the staff and the appointment and dismissal of officers and employees. The Bank's management enjoys a relatively greater degree of autonomy than other international organisations. The autonomy of the management arises from a combination of the Bank's independent financial base, the impressive technical and intellectual reputation of its staff, its pre-eminent position among multilateral lending agencies and the activities of successive presidents to develop and preserve organisational autonomy. John J. McCloy, the second president of the Bank (1947–49), insisted as a condition of his acceptance of the executive head's role that the influence of the executive directors in the operations of the Bank should be curbed.[17]

In common with most international organisations an informal group system exists in the Bank. Informal groups of executive directors meet continuously to exchange positions and coordinate positions. The G24 convened by the G77 in the context of the IMF also meets in relation to the World Bank. The G24 meets in advance of the Joint Ministerial Committee of the Board of Governors of the IMF and World Bank (the Development Committee) and is a counter to the coordination of the AICs.

From this review of the organisational characteristics of the Bank it is possible to discern three constraints on the World Bank Group. First, the Bank is a bank and is constrained by its reliance on private capital markets. It would be unable to retain its high credit rating if it did not pursue policies which the financial community thought were prudent. There is thus an inherent conservative bias to Bank lending. Secondly, Western countries, especially the United States, maintain considerable influence over Bank policy through the weighted voting system. This influence is further enhanced by the Bank's dependence on Western financial institutions. A third constraint arises from the bureaucracy. William Ascher argues that the Bank is slow to change. He argues that although many changes may be proposed by the highest echelons in the organisation, staff at lower levels can obstruct innovations. Often policy is made by staff in the field and they can resist new criteria, such as social pricing as less rigorous, reject or minimise new concerns such as ecology or the role of women, and question their bargaining role.[18] Various presidents have tried to tackle this problem through a reorganisation of the bureaucracy. The current Bank president, Lewis Preston, initiated a major administrative overhaul soon after taking up office.[19]

The IDA, IFC and MIGA

The IDA established in 1960 as the soft-loan affiliate of the IBRD has its own constitution but shares the same offices and staff as the IBRD. In organisational terms the IDA is, in the words of Mason and Asher, an 'elaborate fiction'.[20] Too much time will not, therefore, be spent in detailing the organisation and operations of the IDA. Nevertheless, certain features of the organisation are worthy of mention.

Membership is open to all members of the IBRD, but some IBRD members have chosen not to join the IDA. In 1992, the IDA with 142 members had 18 fewer than the IBRD. The IDA is essentially an instrument for resource transfer. The criteria for project selection, scrutiny of projects, implementation and financial and economic rates of return are identical to the IBRD but IDA credits are reserved for developing countries not capable of borrowing from the IBRD. Some countries, the so-called 'blend countries' are eligible for both IDA credits and IBRD loans. Eligibility for IDA loans – called credits – is based on per capita national income. In 1992 IDA credits were restricted to countries with an annual per capita GNP of $610 (in 1990 dollars) or less. IDA loans are interest-free but carry an annual service charge of 0.75 per cent. The maturity on an IDA credit is 35 to 40 years with a grace period of 10 years. Unlike the IBRD, the IDA is almost wholly dependent on member countries for its finances. The primary source of funding comes directly from grants made by its members in three-yearly replenishments. Further, income accrues from transfers of IBRD income from its retained profits, repayment of principal and special supplementary contributions from members. The dependence of the IDA on the industrialised countries for the periodic replenishment of its resources makes it vulnerable to the changing development assistance priorities of these countries and ensures the existence of a permanent negotiating process between the Bank and donor governments.

The organisational structure of the IDA replicates that of the IBRD but the percentage share of the votes held by the major states varies slightly from the distribution in the IBRD. On 30 June 1992 the five largest individual shareholders were the United States (16.71), Japan (9.82), Germany (6.91), the United Kingdom (5.54) and France (3.95).

The IFC, founded in 1956, is legally a separate entity from the Bank although membership in the IFC is not open to non-members of the IBRD. Membership of the IFC stood at 146 in 1992. The IFC has its own legal and operating staff but draws on the Bank for administrative and other services. The IFC functions like an investment bank. It participates directly in equity as well as loan investments. It participates only in private ventures and its loans are not dependent on government guarantees.

Created in 1988, the MIGA offers investment insurance to mitigate political risk through its guarantee programme and provides promotional and advisory services to assist member countries in their efforts to attract or retain direct foreign investment. MIGA is a legally distinct entity from the Bank or the IFC and has its own Executive Board.[21]

Organisational ideology

Changing Bank policies and approaches to the problem of economic development would appear to suggest that the search for a dominant ideology which conditions Bank thinking is a fruitless task. The contention of this section is that, despite the appearance of difference, the strategies of trickle-down, basic needs and poverty-oriented growth share certain similarities. The dominant ideology of the Bank is inscribed in its Articles of Agreement, articulated by successive presidents, disseminated in its economic and research output and informs its project and programme lending. This ideology, similar to that of the IMF, can best be termed economic neo-liberalism.[22] It is, of course, difficult to summarise an extensive body of writing but it is hoped that the assumptions and policy preferences of neo-liberalism presented here is not a caricature.

Neo-liberals believe in the efficacy of the market in providing the most efficient solutions to the problems arising from economic scarcity. Neo-liberal economic theory insists that the principal route to economic growth is through the market mechanism. Policies favoured by its adherents therefore tend to stress the relaxation of government controls on the economy as the best means of fostering efficiency and contributing to growth. A mixture of policies aimed at liberalising the domestic economy and increasing contact with the external environment are the standard prescriptions. These policies include curbing price and import controls, the promotion of a sound climate for foreign and domestic investment, economic stability and the stimulation of exports.

Another central tenet of neo-liberal theory is the desirability of economic growth. There is a belief that the pursuit of growth can be achieved through the application of certain universally valid principles. Underdevelopment, according to this approach results from the absence of savings and investment, the poor mobilisation of domestic resources and the failure to be more fully integrated into the world economy. The possibilities of rapid growth are constrained by resource gaps and crucial scarcities including capital, savings and foreign exchange flows.

In this view the best method of alleviating poverty or achieving income redistribution is through economic growth. As ex-Bank President Tom Clausen put it,

> The real choice is not between poverty alleviation and adjustment programs; more accurately the choice is between inappropriate programs and policies which aggravate poverty, and effective adjustment programs which will sustain economic growth over the medium term and thereby reduce poverty.[23]

Underpinning the faith in the market and the pursuit of growth as a central objective is a belief in the essentially technocratic nature of economics. Economics is conceived as a value-free science which can provide universal solutions to economic difficulties. An early Bank document encapsulated this belief when it stated, 'For to date, none of man's efforts to repeal the law of supply and demand have been successful.'[24] Ayres in his research discovered that World Bank staff rejected the notion that such ideas are in any sense ideological.[25]

To highlight the capitalist ideology of the Bank is not to engage in explicit or implicit criticism of the institution. The World Bank has never pretended to be anything other than a capitalist enterprise with a commitment to free trade, the optimisation of investment flows and the support of free enterprise. The criticisms of the early Reagan adminis-tration and other right-wing elements in the United States in the late 1970s and early 1980s were always surprising since the basic ideology of the Bank was never threatened by McNamara's reforms. But this dispute over the Bank's role, nevertheless, alerts us to the fact that the neo-liberal paradigm is a broad one and within it different perspectives are possible.

The evolution of the World Bank

From its inception until the present, the growth and development of Bank activities can be analysed in four periods. This periodisation is based on the dominant approach to development and, the focus of the Bank's lending. In the first period (1946–49) the Bank's main interest was in reconstruction. The second phase (1949–73) is coterminous with the financial and organisational expansion of the institution from the IBRD to the World Bank Group. In this period the Bank concentrated on promoting industrialisation. The third phase (1973–79) saw an expansion in Bank lending and a new emphasis on the rural sector. The fourth phase (1980–) is dominated by adjustment lending and a greater role for programme lending. The McNamara years are normally viewed as a specific chapter in the Bank's history reflecting both his dominant personality and imprint on the institution and the movement away from the dominant economic strategy of the previous era. But in the first five years of McNamara's presidency the Bank's orientation was similar to that under the previous president, George Woods, and the move to adjustment lending was made before he stepped down from office.

The early years: 1946–49

No loans were disbursed in 1946, although loan applications were made by seven countries. Eugene Meyer the first president spent the period trying to gain the confidence of the financial community. After repeated conflicts with the US Executive Director Meyer resigned in December 1946. The new president, John J. McCloy, presided over the first four loans totalling $497 million, extended to Denmark, France, Luxembourg and the Netherlands in 1947. These were programme loans and it was not until the following year that the Bank made its first project loan. This loan, to Chile, signalled the major form Bank lending took over the next three decades. By 1947 it was apparent that the Bank's resources were inadequate to cope with the demands of West European reconstruction. With the launch of the Marshall Plan the Bank's role in financing reconstruction was effectively over. It continued to supply financial resources to European countries, particularly to southern Europe, but by 1953 of a total disbursement of $1.8 million, roughly $1 million was for development projects located outside Europe.[26] The reorientation of the Bank's activities towards its poorer clients began at an early stage in its history. When McCloy resigned the leadership in May 1949, his statement that 'the reconstruction phase of the Bank's activity is largely over', was correct but his observation that 'the development phase . . . is under way',[27] was somewhat premature. It was under the presidency of Eugene Black (1949–62) that the Bank made the decisive shift to financing economic development.

Financing economic development: trickle-down, industrialisation and infrastructure 1947–73

This second phase saw the Bank expand its lending and develop a specific approach to economic development. Under Eugene Black's leadership the Bank successfully transformed itself from a focus on reconstruction to one on development.[28] Lending policy was heavily influenced by the prevailing theories of development. The dominant development paradigm perceived underdevelopment to be the result of low savings, high population growth and a series of bottlenecks in the local economy. Development and growth were used interchangeably and it was believed that the successful pursuit of economic growth would lead to development. The path to growth was through industrialisation and the development of infrastructure. With this theoretical underpinning Bank lending concentrated on economic growth-related projects. Investment was targeted to sectors such as infrastructure, transportation and energy. A combination of investment in these sectors, financial stability and sound monetary and fiscal policies provided the key to development according to this perspective. The sectoral allocation of Bank lending between 1949–63 gives a clear indication of the Bank's priorities. Until 1963, 73.7 per cent of Bank lending was allocated to infrastructure (communications, power and transportation). And between 1961 and 1965, 76.8 per cent of all Bank lending went to electrical power and transportation.[29]

This period also witnessed an increase in the activities of the World Bank. Loans increased from $137.1 million in 1949 to $1,332.4 million in 1965 but fell back to $953.6 million in 1968.[30] Increased lending was partly a consequence of the organisational expansion of the IBRD. In 1968, for example, IDA credits accounted for $106.6 million of the total mentioned above. To finance the new lending the Bank capital was increased, in 1959 from $10 million to $21 million.

Moreover, the IFC provided extra assistance to the private sector. In its first five years of operation its commitments were about $18 million per year but under the presidency of George Woods (1963–68), IFC commitments grew to over $50 million in 1967–68.[31] Bank aid to the private sector was also expanded through the use of development finance companies (DFCs). Bank lending to DFCs in this period was larger than its IFC commitments. For example, in 1966, lending to DFCs reached $100 million and increased to $159 million in 1968.[32]

Important though it was to channel funds to the private sector through the IFC and DFCs, it was the creation of the IDA in 1960 which best embodies both the expansion of the Bank and its firm commitment to economic development. Writing in 1971, Robert Asher noted that 'The creation of the IDA can be considered as a major milestone in the as-yet-incomplete transformation of the World Bank Group into a development agency.'[33] The creation of the IDA with its favourable lending conditions enabled the World Bank to reach out to countries unable to afford the tougher IBRD loans and to increase lending to previously neglected sectors like agriculture and education.

Other innovations during this period included the establishment of an Economic Development Institute in 1955 to provide short-term training for administrators in developing countries and the development of a Technical Assistance Program to assist borrowing countries in the preparation of loan applications and development plans.[34] The expansion of the IBRD into the World Bank Group arose partly as a result of the pressures exerted by the developing countries in the UN system in the 1950s. Dissatisfaction with the international economic system led to demands for a Special United Nations Fund for Economic Development (SUNFED). The Third World's quest for increased concessional financial aid was answered by the creation of the IFC and IDA. Western nations rejected the SUNFED concept but compromised by expanding the operational role of an organisation they controlled. In the early part of its second phase, the Bank successfully responded to the wave of decolonisation through institutional expansion but retained its largely conservative lending principles.

In 1968 the World Bank acquired a new president who began to make changes that would eventually lead the Bank to abandon the trickle-down theory. Some of the most dramatic changes in Bank direction took place under the leadership of Robert McNamara (1968–81). During the McNamara presidency, the Bank dramatically increased its lending and developed a new focus on poverty alleviation. It also became a more high profile and controversial organisation as it attempted to grapple with rapid change in the international economic system. This period witnessed the end of the stable exchange rate system established at Bretton Woods, the end of the post-war economic boom, the onset of recession and the oil price rises of 1973–74 and 1979. Most developing countries faced a hostile and unpredictable international economic climate for most of the 1970s. The relative stability of the post-war economic system was shattered by rising inflation, a downturn in economic activity in the major industrial centres and increased turbulence in the international economic system. This unfavourable economic climate coincided with the frustrations felt at the poor results of the First Development Decade (1961–70). The launch of the Second Development Decade seemed an act of despair rather than one of hope. The failure of Third World development strategies, increased economic insecurity and the possibility of increased influence due to the possession of commodity power led to a demand, in 1973, for a radical restructuring of the international economic order. The changes of the World Bank in the 1970s have to be placed in the context of failed Third World development, a turbulent international economic environment and the concerted pressure of the G77 and NAM for the creation of a New International Economic Order.

McNamara's first and most concrete change was to increase drastically the number and amount of loans and to shift the regional focus of lending. By 1969 World Bank financing had increased 87 per cent over the previous year and 86 per cent of all Bank spending up to 1981 occurred during McNamara's tenure.[35] The number of projects also rose dramatically from 62 in 1968 to 266 in 1981 with equivalent costs of $953.5 million and $12.4 billion respectively.[36] World Bank lending to Africa rose from $134.6 million to $2,812.4 million, to Asia and the Middle East from $305.5 million to $5,889.6 million and to Latin America from $385.5 million to $3,153.2 million. In percentage terms, Africa's share increased from 16.3 per cent to 23.7 per cent, that of the Asian and Middle East region rose from 37 per cent to 49.6 per cent, and Latin America experienced a relative decline in flows from 46.7 per cent to 26.6 per cent.[37]

A new-style lending policy: basic needs and redistribution with growth 1973–80

McNamara's presidency will, however, probably best be remembered for reorienting the Bank away from the 'trickle-down theory'. As Hurni put it,

> The new style lending projects can be seen as an attempt to practice a 'trickle-up' strategy in order to help the poor without hurting the rich who generally produce more for their national economies and have higher savings and investment rates.[38]

The idea of redistribution with growth became the dominant theoretical approach to development during this period.[39] McNamara's famous policy speech in Nairobi in 1973 is frequently taken as the turning point in the Bank's new approach.[40] But the 1973 speech, although important in generating political commitment and prioritising rural development projects, echoed themes McNamara had been articulating soon after taking office.[41] Ascher has suggested that the political importance of the Nairobi speech arises from a convergence between US policy-makers' rethinking of development and the World Bank's new approach.[42]

McNamara committed the Bank to poverty-oriented projects because in his view, previous development efforts had failed to reach the absolute poor, defined as the bottom 40 per cent in developing countries. As noted in the *Redistribution with Growth* report, 'although the average per capita income of the Third World has increased by 50 per cent since 1960, this growth has been very unequally distributed among countries, regions within countries, and socio-economic groups.'[43] The aim of the new approach was to raise income levels in developing countries without increasing income inequality or to raise income levels to a level which would lead to an improvement in income equality as a result.[44] The new strategy consisted of two approaches. A basic-needs approach with a focus on investment in human capital and, to complement this an emphasis on rural development. It should be noted that the Bank was not the sole exponent, or indeed the pioneer, of the basic-needs approach to development. Other international organisations, notably the International Labour Organisation (ILO), contributed significantly to the articulation of the basic-needs paradigm.[45] After 1973, rural development became the main lending priority of the Bank. In fiscal year (FY) 1974, loans for rural development projects totalled $500 million but in FY 1979 this had risen to $2,000 million.[46] The integrated rural development strategy covered agricultural credits, new settlements, rural training, visiting and extension services (in cooperation with contract farmers), small-scale enterprises and off-farm employment creation.

This new emphasis on basic needs and rural development was reflected in the sectoral allocation of Bank spending. Agriculture and rural development represented only 18.1 per cent of Bank lending in 1968 but by 1981 it accounted for 31 per cent of the total. Nevertheless, in the context of overall Bank policy it is instructive to note that although the agriculture and rural development programme received the largest share of Bank lending, taken together the traditional sectors of energy, transportation and telecommunications still accounted for the bulk of Bank lending.

The new policies were integrated with old concerns, i.e. funds were channelled to poverty-oriented new-style lending projects within the existing sectors. In agriculture, funds were shifted from infrastructural projects like irrigation to those concentrating on, for example, land settlement and agricultural credit. Between 1974 and 1978, approximately 75 per cent of the 363 agricultural and rural development approved by the Bank contained a small farmer element or component. And over 50 per cent of Bank lending for agriculture and rural development between 1974–78 went to projects in which more than half the direct benefits were expected to accrue to the rural poor.[47]

Bank lending for education increased with a shift in resources to primary and non-formal education. Between 1979 and 1983, 21.2 per cent and 24.6 per cent of Bank lending for education went to primary education and non-formal education respectively.[48] Bank lending for urban poverty alleviation was developed and more emphasis given to health projects.[49]

Internal reorganisation of the Bank's bureaucracy was also undertaken to implement the reforms. New departments were created – Agriculture and Rural Development (1973), Urban Projects (1975) and Population, Health and Nutrition (1979). Furthermore, in 1976 a Project Preparation Facility was initiated to enable the poorest countries to plan and prepare projects capable of meeting the criteria laid down by the Bank.

During this period the Third World countries were concerned about the weighted voting system in the Bank and attempted to increase their influence in decision-making. Under the NIEO banner, the Bank was among a number of international organisations targeted for reform of their decision-making structures. It is not difficult to see why this campaign ended in failure. It is unlikely that the major shareholders in a financial institution are likely to agree to a decision-making formula which fails to distribute voting shares proportionately to paid-in capital.

The Third World also attempted to increase participation in the Bank through increased representation of their nationals on the Bank's staff. The number of officials from developing countries were increased during this period and the proportion of North Americans and Europeans on the Bank's professional staff fell. In fact, the claim that a citizen of a Third World country is somehow likely to be more sympathetic to the aspirations of Third World peasants and workers or to show a greater appreciation of the needs of development than someone from the North is not very convincing. These officials are just as likely, through their education in the West and socialisation into the organisational ideology, to be divorced and alienated from the rural sector and urban poverty as their Western counterparts.

Adjustment lending and policy-based dialogue: 1980–

It was the McNamara presidency which effectively ended the focus on basic needs. In his final year in office, the Bank initiated a new type of programme lending. The structural adjustment loan (SAL), created in 1980, has been the focus of much current criticism of the Bank. The SAL was initiated in response to the deteriorating balance of payments position of a number of developing countries and reflected the desire of the top management in the Bank to exert greater control over the policy environment of Bank lending. The move to adjustment lending shifted the goal of the Bank's activities away from poverty alleviation to policy dialogue. The aim of SAL is to force developing countries to implement policy reforms devised by the Bank. Adjustment lending supports programmes of specific policy changes and institutional reforms in order to achieve improvements in the balance of payments, maintain economic growth in the face of severe constraints and increase inflows of external assistance. The dominant motif of Bank lending in the 1980s and 1990s is policy dialogue or adjustment lending.

Three challenges have confronted the Bank in this period. The onset of the debt crisis in 1982 brought increased demands on Bank resources from the heavily indebted middle-income developing countries. The Bank was slow to respond to this challenge and developed an active strategy only after James Baker, the US Secretary of State, in October 1985 proposed a central role for the Bank in debt management.

The catastrophic failure of development policies in Sub-Saharan Africa compounded by wars, famines and natural disasters with the attendant human and physical degradation, has drawn the attention of the world community to the dire plight of Africa's peoples. The Bank responded to the worsening situation in Africa with a series of special lending instruments and a commitment to increase the flow of financial resources to the continent. The revolutions in Eastern and Central Europe and the end of the Cold War expanded the Bank's membership and brought new clients in search of foreign aid. In this section we will concentrate on the Bank's response to the first two challenges.

In the post-McNamara era, three presidents – A. W. (Tom) Clausen (1981–86), Barber Conable (1986–91) and Lewis Preston (1991–) – have led the World Bank Group. To some extent changes in Bank policy have reflected the interests, talents and personalities of its executive heads. The focus on adjustment lending and greater emphasis on conditionality has provided elements of continuity, but the three presidents have adopted different styles of management.

Tom Clausen stressed the role to be played by the private sector in development. He expanded the role of the IFC and increased the Bank's role in co-financing. In June 1984, for example, the Board of Governors approved a $650 million capital increase for the IFC, bringing its total capital to $1.3 billion. The attempt to increase the involvement of the private sector in the financing of economic develop-ment was enhanced with the launch in 1983 of the 'B' loan scheme. This is a syndicated loan including both IBRD and commercial bank financing.

Clausen steered the Bank away from a focus on poverty alleviation to a reassertion of the importance of economic growth and free market principles. Increased conditionality became an important part of this process.[50] Conditionality featured in SALs and sectoral adjustment loans (SECALs). In the various special programmes devised for Africa disbursement was conditional on borrowing governments undertaking World Bank reform programmes. Similarly, the Special Action Program (SAP), a quick disbursing programme for new and ongoing projects, operative between 1983–85 was designed for countries following Bank advice.

The mood engendered by McNamara was changed through certain other policy decisions. Under Clausen, increased emphasis was placed on graduation, i.e. the process by which borrowers move from IDA credits to IBRD loans to commercial borrowings. Moreover, Bank loans became subject to floating interest rates from 1982 onwards. It is tempting to see these changes as wholly inspired by the Reagan administration and Tom Clausen as a tool of US foreign policy. To do so, however, would be to ignore the policy conflicts between Clausen and the Reagan White House. The most notable clash, perhaps, occurred over the sixth replenishment of the IDA when the Reagan administration initially refused to agree an increase in IDA funding.

Barber Conable, a former Republican Congressman, continued Clausen's stress on the importance of the private sector in the financing of economic development.[51] The role of the IFC and co-financing continued to be emphasised. The Conable presidency marked a departure from the Clausen period in two significant ways. Conable announced in 1987 that greater primacy was to be given to environmental considerations and instituted a thoroughgoing reform of the bureaucracy so the new policies giving more consideration to the environmental impact of Bank projects could be implemented. And in 1990 poverty alleviation was reintroduced as a major focus of Bank activity.

In his brief tenure of the office Lewis Preston has intensified the concern for the distributional impact of Bank projects and programmes and plans to put poverty alleviation at the centre of the Bank's concerns in the 1990s.[52] As part of the new strategy it is planned that the volume of the Bank's lending to a country should be linked to the efforts made by the borrowing government to reduce poverty.[53] Furthermore, he has continued to emphasise the importance of the environment. The 1992 *World Development Report* focused on the development and the environment and committed the Bank to the concept of sustainable development. Economic growth and protection of the environment are seen as compatible rather than conflicting objectives.

In attempting to adapt to the financial needs of its poorer member states the Bank has once again been influenced by the leading ideas on economic development. The 1980s saw the triumph of economic conservatism in the industrialised countries and the forging of a new consensus on economic policy.[54] As we demonstrated in the section on organisational ideology, the Bank's basic economic philosophy is biased in favour of market and private enterprise solutions. From the outset, Bank policy has been in favour of the free flow of goods and services across national boundaries. In the 1980s and 1990s the Bank has given greater support for neo-liberal principles and the argument that market solutions are preferable to intervention. The international economic environment of the 1980s was an uncertain one. For many developing countries it was a period of negative growth with declining export prices, rising import prices, shrinking commercial lending and increased indebtedness. The recession in the industrial countries harmed the export prospects of many developing countries and rising protectionism shut them out of markets in which they were competitive.

The Bank began the 1980s on the defensive from attacks by its principal shareholder, the United States, and ended the decade trying to defend itself from accusations that it was a mere tool of Western interests. Its enhanced role in coordinating creditors' clubs and conditional lending gave it increased leverage over its poorer members and this fuelled the debate on its role in the Third World. The extent to which the Bank pursues independent policies or is merely the instrument of its leading members is a contentious issue and I will return to it in the final section of this chapter. But we can note at this point that the Bank has been a chosen instrument of the United States and its allies in the handling of the debt crisis and the reconstruction of the former communist states of Eastern Europe.

The Third World countries reacted anxiously to changes in Bank policy in the early 1980s. The move away from poverty alleviation was viewed with scepticism. Many saw the reassertion of conservative banking principles, e.g. co-financing, flexible interest rates and graduation, as signalling the retreat of the Bank from its role as a development agency. Nevertheless, the parlous economic circumstances in which the majority of developing countries found themselves led to calls for increased Bank assistance rather than less. For example, the Third World countries proposed that the Bank's gearing ratio be doubled to 2:1. They argued that the 1:1 ratio was too conservative and placed too severe a limit on the Bank's ability to raise capital. Third World governments were also against the increase in conditionality which was seen in some cases as an infringement of sovereignty.

The World Bank as development agency

The World Bank is the leading international agency concerned with the promotion of economic development. It is the single largest provider of credit to the Third World. The objective of the World Bank is to assist poor countries to accelerate economic growth and reduce poverty through channelling financial aid from the developed world to the developing countries. Competing perspectives on the meaning of development ensures the existence of different assessments of the World Bank's role as a development agency. Conservative critics dismiss multilateral aid as ineffective and tend to argue that the Bank fails to promote neo-classical economic principles with sufficient vigour. Radical critics see the Bank as a capitalist institution which perpetuates dependence and obstructs genuine development. Centrist critics believe that, on balance, the Bank has been effective in promoting development despite the existence of political and organisational constraints.[55]

The World Bank's dominant position in the aid regime arises from the mutually reinforcing activities it undertakes. First, it provides loans to finance economic development. Bank and IDA lending in the 1980s and 1990s is shown in Table 5.1. The Bank considers investment in the private sector one of its main goals. Table 5.2 shows IFC operations between 1983 and 1992. It shows that the number of payments and the

Table 5.1 IBRD and IDA loans approved and disbursed, Fiscal Years 1981–92

	1981	1985	1991	1992
IBRD				
Loans approved	8,609	11,356	16,392	15,156
Disbursements	5,063	8,645	11,431	12,666
Operations				
approved	140	131	103	. . .
IDA				
Loans approved	3,482	3,028	6,293	6,550
Disbursements	1,876	2,491	4,549	4,765
Operations				
approved	106	105	103	. . .

Source: World Bank, *Annual Reports 1981–1992*.

Table 5.2 IFC operations, Fiscal Years 1983–92

Year	Amount	Number of payments
1983	2,894.1	58
1985	937.2	75
1990	1,500.0	122
1991	1,500.0	152
1992	1,800.0	167

Source: World Bank, *Annual Report 1992*.

Table 5.3 IBRD and IDA cumulative lending operations, by region, 30 June 1992

Region	IBRD	IDA
Africa	16,765.3	25,854.4
East Asia & the Pacific	51,344.5	8,665.1
Middle East & North Africa	21,037.4	2,499.1
Latin America & the Caribbean	71,666.7	2,045.0
Europe & Central Asia	31,756.8	219.6
South Asia	25,639.2	31,781.8

Source: World Bank, *Annual Report 1992*.

amount of funds committed have been increasing in the past three years. The cumulative distribution of Bank and IDA lending by geographical region is shown in Table 5.3. Over the whole period of the Bank's operations, Latin America has been the main beneficiary of loans from the Bank and, most IDA credits have been granted to South Asia. The World Bank's role as a provider of finacal resources is not limited to the funds it provides directly to governments and other institutions. It plays a catalytic role in generating financial flows from other sources.[56]

The World Bank's resources are not only financial. Crucial to the Bank's role as a development agency is its function as a research institute. The Bank is in the forefront of thinking on development issues and its expert staff of economists, engineers and other professionals produce highly valued country studies, sectoral analyses and influential research publications on issues such as debt, capital flows and trade liberalisation. The Bank's output on development issues are frequently at the forefront of development thinking and set the trends in thought.

The Bank is actively engaged in conceiving and implementing projects, giving technical advice to governments, and engaging in policy dialogue with borrowers. It is thus in a position to promote its particular approach to development through a variety of activities. I will now focus on two controversial aspects of current Bank policy. Closer collaboration with the IMF and the move to structural adjustment lending in the early 1980s increased the Bank's political profile and it found itself increasingly accused of sacrificing development for the repayment of debt. The controversial issues surrounding conditional aid lending and the impact of Bank policy will be considered in the next section. This will be followed by an examination of the World Bank's environmental policy. Environmental issues came to the fore of the international agenda in the late 1980s bringing the environmental aspects of Bank lending under intense scrutiny.

Aid, conditionality and economic development

In the 1980s and 1990s the debate on World Bank lending shifted from discussion of basic needs and rural development to structural adjustment lending. Project lending remained the main type of lending initiated by the Bank but the political and economic impact of adjustment lending gave it a higher profile in discussions of the Bank's activities. This section will chart the origins and development of adjustment lending and examine the evidence pertaining to its effectiveness.

It is widely agreed that adjustment lending was initiated in 1980 in response to the worsening balance of payments position of the developing countries.[57] Poor economic performance and a worsening trade balance were the consequences, it was argued, of external shocks and domestic policy errors. The development of adjustment lending is thus solely linked to movements in the world economy. Mosley, Harrigan and Toye dispute this orthodox interpretation and stress the role of institutional factors in the move to a greater reliance on programme lending and emphasis on policy change. They argue that the move to adjustment lending was, first, signalled by McNamara in a speech to UNCTAD in May 1979 and arose from internal pressures in the Bank, including dissatisfaction with the use of project lending as an instrument with which to initiate policy reforms in developing countries and McNamara's doubts concerning the effectiveness of his poverty allevia-tion strategy.[58] These two accounts of the origin of adjustment lending are not mutually exclusive. The decision to increase programme lending, although made before the second oil shock in late 1979, was given greater credence by changing external circumstances. The deteri-oration of the balance of payments positions of many developing countries in 1980 helped to create the conditions under which policy implementation became more feasible. Adverse terms of trade, high interest rates, falling concessional assistance and restrictions on lending by commercial banks, especially after the beginning of the debt crisis in 1982, made many developing countries more receptive to adjustment lending as the severe structural weaknesses of their economies were exposed. Or to put it another way, an unfavourable economic climate circumscribed their freedom of choice. Moreover, the election of conservative governments in the United Kingdom and United States in 1979 and in Germany in 1980 increased pressures for the linkage of development assistance with policy reform. The quest for change embarked on by the Bank's management thus coincided with external factors helpful to the new policy direction. The change was not automatic and resistance within the Bank and in the Executive Board still had to be overcome.[59]

In one sense, policy-based lending is not a new departure since certain policy conditions have customarily been attached to Bank loans and a policy dialogue between the borrower and the Bank was a central feature of this process.[60] The difference after 1980 lies both in the scope and focus of conditionality. Prior to 1980, the Bank required policy reforms of largely a sectoral kind. These conditions were necessary to ensure the successful completion of the project and as such were a limited instrument for achieving wider macro policy reform. Moreover, as a Bank review concluded, 'On the basis of experience it would be reasonable to conclude that individual projects in general are inefficient instruments for inducing policy change.'[61]

Structural adjustment lending initiates a wide ranging dialogue over all areas of economic policy in a borrowing country. In other words, the focus of the dialogue moved from the sectoral and sub-sectoral levels to the entire national economy. The aim of adjustment lending is to support policy and institutional reforms designed to increase economic efficiency, stimulate sustainable economic growth and improve the balance of payments. Since 1990, an increasing emphasis has been placed on the role of adjustment lending in alleviating poverty.

Adjustment programmes have, as Please outlined, three interrelated components:

1. a financial program designed to monitor and exert discipline over the level of aggregate demand for goods and services;
2. an external borrowing program to monitor and discipline the extent to which the supply of goods and services should be augmented from abroad in the light of creditworthiness considerations;
3. a program of structural adjustment measures designed to monitor and discipline the use to which resources are put.[62]

The World Bank uses two instruments of adjustment lending, namely structural adjustment loans and sectoral adjustment loans. The distinction between SALs and SECALs lies not in the nature but the breadth of policy and institutional reforms proposed.[63] Both SALs and SECALs may support sectoral and national reforms, provide balance of payments support and endorse institutional change. The decision on whether to use a SAL or SECAL in a particular borrowing country depends on the perceived operational effectiveness of the instrument.

Adjustment programmes typically cover the following:

1. External trade – measures include devaluation, removal of quantitative restrictions, tariff cuts and improved export incentives.
2. Resource mobilisation – measures include interest rate adjustments, tax or budget reforms, cost recovery systems for public enterprises and greater control over the level and administration of external borrowing.
3. Efficient use of resources – including the reduction or elimination of food subsidies, the restructuring and rationalisation of state marketing boards, changes in public expenditure, e.g. a shift away from transport and government buildings to agriculture, health and education, and measures to improve energy efficiency.
4. Institutional reforms – including privatisation of publicly owned companies, increased efficiency for public enterprises and a better targeted support for agriculture and industry programmes to improve project evaluation and the management of public enterprises.

Initially the Bank concentrated on SALs with a country designated to receive a series of loans, of 12 to 18 months over a 3 to 5-year period.

Table 5.4 IBRD and IDA adjustment lending

Year	SAL		SECAL	
	volume	percentage	volume	percentage
1989	1,825.7	18	4,615.5	27
1990	1,434.0	17	5,534.6	25
1991	2,238.9	21	3,432.5	25
1992	3,159.8	26	2,687.5	22

Source: World Bank, *Annual Reports 1989–1992*.

But the deterioration in the external environment faced by developing countries since 1982 led to a change of policy whereby it was accepted that adjustment lending can be for longer periods.[64] Furthermore, the Bank shifted the burden of adjustment lending to SECALs. Between 1984 and 1991, the SAL was overtaken by the SECAL as the main form of adjustment lending. In 1992, however, SAL represented a higher proportion of Bank lending (see Table 5.4). It is too early to say whether this heralds a new change of direction.

In order to assess the effectiveness of adjustment lending it is necessary to examine the suitability of the policies proposed for the borrower and the extent to which the policies have been implemented. Assessment of the effectiveness of Bank policy is further compounded by the difficult problem of attempting to decide what would have happened in the absence of Bank-sponsored adjustment policies. Failure to adjust can be as costly, and in some circumstances more costly in the short run than following the prescriptions of adjustment lending. John Toye expressed this point succinctly when he observed, 'Ghana's sad history between 1973 and 1983 shows vividly that doing nothing is an option which can inflict terrible social costs . . . .'[65] In examining the impact of policy measures it is important that some agreement is reached on the methodology to be employed and the criteria for evaluation. It is difficult to establish causality since the results obtained by any method may have been caused by extraneous factors. Even, however, if agreement is reached on the most salient criteria by which to judge a programme this does not guarantee consensus on the weight to be attached to different objectives. For example, is restoration of the external balance more important than poverty alleviation? Is increased efficiency of government enterprises more important than the provision of employment? No easy answers exist to these questions and judgement on the outcome of World Bank adjustment programmes will reflect the value biases of the analyst. Acceptance of the inherently subjective nature of judgements on the impact of Bank programmes does not in itself remove the obligation to develop an approach which can be tested by others.

World Bank evaluations of the effectiveness of its adjustment programmes are, not surprisingly, more positive than independent studies. A recent Bank study concluded that 'Adjustment lending through both SALs and SECALs has contributed to successful stabilisation and structural adjustment in many cases.'[66] In support of this claim it referred to a cross-country comparison of 93 countries which showed that the 30 countries in receipt of structural adjustment lending before 1985 outperformed the 63 non-recipient countries even though the countries receiving adjustment lending experienced more severe external shocks.[67]

A joint World Bank/United Nations Development Programme (UNDP) study on Africa's adjustment experience during the 1980s concluded that adjustment with growth was a viable strategy for Africa.[68] The study argued that countries with strong reform programmes produced a better overall economic performance than those without. Specifically, it cited seven benefits of policy reform. Inflation rates were lower in the second half of the 1980s than they had been in the first half. Secondly, governments had achieved success in substantially reducing fiscal deficits without sacrificing capital expenditure. The study noted, thirdly, improved investment performance and improved performances also in agricultural production, exports and gross domestic product (GDP). Fourthly, real consumption growth rates in the reforming countries were three times higher in 1986–87 compared with 1980–86. The report also pointed to the ways in which the decision to undertake reforms influences external creditors. Aid donors had shifted aid to Africa away from non-reform countries to those countries implementing reforms. Furthermore, in 1986–87 official creditors increased the annual amount of debt relief for countries undertaking reform by some 50 per cent compared with the previous six years. On the other hand, debt relief was virtually eliminated for the non-reform group of countries.[69]

Initially the Bank paid little attention to the distributional impact and social welfare consequences of its adjustment programmes believing that growth would automatically take care of such concerns given that it is the failure to adjust which is of greater harm to the poor.[70] Recently, the Bank has demonstrated greater awareness of the importance of the social costs of adjustment. This is partly in response to vociferous criticism from a number of sources[71] and the resistance to adjustment policies by Third World peoples. Moreover, analyses undertaken by Bank staff have addressed the shortcomings of the strategy. For example, Uma Lele's analysis of the impact of structural adjustment policies on agricultural development in Malawi noted that structural adjustment policies worked against growth and equity since the policies had failed to promote growth and to avoid adversely affecting the poor.[72] In the light of these and other findings the Bank has devised three strategies for improving the impact of its programmes on the poor. The first strategy seeks to involve the poor in the growth process through asset creation and redistribution. The second strategy concentrates on ensuring that measures are included to mitigate the short-term costs borne by the temporary new poor. The third strategy lies in the attempt to encourage social targeting, e.g. the recognition that desirable cuts in food subsidies have a negative impact on the poor can be countered not by the reintroduction of subsidies but through the provision of alternative devices, such as food stamps, school lunches and direct food aid. These measures reach the poor and also improve efficiency.[73]

A recent study on measures to help the poor during structural adjustment envisaged three key tasks to be performed by the Bank. The first task involves participation in funding the transition costs borne by the most vulnerable members of society during the adjustment period. The Bank should, secondly, provide assistance for the design and implementation of measures during the adjustment process of benefit to the poor, e.g. labour market reforms, retraining programmes and the reallocation of resources in favour of ministries of education and health. A third task for the Bank is the provision of assistance for the creation of evaluation mechanisms to monitor progress in certain social sectors, e.g. health, literacy and income distribution.[74] It is too early to say whether these reforms will be carried out and what effect they will have on the most vulnerable groups in developing countries.

Much criticism of World Bank structural adjustment lending differs marginally from that levelled at the IMF. I will not rehearse those arguments here, but will summarise the findings of a recent critical evaluation of Bank policy. A major study of World Bank adjustment lending found serious flaws in the design, implementation and effectiveness of these programmes. Mosley, Harrigan and Toye applied three different analytical methods in order to evaluate the effectiveness of structural adjustment lending.[75] They concluded that the implementation of structural adjustment programmes had a positive impact on exports and the external account, a neutral effect on national income and foreign private capital inflows, but a negative impact on investment.[76] They agreed with the contention that the living standards of the poor had fallen under adjustment programmes but felt that the distributional impact of Bank policies was probably neutral.[77]

The case studies conducted by Mosley and his associates showed that adjustment experience varied widely between countries. They argued that, structural adjustment policies of the Bank's chosen variety constitute in very poor countries a gratuitous obstruction, just as in the NICs they constitute a welcome acceleration, of [the] policy evolution . . . in very poor countries, privatisation and removal of infant-industry protective structures are at best an irrelevance. True structural adjustment requires the building up of a country's export sectors and associated infrastructure, which in the short term may require more rather than less state intervention.[78]

The case studies clearly show that the appropriateness of Bank policy depends on the stage of development reached by the recipient country. In Turkey and the Philippines, Bank policies proved successful because internal institutional change and level of development created conditions favourable to the Bank's prescriptions. At the other end of the scale, Bank policy in Guyana and Ghana in the early 1980s were dismal failures.[79]

The foregoing discussion of the impact of Bank lending for adjustment assumes that Bank policy reforms are implemented. But the available evidence suggests that Bank conditionality is not always rigidly adhered to by the borrower. In so far as the impact of Bank programmes depends on the degree of implementation it is therefore necessary to examine the record on this issue.

Two attempts have been made to quantify the implementation of conditionality. This is a process which relies more on judgement than the raw scores suggest and tells us little about the conditions under which the reforms were attempted. Mosley and his collaborators reported a compliance rate of 54 per cent in their sample of 9 countries.[80] A World Bank study of 51 SALs and SECALs in 15 countries discovered a compliance rate of 60 per cent.[81] These results are very crude and the only conclusion that can be derived from them is the knowledge that in many programmes slippage from the policy conditions occurs.

Successful implementation is a function of a number of factors including the design of the programme and the social, political and economic environment of the borrower country. Programme design is critical since a poorly designed programme has little chance of being implemented effectively. Three elements of programme design can be identified.[82] First, the areas for action must be specified. The structure of conditionality as evidenced by Table 5.5 shows that the Bank possesses a general diagnosis of the problems affecting its clients. However, the application of conditions depends on the bargaining relationship between the borrower and the Bank. Mosley, Harrigan and Toye came to the conclusion that the 'average number of conditions negotiated with low-distortion countries . . . is insignificantly different

Table 5.5 The structure of conditionality

Item	Sub-Saharan African countries a.	Highly indebted countries b.	Other developing countries c.	All 15 countries
Fiscal policy	8	11	15	11
Budget and public expenditures	12	9	10	10
Public enterprises	19	17	12	16
Financial sector	4	13	13	11
Exchange rate	4	2	0	2
Trade policy	25	32	25	28
Industrial policy	7	2	2	3
Energy policy	1	3	15	6
Agricultural policy	17	1	2	2
Other	2	1	2	2

a. Ghana, Kenya, Malawi, Zambia.
b. Chile, Colombia, Côte d'Ivoire, Jamaica, Mexico, Morocco and the Philippines.
c. Republic of Korea, Pakistan, Thailand and Turkey.

Source: IMF/IBRD Development Committee, *Problems and Issues in Structural Adjustment* (1990) based on an analysis of 51 SALS and SECALS in 15 developing countries.

from the number negotiated with high-distortion countries'.[83] It is likely that governments in weak bargaining positions are likely to be more vulnerable to Bank pressure on the number of areas to be reformed.[84] One problem with Bank lending has been the excess of conditionality, i.e. the imposition of too many conditions.[85]

A second element of programme design concerns the policy reform to be recommended. The belief in a technocratic solution is misguided since even if the diagnosis is correct competing measures to achieve the same goal are likely to exist. The third element in programme design concerns the sequence in which actions should be taken. For example, tax reform requires new or reorganised administration and policy reform can be hampered by institutional deficiencies, skill shortages and inadequate infrastructure in the borrowing country. Thus, programme design creates the possibility of conflict between the borrowing country and the Bank and cannot guarantee effective implementation.

The sustainability of effective implementation depends on the existence of an appropriate social and political environment in the borrowing country. Adjustment lending will provide benefits for some sections of the population and create costs for others. Unless the local elite in favour of implementing reform can harness a political coalition to support the proposed changes, discover ways of mitigating the social effects of adjustment the tendency will be for governments to renege on implementation.[86]

The World Bank and the international environmental agenda

In this section I will examine the Bank's response to the environmental challenge. This section will also attempt to assess the effectiveness of the Bank's environmental policy. The World Bank was the first of the multilateral development banks to express an interest in the environmental consequences of development.[87] The creation of the post of Environmental Adviser in 1970 marked the Bank's first attempt to address environmental issues. The evolution of its environmental policy over the past two decades has been shaped by internal bureaucratic politics and external actors – donor countries, borrowing members and Non-Governmental Organisations (NGOs).[88]

Until the creation of an Environmental Department in 1987, as part of Conable's reorganisation of the Bank, environmental concerns were addressed through the Office of Environmental and Scientific Affairs (OESA). This was an inadequately staffed section which focused primarly on assessing the environmental impact of projects.[89] In addition to identifying and preparing environmental projects, OESA's tasks included generating greater awareness inside and outside the Bank about the ecological and resource management impact of development projects; reviewing project implementation in order to assess the environmental consequences; and cooperation with other agencies such as UNDP and UNEP to develop research and operational policy.[90] OESA was given a broad mandate but limited resources with which to implement it.

In a speech to the World Resources Institute in May 1987, Barber Conable acknowledged mistakes in previous Bank environmental policy. For instance, he described the controversial Polonoreste project in Brazil as 'a sobering example of an environmentally sound effort that went wrong'.[91] He announced a number of organisational reforms and new initiatives designed to increase the effectiveness of the Bank's environmental policy.

A new central Environment Department was established with 30 staff members in three divisions. Its role is to conduct policy and research in technical, economic and social areas, to provide conceptual guidance or specialised expertise for staff in the regional offices, to establish and maintain information systems and databases and to train and educate Bank staff on environmental issues. Environmental units were created in each of the Bank's regional units to review Bank-supported projects and liaise with national officials in identifying more general tasks related to resource management.

New initiatives designed to integrate development planning and environmental management following the suggestions of the Brundtland

Commission have been taken. A five-year programme to conduct in-depth environmental assessments of 30 countries is currently underway. A less detailed but, nevertheless, important environmental statement for each borrowing country, an environmental issue paper, is also in preparation. Furthermore, specific regional projects examining inter-related environmental issues have been undertaken. For example, the Bank is participating in an Environmental Program for the Mediterranean along with UNEP, the European Investment Bank and the Mediterranean countries. And in conjunction with UNDP and the Economic Commission for Asia and the Pacific has embarked on the Capital Cities Clean-up Project to counter the damaging environmental effects of rapid urbanisation, industrial pollution and environmental neglect in the main Asian cities.

Since 1987 the Bank has attempted to develop ways of integrating environmental issues into development policy-making. From the Bank's perspective its lending activities have become much more sensitive to ecological concerns. It has expanded its efforts to address the environmental consequences of aid projects and to identify projects specifically aimed at environmental problems. In 1989, approximately one-third of Bank projects contained significant environmental components. This figure rose to 48 per cent in 1990, remained roughly the same in 1991 but fell back to under 25 per cent in 1992.[92] To assist in the identification of the environmental consequences of a project, in 1990 the Bank developed a fourfold classification of projects based on their environmental impacts. A systematic environmental screening of all new projects was introduced in 1990. This enables staff to undertake full environmental impact assessments on every project with the potential for substantial environmental effects.

Furthermore, from 1989 the Bank began to pay closer attention to the environmental impact of structural adjustment lending.[93] In examining the environmental consequences of project approval and adjustment lending the Bank is trying to ensure that environmental assessment becomes an inseparable part of its operations. The Bank felt sufficiently confident of its progress on these issues to claim in 1989 that, 'considerable progress was made in fiscal year 1989 in integrating environmental concerns into the mainstream of the Bank's operational and policy work; these concerns now pervade Bank operations, policy, research evaluation, training and information activities.'[94]

The preparation of Environmental Issue Papers (EIPs) and EAPs are part of the Bank's strategy to devote explicit attention to environmental issues and to stress the development of policies capable of influencing environmentally related behaviour. EIPs are prepared by the Bank and seek to identify key problems and their underlying causes for each borrower. EAPs are prepared by national governments, Bank staff and other external agencies. They aim to provide a framework for integrating environmental considerations into a country's economic and social development programmes.

An important source of the Bank's influence in the development aid regime arises from its control over intellectual ideas. The Bank serves as a generator of new ideas on development, new strategies for development and plays an important role in reappraising past experience. The Bank has been in the forefront of the intellectual challenge to investigate the links between the environment and development. The World Bank currently stresses the interdependence between development and the environment but this has not always been the case. Early Bank policy tended to prioritise development over the environment. Robert McNamara is quoted as asserting that 'There is no evidence that economic growth which the developing countries so desperately require will necessarily involve an unacceptable burden either on their own or anybody's environment.'[95]

The causes of environmental degradation according to the Bank are twofold. First, environmental problems can arise from the absence of economic development. Increased population growth in the context of widespread poverty places untold pressure on the land and resources. Environmental problems arising from the persistence of poverty include poor sanitation and lack of clean water; desertification; devegetation and soil erosion.

Environmental degradation is also, in the Bank's analysis, the consequence of rapid and uncontrolled economic growth. Unfettered urbanisation can cause environmental pollution. Air and water pollution is a serious hazard in cities in Africa, Asia and Latin America.[96] From the Bank's perspective a mutually reinforcing link exists between environmental degradation and the development process. As Le Pestre noted, for the Bank, 'environmental problems are linked to the development process in three ways: they are caused by a lack of development; they arise from development activities; and they can impair the future development prospects of a country.'[97] The protection of the environment is thus not inimical to development and development need not be harmful to the environment. The influential paper issued in 1987 by the Development Committee of the IMF and World Bank echoed this sentiment in its insistence that, 'Promoting growth, alleviating poverty, and protecting the environment are mutually supportive objectives in the long run.'[98]

The complementarity between the pursuit of development and the preservation of the environment is now reconciled in the concept of sustainable development. Sustainable development, first successfully articulated by the Brundtland Commission,[99] is now accepted by the World Bank as the method by which the goals of development and conservation can be integrated. The Brundtland Commission defined sustainable development as a policy which 'meets the needs of the present without compromising the ability of future generations to meet their own needs'.[100]

This record of the evolution of the Bank's environmental policy could be interpreted as an example of a successful process of adaptation to the task environment by the organisation. Such an assumption would be unwarranted without a further examination of external pressures on the Bank and a consideration of the views of critics of the Bank's environmental policy.

The World Bank became the focus of criticism by environmental NGOs and independent analysts in the 1970s and 1980s when it appeared that the Bank disregarded the negative ecological consequences of its project and programme lending. The critics accused the Bank of sins of commission and sins of omission. The development by the Bank of policies on issues such as involuntary resettlement (1980), tribal peoples (1982), wildlands (1986) and biodiversity (1986) failed to impress critics who applauded the intentions behind these policies but deplored the lack of specialists and resources to apply such principles effectively to Bank lending policy. World Bank support for colonisation schemes such as the Polonoreste project in Brazil and the trans-migration project in Indonesia, which contributed to deforestation, came under fierce attack. A number of Bank-financed projects were detrimental to the environment. Bank finance for hydroelectric projects, for example, destroyed watersheds and flooded wildlife sanctuaries and portions of parks in Thailand, Malaysia, Brazil and Zaire. The Bank participated in cattle ranching schemes in Latin America which were destructive of forested areas, and financed a cattle development project in Botswana which contributed to desertification.

These activities produced the image of an organisation willing to sacrifice environmental goals for economic growth. This was further supported by the failure of the Bank to coerce borrowers sufficiently forcefully to take account of environmental issues and the continuation of projects which had clearly breached the Bank's own environmental guidelines.[101] Even the Bank's attempt to respond to criticism of its forestry policies through the creation in conjunction with the Food and Agriculture Organization (FAO) of a Tropical Foresty Action Plan in 1985 failed to appease the critics.[102]

The new strategy employed since 1987 is partly a response to the criticisms made by NGOs and others. The Bank's much vaunted cooperative stance towards NGOs in this later period is an attempt to stem the flow of criticism as much as a genuine desire for cooperation. The Bank has attempted to strenghten cooperation with major environmental NGOs based in the West, like the International Union for the Conservation of Nature and Natural Resources (IUCN), the World Wide Fund for Nature (WWF) and the World Resources Institute (WRI). It has also sought to engage collaboratively with NGOs based in developing countries.[103]

The Bank's policy has also been shaped in response to the role of international organisations, most notably UNEP, UNDP, FAO, WHO and UNESCO. One result of this collaboration was the creation in 1991 of the Global Environmental Facility (GEF) which is jointly administered by the Bank, UNEP and UNDP. Based on a proposal by France to the Development Committee in 1989, agreement was reached on the establishment of the GEF in November 1990 and it became operational in March 1991. As of 30 June 1992 more than 30 countries were participants in the GEF. Although many developing countries are sceptical of the scheme, nearly half of the participating countries are from the developing world. The developing countries wanted the GEF to be an independent agency, rather than one run by the World Bank, where the dominance of the rich countries over decision-making will be decisive in shaping GEF priorities. In 1992, the GEF was considering more than 70 projects with a net value in excess of $580 million.

As we have seen, the World Bank's environmental policy addresses a variety of issues, and has been evolving in a positive direction since 1987. However, although it is clear that ecological factors have been included in the Bank's development projects in the recent past there is still considerable room for improvement by the Bank, and convincing grounds to doubt whether the Bank can fulfil its environmental mandate satisfactorily. The Bank gives the impression that its concern for the environment is internally driven but the evidence suggests that external pressure plays a crucial role. The Bank is particularly sensitive to the demands of the US Congress which, in 1991, threatened to withold 25 per cent of the American contribution to the Bank's budget unless the Bank improved its record in implementing environmental reforms in its lending policy.[104] The recent case in which the Bank persisted in its decision to provide financing for the Narmada dam project in India despite a damning report by an independent enquiry set up by the Bank,[105] is a sign that it has not accepted the logic of a genuine ecological perspective on development. This appears to be another example of an inherent flaw in Bank lending policy. Bank staff have an interest in promoting spending rather than curtailing it. Unlike the IMF, where failure to meet target conditions results in the suspension or cancellation of a loan, the Bank's goal is to spend its budget. This organisational politics explanation of the Bank's failure to be more ecologically conscious is not incompatible with the view that the Bank's capitalist ideology is incompatible with an environmentally sound approach, but in the literature they tend to be given as competing explanations.

Conclusion

The World Bank shows a remarkable ability to adapt to the changing international economic environment. Its pre-eminent position in the aid regime stems as much from this flexibility, as from its command over financial and intellectual resources. As this chapter has demonstrated, the World Bank is a constantly evolving organisation. It has undergone widespread organisational change since its creation at Bretton Woods. Its development strategy also has shifted with changes in the dominant orthodox perception of development. The Bank is not a passive recipient of development thinking; on the contrary, it is in the forefront of research on the causes of and solutions to global poverty. The Bank's unrivalled expertise and resources gives it a very powerful position in the arena of development diplomacy. But, the Bank's relationship with its Third World clients is not a calm and harmonious one.

Third World states welcome the aid provided by the Bank, and recognise that aid from multilateral organisations like the World Bank have less political strings attached than bilateral aid. Nevertheless, Third World states voice two major criticisms of the Bank and its activities. First, they want to reform the decision-making process in the organisation so that it better reflects their views. The dominance of the rich countries, especially the United States, over the Bank, shapes its overall approach and affects the level of its funding. The rich countries are unlikey to relinquish control as long as they continue to bear the major cost of direct financing of the organisation. Secondly, the developing countries resent the application of conditionality to Bank loans. This is both an issue of principle and one of substance. The discussion of adjustment lending showed that many borrowing countries are either unwilling or unable to implement Bank recommendations. This highlights a major flaw in the design of Bank projects and programmes, and the fact that recipient governments are not pawns of the Bank. The leverage the Bank exercises will vary on an individual basis.[106]

The Bank is a reformist organisation and judgements on its role in meeting the needs of the Third World will differ depending on whether one accepts the reformist goals of the organisation. The Bank has adapted to changes in the global political economy but it has done so within a framework determined by its organisational ideology and the interests of the leading donor states. The main objective of the Bank remains 'the goal of modernizing the international economy in its capitalist variant for the sake of its long term preservation'.[107] Widespread disagreement exists on the extent to which that goal is compatible with promoting economic development and reducing poverty in Third World countries. The development strategies pursued by most Third World elites in the post-World War II period reveals a willingness to accept the basic premise on which the World Bank was established, even if disagreement exists on precise policies to be adopted.

Notes

1. See Robert E. Wood, *From Marshall Plan to Debt Crisis: Foreign Aid and Development Choices in the World Economy* (Berkeley: University of California Press 1986) pp. 104–137 for a discussion of the concept of aid regime.
2. See the comments of David Stockman (US Budget Director in the Reagan Administration) quoted in Robert L. Ayres, *Banking on the Poor* (Cambridge, Mass.: MIT Press 1983) p. 12.
3. Perhaps the best exponent of this argument is Peter Bauer. Among his numerous publications the following are particularly relevant in this context: *Equality, the Third World and Economic Delusion* (London: Weidenfeld & Nicolson 1981) and *Reality and Rhetoric* (London: Weidenfeld & Nicolson 1984).
4. Cheryl Payer, *The World Bank: A Critical Analysis* (New York: Monthly Review Press 1982) p. 19.
5. *Ibid.* p. 20.
6. Teresa Hayter, *Aid as Imperialism* (London: Penguin Books 1971).
7. Edward Mason & Robert Asher, *The World Bank since Bretton Woods* (Washington DC: Brookings Institution 1972).
8. Ayres, *op. cit.* p. xi.
9. Mason & Asher, *op. cit.* p. 13.
10. Uner Kirdar, *The Structure of United Nations Economic Aid to Underdeveloped Countries* (The Hague: Martinus Nijhoff 1966) p. 103.
11. Article III, section 1(a).
12. IBRD, *The International Bank for Reconstruction and Development 1946–1953* (Washington DC: 1954) p. 6.
13. Payer, *op. cit.* pp. 73–74 argues that this gives power to private sponsors and the Bank over the borrower.
14. Aart van de Laar, *The World Bank and the Poor* (The Hague: Martinus Nijhoff 1980) p. 36.
15. See, for example, Teresa Hayter & Catherine Watson, *Aid: Rhetoric and Reality* (London: Pluto Press 1985) pp. 195–227; Ayres, *op. cit.* pp. 57–58, 71–72; Payer, *op. cit.* pp. 42–44.
16. See Peter Bachrach & Morton Baratz, 'The Two Faces of Power',

American Political Science Review vol. 56 (1962) pp. 947–952; and Peter Bachrach & Morton Baratz, 'Decisions and Non-Decisions: An Analytical Framework' *American Political Science Review* vol. 57 (1963) pp. 641–651.
17. Mason & Asher, *op. cit.* p. 87.
18. William Ascher, 'New Development Approaches and the Adaptability of International Agencies: The Case of the World Bank', *International Organization* (Summer 1983) pp. 419, 429.
19. See Michael Prowse, ' "Tough manager" stamps authority on World Bank', *Financial Times* 19 September 1991, p. 4.
20. Mason & Asher, *op. cit.* p. 380.
21. See Ibrahim F. I. Shihata, *MIGA and Foreign Investment: the Origins, Operations, Policies and Basic Documents of the Multilateral Investment Guarantee Agency* (Dordrecht: Martinus Nijhoff 1988) for an analysis of MIGA.
22. Ayres, *op. cit.* p. 74 reaches a similar conclusion.
23. A. W. Clausen, 'Adjustment with Growth in the Developing World: a World Bank Perspective' in World Bank, *The Development Challenge of the Eighties: A. W. Clausen at the World Bank. Major Policy Addresses 1981–1986* (Washington DC: World Bank 1986) p. 487.
24. 'Findings and Recommendations of an Economic and Technical Mission Organised by the IBRD in Collaboration with the Government of Cuba (1951), quoted in van de Laar, *op. cit.* p. 158.
25. Ayres, *op. cit.* pp. 74–75.
26. IBRD (1954), *op. cit.* p. 9.
27. Quoted in Mason & Asher, *op. cit.* pp. 60–61.
28. See Eugene Black, *The Diplomacy of Economic Development* (Cambridge, Mass.: Harvard University Press 1960) for an outline of Black's approach to economic development.
29. Mason & Asher, *op. cit.* p. 833.
30. *Ibid.* p. 192. These figures are inclusive of IBRD loans and IDA credits.
31. *Ibid.* pp. 373–374.
32. Winsome J. Leslie, *The World Bank and Structural Transformation* (Boulder & London: Lynne Reinner 1987) p. 22.
33. Robert Asher, 'Comment: The Leopard's Spots' in John P. Lewis & Ishan Kapur (eds), *The World Bank Group: Multilateral Aid and the 1970s* (Toronto: Lexington Books 1973) p. 25.
34. Leslie, *op. cit.* p. 21.
35. Ayres, *op. cit.* p. 3.
36. *Ibid.* p. 4.
37. See World Bank, *The World Bank Annual Report 1968* (Washington DC 1968) p. 6; and World Bank, *The World Bank Annual Report 1982* (Washington DC 1982) pp. 120–121.
38. Bettina S. Hurni, *The Lending Policy of the World Bank in the 1970s: Analysis and Evaluation* (Boulder: Westview Press 1980).
39. See H. Chenery, M. S. Ahluwalia, C. L. G. Bell, J. H. Duloy and R. Jolly, *Redistribution with Growth* (London: Oxford University Press 1974) for an elaboration of this approach to development.
40. See, World Bank, *The McNamara Years at the World Bank: Major Policy Addresses of Robert S. McNamara 1968–1981* (Baltimore: Johns Hopkins University Press 1981) for this and other speeches outlining McNamara's approach to development.

41. William Clark, 'Robert McNamara at the World Bank', *Foreign Affairs* (Fall 1981) pp. 167–184.
42. William Ascher, 'The World Bank and U.S. Control' in Margaret P. Karns & Karen A. Mingst (eds), *The United States and Multilateral Institutions* (Boston: Unwin Hyman 1990) p. 121.
43. Chenery *et al.*, *op. cit.* p. xiii.
44. Hurni, *op. cit.* p. 29.
45. See Diana Hunt, *Economic Theories of Development: An Analysis of Competing Paradigms* (Hemel Hempstead: Harvester Wheatsheaf 1989) ch. 9 for a succinct summary and critique of the basic-needs paradigm.
46. Hurni, *op. cit.* p. 45.
47. World Bank, *World Bank Annual Report 1978* (Washington DC 1978) p. 18.
48. Ayres, *op. cit.* p. 263, fn. 18.
49. *Ibid.* p. 263, fn. 17 & 19.
50. See *A. W. Clausen at the World Bank*, *op. cit.* for an indication of his approach to development.
51. See World Bank, *The Conable Years at the World Bank: Major Policy Addresses of Barber B. Conable 1986–1991* (Washington DC: 1991) for his views on development.
52. *Financial Times* 11 May 1992 p. 4.
53. World Bank, *Assistance Strategies to Reduce Poverty* (Washington DC: 1991).
54. See John Toye, *Dilemmas of Development* (London: Basil Blackwell 1987) for an excellent critique of this counter-revolution in development thinking.
55. See Leslie, *op. cit.* for an elaboration and critique of the three perspectives.
56. See Barend A. De Vries, *Remaking the World Bank* (Washington DC: Seven Locks Press 1987) p. 79.
57. See Stanley Please, *The Hobbled Giant: Essays on the World Bank* (Boulder: Westview 1984) pp. 17–18; and World Bank, *World Bank Annual Report 1986* (Washington DC 1986) p. 32.
58. Paul Mosley, Jane Harrigan & John Toye, *Aid and Power: The World Bank and Policy Based Lending vol. 1* (London: Routledge 1991) pp. 33–34.
59. See *ibid.* pp. 34–38 for a discussion of the struggle with the Executive Board.
60. See De Vries, *op. cit.* pp. 63–64.
61. World Bank Operations Evaluation Department, 'Eighth Annual Review of Project Performance Audit Reports 1982' para 306; quoted in Please, *op. cit.* p. 27.
62. Please, *op. cit.* pp. 18–19.
63. World Bank, *Problems and Issues in Structural Development* (Washington DC: IMF/IBRD Development Committee Pamphlet No. 23, April 1990) pp. 17–18.
64. *Ibid.* p. 17.
65. John Toye, 'Ghana' in Paul Mosley, Jane Harrigan & John Toye, *Aid and Power: The World Bank and Policy Based Lending vol. 2* (London: Routledge 1991) p. 188.
66. *Problems and Issues in Structural Development*, *op. cit.* p. 44.

67. *Ibid.* p. 39.
68. World Bank/UNDP, *Africa's Adjustment and Growth in the 1980s* (Washington DC: IBRD/UNDP 1989).
69. *Ibid.* pp. 27–31.
70. For example, 3 SAL programmes for the Côte d'Ivoire (1981, 1983 and 1986) did not refer to income distributional aspects. See Ravi Kanbur, 'Poverty and Social Dimensions of Structural Adjustment in Côte d'Ivoire' *Social Dimension of Adjustment in Sub-Saharan Africa Working Paper no. 2* (Washington DC: World Bank 1990) p. 12.
71. See, for example, Kathy McAfee, *Storm Signals: Structural Adjustment and Development Alternatives in the Caribbean* (London: Zed Books 1991) for a scathing attack on the social consequences of World Bank lending.
72. Uma Lele, 'Structural Adjustment, Agricultural Development and the Poor. Lessons from the Malawian Experience' *MADIA Discussion Paper No. 9* (Washington DC: World Bank 1989).
73. *Problems and Issues in Structural Development, op. cit.* pp. 26–27.
74. World Bank, *Egypt – Alleviating Poverty During Structural Adjustment* (Washington DC 1991).
75. See Mosley *et al.* vol. 1, *op. cit.* chs 6–8.
76. *Ibid.* pp. 301–302.
77. *Ibid.* p. 302.
78. *Ibid.* p. 304.
79. See Mosley *et al.* vol. 2, *op. cit.*
80. Mosley *et al.* vol. 1, *op. cit.* p. 136.
81. World Bank, *Report on Adjustment Lending 1988* (Washington DC: Country Economics Department, document R88–199) quoted in *Finance and Development* (March 1989) pp. 32–34; and Mosley *et al.* vol. 1, *op. cit.* p. 134.
82. Mosley *et al.*, *ibid.* pp. 103–104 specify four elements of programme design.
83. *Ibid.* p. 104.
84. See the comments of African policy-makers in Cadman Atta Mills, 'Structural Adjustment in Sub-Saharan Africa' *EDI Policy Seminar Report No. 18* (Washington DC: World Bank 1989).
85. Please, *op. cit.* p. 43 noted this in respect of project lending, before the move to adjustment lending. It has remained a problem in adjustment lending.
86. See Joan Nelson (ed.), *Fragile Coalitions: The Politics of Economic Adjustment* [Overseas Development Council US-Third World Policy Perspectives No. 12] (New Brunswick: Transaction Books 1989).
87. The first signal that the Bank had an interest in the environment came in a speech McNamara made to ECOSOC in November 1970.
88. See Phillipe Le Pestre, *The World Bank and the Environmental Challenge* (London & Toronto: Associated University Press 1989.) ch. 2 for an extended discussion of internal constraints on Bank policy.
89. OESA had three environmental specialists to review over 300 new project proposals per annum. See Gareth Porter & Janet Welsh Brown, *Global Environmental Politics* (Boulder: Westview Press 1991) p. 54.
90. Jeremy Warford & Richard Ackermann, 'Environment and Development: Implementing the World Bank's New Policies', *Development Committee Pamphlet No. 17* (Washington DC: World Bank July 1988) pp. 2–3.
91. *The Conable Years, op. cit.* p. 22.

92. See World Bank, *World Bank Annual Reports 1981–1992* (Washington DC: 1981–1992).

93. Jeremy J. Warford & Zeinab Partow, 'World Bank Support for the Environment: A Progress Report' *Development Committee Pamphlet No. 22* (Washington DC: World Bank Sept 1989) pp. 23–26.

94. World Bank, *World Bank Annual Report 1989* (Washington DC: 1989) p. 50.

95. Quoted in Le Pestre, *op. cit.* p. 25.

96. See World Bank, *World Development Report 1992* (New York: Oxford University Press 1992) p. 7; Jeremy Warford, 'Environment Growth and Development', *Development Committee Pamphlet No. 14* (Washington DC: World Bank Aug/Dec 1987) pp. 2–3.

97. Le Pestre, *op. cit.* p. 26.

98. *Development Committee Pamphlet No. 14, op. cit.* p. 5.

99. World Commission on Environment and Development (The Brundtland Report), *Our Common Future* (Oxford: Oxford University Press 1987).

100. *Ibid.* p. 8.

101. See Le Pestre, *op. cit.* ch. 5 for a detailed examination of criticisms of the Bank during this period.

102. See, for example, Larry Lohmann & Marcus Colchester, 'Paved with good intentions: TFAP's road to oblivion', *The Ecologist* (May/June 1990) pp. 91–98.

103. See *Development Committee Pamphlet No. 22, op. cit.* pp. 38–39 for an elaboration of the various forms of cooperation between the Bank and NGOs.

104. Iain Guest, 'Washington demands the earth from the World Bank', *The Guardian* 31 May 1991, p. 27.

105. *Financial Times* 20/21 June 1992, p. 4.

106. See Leslie, *op. cit.* p. 162.

107. Ayres, *op. cit.* pp. 10–11.

6

The General Agreement on Tariffs and Trade and the Third World

The General Agreement on Tariffs and Trade (GATT) is the principal organisation concerned with creating and preserving a liberal international trade regime.[1] The system of rules and regulations embedded in the GATT are based on a neo-classical analysis of international trade but also reflect the realities of differential power in the global political economy. Until recently, Third World countries took a sceptical attitude towards GATT. The standard Third World critique of GATT emphasised a number of deficiencies, which, they claimed, limited GATT's role in the international trading system. First, GATT's mandate is perceived as being too limiting. Unlike the stillborn International Trade Organisation (ITO) the original Articles of Agreement omitted any mention of economic development and failed to provide coverage in respect of commodity trade. Secondly, the very premises of GATT have been challenged by many Third World states. The liberal theory of free trade and the emphasis on non-discrimination is rejected in favour of a more mercantilist and interventionist posture. Thirdly, Third World countries have pointed out the relative weakness of the GATT and its inability to impose controls on the major trading states. Powerful states have shaped the international political economy so that liberal policies do not apply in areas of particular interest to developing countries, e.g. agriculture and textiles.

In the 1980s, the developing countries began to take a more active interest in the GATT. This appears to be less a response to changes in GATT policies and more the consequence of a redirection in economic policy by many Third World governments. The traditional Third World reservations concerning GATT have been set aside in recent years as many governments in the developing world embraced market-oriented policies. This change in approach is clearly symbolised by increased Third World membership of GATT. In 1970, 49 members of the Third World coalition were Contracting Parties to the GATT, but by 1991, 71 such countries had become full members of the GATT. A good indication of this turn-round in thinking is the fact that Mexico, for so long a fierce critic of GATT's liberal ideology joined the organisation in 1986.

GATT's role in the international trade regime is controversial, with some of its potential supporters emerging as trenchant critics. Attitudes to the GATT arise from views held on two distinct issues. The first concerns the gains from trade and the benefits and costs of international trade. Neo-classical economists stress the beneficial aspects of participating in the world economy and support efforts to liberalise trade. Mercantilist writers do not deny the operation of the law of comparative advantage but believe that market intervention is necessary in certain cases to protect domestic producers. Theorists from the unequal exchange or imperialist perspective argue that international trade is inherently exploitative. Support for GATT's aims comes mainly from liberal trade theorists. The second issue relates to the view held on the role of international organisations. Critics of GATT concentrate on its weak enforcement powers and the unequal structure of power in the organisation. Supporters of the GATT, on the other hand, whilst aware of its limitations, nevertheless believe that GATT has been influential in curbing protectionist demands in the international trading system.

This chapter will begin with a discussion of GATT's origins. This will be followed by an analysis of GATT as an international organisation. The third part of the chapter will examine GATT's role in the international trading system and the organisation's contribution to the liberalisation of world trade. The specific demands of the developing countries for reform of the GATT and the liberal trade regime will be the concern of the next section of the chapter. This will be followed by a discussion of the Uruguay Round of trade negotiations.

The origins of GATT

Like the IMF and the World Bank, GATT is the outcome of the interwar dialogue on the shape of the post-war world economy which took place between the American and British governments. Unlike the IMF and the World Bank, GATT was not negotiated at Bretton Woods but can, nevertheless, be seen as part of the Bretton Woods system of global economic management. Two strands of thought influenced the institutionalisation of world trade in the post-war period. First, political and business elites in the United States supported moves to freer trade as a means of guaranteeing export markets for American goods. A liberal trade order was a way of legitimating American economic supremacy. Secondly, it was widely believed in the US and Europe that the rise of protectionism in the 1930s had been harmful both to prosperity and peace. The economic nationalism of the interwar period, economic crisis and political instability led to an increased awareness of the necessity to coordinate national commercial policies in an increasingly interdependent global economy. It was hoped that the creation of a more open trade regime would establish a model of economic interdependence and so ensure peace through internationally shared prosperity. Free trade would allow countries to specialise according to comparative advantage and thereby achieve higher standards of growth. The consensus was that economic prosperity would form the basis of a more stable world order.

The US administration which had taken the lead in the reconstruction of the international monetary and financial systems was the main actor in the attempt to restructure international trade after World War II. Subsequent to its proposals in the monetary and financial fields, the US government published proposals for the creation of an international trade organisation on 6 December 1945.[2] These proposals were taken up within the UN, and the Economic and Social Council (ECOSOC) in February 1946 proposed the convening of an International Conference on Trade and Employment, 'for the purpose of promoting the expansion of the production, exchange and consumption of goods'.[3] A 19-nation preparatory committee was established[4] and it held two sessions – 15 October–22 November 1946 in London, and 4 April–22 August 1947 in Geneva. This led to the convening of the United Nations Conference on Trade and Employment held in Havana, Cuba from 21 November 1947 to 24 March 1948. Attended by 53 states the conference produced the Havana Charter for an International Trade Organisaton which comprised an outline for an International Trade Organisation and a code of conduct for ITO members.

The ITO failed to achieve ratification by sufficient signatories to the Havana Charter and never came into existence.[5] The success of the ITO depended on US participation but domestic opposition to the proposed organisation created a climate in which President Truman's efforts to win Congressional approval were unlikely to achieve success. Opponents of the ITO in the American business community were effective in securing Congressional support for their case.[6] The Charter was criticised for failing to give adequate protection to US foreign investments and for inadequate recognition of American interests in its voting arrangements. Congressional opposition to the ITO resulted in President

Truman's decision in 1951 not to submit the Havana Charter to Congress for ratification. This move signalled the end of the ITO, and pushed GATT, an interim arrangement, to the centre stage.

In an effort to hasten the moves towards liberal trade in the post-war world, and with the prospect of a successful conclusion to the forthcoming Havana Conference, 23 nations met in Geneva in March 1947 to negotiate tariff concessions.[7] In January 1948 the agreed tariff cuts, based on the most-favoured nation (MFN) principle, were implemented. Appended to the schedule of tariff cuts was a set of rules outlining the obligations of the parties with respect to the management of international trade. The General Agreement on Tariffs and Trade signed on 30 October 1947 consisted of three parts. The first, a Schedule of Concessions contained the commitments to reduce tariffs taken by the 23 governments and the MFN clause. A legal code of behaviour designed to provide a framework in which the tariff concessions would be protected was incorporated in two parts. The second part contained the commercial policy regulations and the third listed *inter alia* the provisions on territorial applications and regional arrangements.

Thus GATT, designed as a provisional instrument and in many respects ill-equipped to provide the framework in which a multilateral trade regime would be established, became the central instrument for the management of international trade. GATT developed from a multilateral treaty administered by conferences to a body performing the duties and functions of an international trade organisation.[8] It is to a consideration of GATT as an international trade organisation that we now turn.

GATT: organisational structure and political process

The GATT framework

Although some doubt may be cast on its status as an international organisation GATT is more than a multilateral treaty. It is an international organisation with headquarters, a secretariat and an executive head called the director-general. It monitors trade flows, provides its members with information and possesses a research department that investigates current trade problems. The Contracting Parties meet annually and have entrusted the day-to-day running of the organisation to the GATT Council. The Council, which meets about every six weeks, acts as the management board of the GATT. A network of specialised committees, panels, working parties and *ad hoc* bodies report to it. In organisational terms GATT has three separate but interrrelated aspects.

First, it is a contractural document which provides a framework of rules and principles to govern the behaviour of states in the international trading system. Secondly, it is a forum for multilateral trade negotiations. And thirdly, it acts as a centre for the settlement of trade disputes.

The General Agreement consists of 38 Articles and enshrines four key principles. The most important principle of GATT is that of non-discrimination, embodied in the MFN clause. The provision for equality of treatment is articulated in Article I of the General Agreement. It states that,

> with respect of customs duties, any advantage, favour, privilege or immunity granted by any Contracting Party to any product originating in or destined for any other country shall be accorded immediately and unconditionally to the like product originating in or destined for the territories of all other Contracting Parties.

The MFN principle ensures that any concession granted to one Contracting Party must be extended to all other Contracting Parties. The MFN principle is therefore the cornerstone of the liberal multilateral payments system.

The second principle is that of reciprocity. This principle is intended to ensure that when one country lowers its tariffs against another's exports, it will in return be granted concessions of equal importance. The principle of reciprocity applied through multilateral bargaining means that in theory one country's concessions are 'paid for' by a third country which in turn passes it on to another and the process continues to repeat itself. Thirdly, GATT supports a system in which the only permissible protectionist devices are tariffs. Non-tariff barriers (NTBs), such as import quotas are banned and countries are urged to replace NTBs with tariffs. This is the principle of transparency and is based on the fact that tariffs are a more visible source of protection. The fourth principle is that of multilateralism and reflects the commitment to the creation of a multilateral trade regime and participation in periodic rounds of tariff cutting.

From the outset the need to balance national interests against international commitments resulted in a number of important exceptions and deviations from these underlying principles. The GATT is a compromise between protectionist and liberal sentiments and is best conceived as a framework for managed trade rather than an instrument of free trade.[9] Members are allowed to use protective measures in certain circumstances. Members may apply anti-dumping duties to combat an unfair purchase of market share by another country. They are also authorised to institute protective measures to protect the overall balance of payments and to apply quotas in the event of market disruption in a particular industry. Such measures are supposed to be applied on a non-discriminatory basis. Moreover, the preferential trading systems established by France and the United Kingdom were excluded from the non-discriminatory principles of GATT.

It is, however, the exclusion of agriculture and textiles from the GATT rules and the development of forms of protection contrary to the spirit of the GATT which calls into question the status of the rules. The most striking departure from free trade rules has been in agriculture. In allowing quotas to be imposed, in special circumstances, on agricultural imports the original Agreement created a situation whereby agriculture was treated differently from industrial products. The original exception was granted so that the US Congress could continue its price support programme. In 1955 the United States was granted a waiver enabling it to legalise import controls on agricultural products. This waiver covered a substantial part of US agricultural imports and was responsible for the creation of a climate favourable to agricultural protectionism.[10] The advent of the European Community and the establishment of the Common Agricultural Policy (CAP) consolidated opposition to the liberalisation of trade in agricultural products. The Uruguay Round marks the first serious attempt to address the problem of agricultural protectionism.

Textiles form the second major exclusion from the GATT system. The treatment of textiles has contravened two of the basic principles of GATT. The approach taken allows discrimination against specific countries, and uses quotas instead of tariffs. When Japan acceded to the GATT in 1955 some members maintained import controls against some Japanese goods, especially textiles. The competitive position of Japan and some Asian developing countries, e.g. Hong Kong, India and Pakistan, in textiles and clothing led to the creation in 1961 of the Short-Term Arrangement (STA) on textiles. This lasted for one year and was replaced in 1962 by the LTA, renewed twice, in 1967 and 1970. The MFA, first implemented in 1974 and renewed three times, has since governed North–South trade in textiles. Both agriculture and textiles will be discussed in more detail later in the chapter.

The rules and principles of the GATT provide a framework for the negotiations which take place on the reductions of barriers to trade. As a forum for trade negotiations GATT operates through bargaining rounds. To date, seven rounds of trade negotiations have been completed and the eighth round has been under way since 1986. The first five rounds of negotiation (Geneva, 1947; Annecy 1949; Torquay 1950–51; Geneva 1956; and Dillon 1960–61) concentrated on tariffs, and reductions were negotiated on an item-by-item basis. The Kennedy Round (1963–67) was the first round to adopt a linear approach to tariff liberalisation. With the Tokyo Round (1973–79) an assault was made on non-tariff barriers which had increased considerably since the inception of GATT. The current Uruguay Round launched in 1986 marks the first attempt to bring agricultural trade under GATT auspices and to address the problem of trade in services.

One of the reasons why members value the organisation is the existence of dispute settlement procedures. In the event of a trade dispute between two members, any member can call for the establishment of a panel of experts to rule on the dispute. These panels consist of three experts drawn from member countries with no interest in the subject matter. The findings of the panel are binding on the plaintiff and defendant if a consensus decision is reached by the experts. In the event of non-compliance with the panel's ruling members are allowed to take retaliatory action. GATT panels have managed to resolve a number of dangerous trade disputes and the available evidence suggests that the GATT dispute settlement system has worked better than is generally perceived.[11]

Membership and decision-making

Countries can become members of the GATT through two different methods. The usual method of accession requires the approval of two-thirds of the existing members. On entry a member must negotiate tariff reductions commensurate with previous GATT practice. Some developing countries have become members through the second route. A newly independent country can automatically become a member of GATT if the former metropole had applied GATT provisions to the colony. This form of entry is not subject to vote or to a negotiation of tariff concessions of equivalent value. More than 30 developing countries have attained GATT membership in this manner.[12]

Decisions in GATT are taken by majority vote and this in theory increases the influence developing countries have over the organisation since they account for over two-thirds of its membership. In practice, decisions are taken by consensus. The development of consensus in GATT reflects developments in other international organisations. And like the decision-making process in other organisations the consensus mode of decision-making hides the real power relations behind the outcomes. Although the search for consensus does require the dominant economic nations to consult other states on certain issues they can nevertheless ignore conflicting interests unless a reconciliation of divergent views is essential for a solution. Moreover, the weaker states are aware that the recourse to voting against the wishes of the major trading states will achieve nothing, except, perhaps, to marginalise the organisation.

Negotiations in GATT rounds definitely reflect the strength of the parties. Negotiations typically take place between principal suppliers and principal consumers. This effectively diminishes the impact that developing countries can have on the negotiations since they rarely account for major market share either as producers or consumers. The most effective participants in GATT negotiations have therefore been the representatives of the OECD countries. Indeed the stimulus for GATT negotiations have always come from the United States. As previously mentioned, the original meeting in Geneva was convened so that President Truman could use the powers granted him in the Reciprocal Trade Agreements Act before they expired in 1948. Successive GATT rounds have been tied to enabling American legislation in the field of international trade. Moreover, the delegations from developing countries often lack the expertise and coverage of those from the industrialised world. For example, at the December 1990 Brussels GATT summit the US delegation consisted of over 400 delegates, which was more than the combined total of the staffs of the Sub-Saharan African and Latin American trade missions.[13]

Organisational ideology

In common with the IMF and the World Bank, GATT was founded on liberal principles. The case for free trade rests on the theory of comparative advantage. Initially propounded by David Ricardo in the nineteenth century the theory has since been updated. Ricardo argued that specialisation and trade are worthwhile even when a country can produce all goods more efficiently than other countries. What matters is the comparative relative efficiency of production in different countries rather than their absolute efficiency. Complete specialisation in products in which countries enjoy a comparative advantage results in increased efficiency and welfare gains for the country and the world. Trade leads to both increased productivity and higher incomes in the national economy and the international economy. Modern trade theory emphasises differences in factor endowments rather than costs as determining comparative advantage. For example, a country with a relative abundance of capital compared with other factors will tend to specialise in goods which are relatively capital-intensive.

The official GATT ideology rests on free trade arguments. The gains from trade outweigh the disadvantages according to this perspective. Trade provides developed and developing countries with mutually advantageous exchange. Neo-classical economists point to a number of benefits arising from international trade. Apart from the exchange gain from trade, two further static gains arise if trade is organised according to the law of comparative advantage: first, the ability to consume more because of international specialisation; and secondly, the export of surplus production.

For developing countries the dynamic gains from trade are greater than the static gains. By definition developing countries suffer from an absence of capital and technology. Liberal economists argue that trade provides an opportunity to gain much needed foreign expertise, to raise the productivity of the work force and force local firms to become more competitive. So, far from resorting to protection in order to protect domestic industries developing countries should welcome the opportunities and discipline imposed by market forces. Without trade developing countries are unlikey to generate sufficient investment to facilitate a satisfactory rate of economic growth.[14]

The liberal view of the benefits of free trade and the organisation of the international trading system is challenged by mercantilist and unequal exchange perspectives. Mercantilists tend to point to the gap between the liberal ideal of free trade and the reality of protection in the real world. Mercantilist theorists do believe that trade can be the engine of growth but focus on power relations in the international economy and do not subordinate national goals to those of the world economy. They stress that in the real world sectional and national interests predominate, and protectionism rather than free trade is the norm. Mercantilist theorists argue that free trade tends to benefit the more economically powerful states and that protection is necessary to maintain employment or to protect infant industries. The separation between the economic and political and/or the subordination of the political to the economic so common to liberal economic thinking is challenged in realist mercantilist writing. As Susan Strange makes clear, 'The basic premise that state policy should, or even can, be based on the single criterion of maximising efficiency . . . is demonstrably false. Efficiency never has been, and never can be, the sole consideration in the choice of state policies.'[15]

The Marxist or unequal exchange perspective argues that far from being an engine of growth, trade can retard the development process in poor countries. According to this view the structural inequality in the world system is an inevitable product of capitalist relations of production. Advanced capitalist states use trade to control the international economic system and so maintain and increase inequalities between the North and the South. In this approach the imperialism of free trade stifles productive forces in the peripheral countries.[16]

In the next section I will consider the impact of GATT on the world trading system. The ideology of free trade has played a major part in defining GATT's role. But in reality GATT is not a *laissez-faire* organisation. The post-war international trading regime in Ruggie's felicitous phrase is one of embedded liberalism.[17] The trade regime as constructed in the GATT is a mixture of bilateralism and multilateralism. The GATT rules strike a compromise between global economic integration, multilateralism and a reliance on market forces on the one hand, and the quest for domestic stability, economic expediency and bilateralism on the other. In this context appeals to liberal values serve a distinct ideological function and the use of liberal economic theory to support the functioning of the order is an attempt to render free trade as objective and value-free. The history of the post-1945 international trading system should therefore be interpreted from the perspective of this balance between a commitment to multilateralism and the need to guard against excessive domestic costs resulting from a liberal order. The exceptions and exclusions in the GATT are therefore to be seen not as unfortunate deviations from a free trade ideal but as essential components of a system of managed trade.

GATT and the international trading system: trade liberalisation and the 'new protectionism'

Trade liberalisation

Two features of the trade liberalisation which has taken place in the post-war period are worthy of note. The first is the significant reductions in tariffs achieved through GATT rounds. The 23 original contracting parties agreed tariff reductions on some 45,000 products which constituted approximately half of world trade at the time. This initial momentum was continued in the next two rounds at Annecy in 1949 and Torquay in 1951. By the end of the Torquay Round in 1951 over 58,000 individual items had been the subject of tariff concessions.[18] The third round, in Geneva, in 1956 and the Dillon Round (1960–61) achieved little in the way of further liberalisation. Three factors can be adduced to explain the slackening off in trade liberalisation in this period. First, the recovery of the European economies was slower than expected and these countries were not yet ready to face the full force of international competition. The second is the interest taken in customs unions and free trade areas during the late 1950s and early 1960s, e.g. the creation of the EEC, the European Free Trade Area, the Latin American Free

Trade Area and the Central American Common Market focused attention on regional tariff-cutting and away from the GATT. A third factor was the approach used in negotiations. The item-by-item method of negotiating tariff cuts was unsatisfactory and impeded trade liberalisation.

The Kennedy Round (1963–67) revived the flagging GATT system through its attempt to tackle issues previously ignored, e.g. agriculture and non-tariff barriers; an increased number of participants; and the adoption of the principle of across-the-board cuts in tariffs in preference to the item-by-item approach. By the end of the Kennedy Round, agreement had been reached on tariff reductions covering some $40 billion worth of world trade, equivalent to some 75 per cent of total world trade. The average reduction in tariffs amounted to between 36 and 39 per cent.[19]

The Tokyo Round, although conducted in a less favourable world economic climate than the Kennedy Round, nevertheless maintained the momentum in respect of the dismantling of tariff barriers. Tariffs were successfully reduced by an average of between 33 and 38 per cent covering over $100 billion worth of world trade. The significance of the Tokyo Round, however, lay not in its efforts over tariff-cutting but in its results in other areas. The Tokyo Round was at the time the most comprehensive multilateral trade negotiations ever undertaken and attempted to deal with the problems created by the rise of NTBs. Six voluntary codes to prohibit the use of NTBs were agreed on but the resulting implementation has been poor. In addition a sectoral code for trade in aircraft and a 'framework agreement' covering subjects primarily of interest to developing countries were agreed.[20] The current Uruguay Round will be discussed in a separate section below.

The second noteworthy feature of trade liberalisation under GATT is the uneven nature of the process. In other words, GATT's effectiveness has been limited mainly to trade in manufactured products. GATT has been successful in maintaining the commitment of the leading Western countries to a system of embedded liberalism by skewing the benefits of trade liberalisation in their favour. The range of manufactured products that have benefited most from trade liberalisation are products produced in the AICs.

The claim that the main beneficiaries of the tariff cuts in the seven completed rounds are the developed countries is clearly borne out by the evidence. In 1947 at the first round of GATT negotiations, the average tariff on manufactured goods was around 40 per cent. By the end of the Kennedy Round these tariffs had been lowered to an average of 10 per cent. The tariffs of the industrial countries were reduced by about 35 per cent as a result of the Tokyo Round.[21] Average nominal tariffs on industrial products in the United States declined from about 50 per cent to about 4 per cent and those in the United Kingdom from around 40 per cent to around 4 per cent between the 1947 round of negotiations and the conclusion of the Tokyo Round in 1979.[22]

The role of GATT in facilitating trade liberalisation and the expansion of trade is contested in the literature. Liberal theorists argue that GATT provides an economic climate generally conducive to trade liberalisation which in turn has contributed to the expansion and growth of the world economy. The opposing viewpoint argues that GATT was irrelevant to the reductions in trade barriers which have taken place and that the extent of actual liberalisation has been exaggerated by liberal theorists. A third perspective rejects both the above arguments and proposes that GATT has been influential in regulating world trade but only in the context of the structural constraints of a changing world economy.

World output in the period since 1945 has grown faster than at any other period in history. But the increase in world trade has been more rapid than that in world output. Between 1950 and 1985 world output increased roughly fivefold in volume terms but the volume of world trade increased almost ninefold.[23] Liberal theorists argue that the GATT multilateral framework was one of the key factors behind these developments. Finlayson and Zacher delineate four interdependent and mutually reinforcing functions of the trade regime responsible for this result.[24] First, GATT provides a 'facilitative function' through serving as a forum for communication, negotiation of treaties and trade liberalisation in a multilateral framework. Secondly, GATT provides a 'constraint function' through its rules and procedures for compliance. The dispute settlement process, the codes of conduct and the binding of tariffs all form part of this function. Thirdly, GATT fulfils a 'diffusion of influence function' through the spread of liberal economic principles and practices. Finally, the 'promotion of interaction function' allows smaller states better scope for negotiating access to markets abroad and more influence over the regulation of trade barriers than would be possible under a self-help system.

Susan Strange rejects the view that GATT has been a major influence on trade liberalisation and the growth in world output. She argues that statistical demonstrations which ascribe successful trade liberalisation to GATT and link this with global economic expansion are 'apt to confuse correlation and cause and to make exaggerated claims for trade liberalisation as the major cause of trade expansion and growth in the world economy'.[25] Strange argues that the multilateral regime model of the world trading system is inadequate and fails to capture the reality of a world in which governments actively intervene in international trade.

She suggests that the liberal approach should be replaced with a web-of-bilateral-contracts model. One weakness of the liberal model according to Strange is its focus on states. GATT was created to regulate trade between states but today a great deal of trade is intrafirm trade within the transnational corporation. Reliable statistics on the growth and size of intrafirm trade have been produced for the United States and a limited number of industrialised countries. The evidence suggests that this is an increasing trend in the international trading system.[26]

For Strange the explanation of the post-war economic boom lies in the creation of international credit. In a recently co-authored book the argument is put that 'the real engine of growth has been credit creation begun by governments through the Marshall Plan and other state initiated measures but continued through the combined efforts at financial innovation of TNCs and banks in issuing tradeable commercial paper.'[27]

It is difficult to determine whether trade liberalisation led to economic growth or whether the reverse proposition is correct. Moreover, it is problematical whether increased production necessitated trade liberalisation under GATT. It does appear, however, to be the case that increased protection tends to accompany and follow recessionary periods. In order to study the influence of GATT on trade liberalisation and world output it is necessary to place GATT within the context of a changing world economy and to assess the importance of the organisation to its dominant members.

As stated earlier, GATT has never presided over a free trade regime. GATT exists in a world with both liberal and protectionist interest groups vying for control of state policy. It has therefore always represented a departure from textbook *laissez-faire* in the direction of managed trade. In practice GATT has only brought about limited freer trade in selected sectors. Important sectors in the world economy such as agriculture and textiles have been organised outside of GATT's scope. The success of the GATT arises from the important role it plays in securing the interests of the dominant actors in the international political economy. The ideology and principles of the institution have played a crucial role in maintaining support for the international trade regime. Thus GATT helps to structure the negotiations and their outcomes by focusing trade liberalisation in certain areas and excluding others. The GATT provides a mechanism whereby states and transnational corporations (through their influence on state policy) can adapt to the demands of an evolving international economy.[28] In the next section I will examine the rise of the new protectionism and link the increasing resort to protectionist measures to developments in the structure of international trade.

The new protectionism

Many writers assert that sometime in the 1970s GATT began to lose its effectiveness as the bulwark of the liberal trade regime. The positive achievements of the GATT in achieving unprecedented levels of tariff reductions was now threatened by the rise of what is called the new protectionism. This new protectionism impeded the drive towards trade liberalisation. Such protectionist measures have exploited the grey area between what was legal and illegal in GATT. A variety of studies pointed to the growing incidence of protection in developed countries.[29] The new protectionism is mainly practised by the US, EC and Japan. The new protectionism differs from old protectionist measures through a greater reliance on NTBs and the resort to bilateralism. The most widely used NTBs include quotas, voluntary export restraints (VERs), customs valuation procedures, administrative authorisations to import, subsidies and health standards.

Protectionism gained momentum in the 1970s as domestic interest groups in the major capitalist states promoted their sectional interests (and, they argued, the national interest). The US and the EC have endorsed and popularised the concept of fair trade and the policies of bilateralism and market management in contravention of GATT rules. Such arrangements implicitly break GATT's MFN rules which only prohibit discriminatory import controls. The EC, US, Canada and Australia have also established their own anti-dumping and countervailing duties procedures which often amount to thinly disguised protection.

Since 1974, US trade law have been updated to threaten to undertake retaliatory action against unfair trade practices if an agreement suitable to US interests is not concluded. The resort by the United States to Section 301 and Super 301 of its trade law allows the American president to retaliate against foreign trade practices that unfairly discourage American exports. It is, however, solely American officials who decide what is unfair! Between 1974, when the Trade Act became law, and 1985, 27 cases involving unfair barriers were brought. Since 1986, the law has been used more aggressively. By 1988, $4 billion worth of trade was subject to Section 301.[30] In 1988 the Omnibus Trade and Competitiveness Act increased the scope of Section 301 to Super 301. Whereas Section 301 dealt with disputes about specific products, Super 301 has been used to accuse countries of a wide range of unfair practices.[31]

VERs are perhaps the most symbolic of the measures taken under the guise of the new protectionism. Under such arrangements which are usually bilateral and sometimes secret, low cost exporters 'voluntarily' restrict sales to countries where their goods are threatening industry and employment. Countries have resorted to these measures outside the framework of the GATT, which was designed to cope with quantitative restrictions and tariffs but not non-tariff barriers and voluntary export restraints.

Not only are NTBs difficult to identify, the GATT lacks adequate rules to cope with the problem. The resort to bilateralism, especially the frequent use of VERs in sectors such as automobiles, steel and electronic products, effectively circumvents the GATT system. The reliance on NTBs has meant that many of GATT's rules have been frequently bypassed or violated. The greater the recourse to non-tariff measures, the greater is the erosion of GATT's ability to regulate international trade. Voluntary trade restraints signal a retreat from multilateralism and non-discrimination.

The rise of the new protectionism is a response to a number of changes in the international political economy. The compromise between global economic integration and the political costs of domestic adjustment became much harder to resolve in the context of recession and international economic instability. The rise in protectionism is linked to rising unemployment in weak industrial sectors in the AICS. Secondly, many AICs found it hard to cope with the shift in comparative advantage to the NICs and the consequences of Japanese competition, particularly in labour-intensive industries. Thirdly, national governments have attempted to protect domestic economic policies from the exigencies of the market place. The transnational corporations and a liberal world order is seen as a threat to the pursuit of domestic growth and welfare objectives.[32] The new protectionism has also been blamed on the tendency of oligopolies in traditional industries, like steel and shipbuilding to restructure international production through market-sharing arrangements and coordinated actions among producers.[33] Other explanations for the new protectionism include responses to exchange rate policies[34] and the declining mobility of labour in the industrial countries.[35]

The developing countries in GATT

The developing countries form a less structured and coordinated group in GATT than in either the IMF or the World Bank. This is partly a consequence of the different stages of economic development, dissimilar comparative advantages and specific interests in international trade. It is also caused by the GATT negotiating structure, which is not conducive to group politics.[36] Nevertheless, a distinct Third World perspective and set of interests is evident in an examination of GATT's historical record. Developing countries have mounted a sustained campaign for the reform of GATT and articulated a set of specific interests in the context of GATT negotiations. Despite increased fragmentation in the Third World coalition in recent years the developing countries do still have common interests on a wide range of trade issues. Three main themes emerge from a review of developing countries' participation in the GATT. In the first, the developing countries have consistently presented a case for special and differential treatment.[37] Secondly, the GATT rules have been applied in a discriminatory manner with two areas of major interest to the developing countries, viz. agriculture and textiles and clothing exempt from the post-war trend towards freer trade. A third feature of Third World participation in the GATT is the manner in which these countries, while protesting at their marginalisation from decision-making in GATT, did little to increase their involvement in the rounds of tariff cuts. The next three sections will discuss these issues in the period 1947–86. Developments in the Uruguay Round will be analysed separately.

Special and differential treatment

The demand for special and differential treatment is based on the claim that the demands of development are incompatible with the untrammelled operation of market forces. The GATT's free trade approach is, according to this perspective, incapable of supporting the development aims of the Third World. Furthermore, the developing countries argued that the original GATT as an instrument of trade liberalisation was seriously flawed since it omitted consideration of their special problems. The developing countries mounted a campaign in the 1950s and 1960s in order to reform GATT to reflect better their developmental needs. Criticism of GATT's organisational ideology and attempts to reform the GATT structure were conducted simultaneously.

For most of the post-war period the governments of the developing countries have pursued interventionist trade policies. Whereas industrial countries reduced tariffs on a wide range of products trade liberalisation was seldom undertaken by developing countries. Import-substitution industrialisation was seen as the fastest route to economic development. This doctrine, originally espoused and applied in Latin America through the influence of the Economic Commission for Latin America (ECLA) and its executive-director, Raul Prebisch, was accepted by newly independent governments in Africa and Asia. Developing countries also felt that persistent balance of payments deficits necessitated the resort to selective import controls.

The campaign for different and more favourable treatment begun in the 1950s finally resulted in the acceptance, by GATT, that 'equal treatment of unequals begets inequity'. The extent to which the derogations in favour of developing countries assists their development prospects and boosts their exports is, however, open to question.

The developing countries first identified a collective interest with respect to the shortcomings of the original General Agreement. Whereas the Havana Charter had included eight articles on development and provisions dealing with commodity trade GATT omitted special provisions for trade in raw materials and only one article (Article XVIII) was devoted specifically to the problem of economic development. This sanctioned the use of quantitative restrictions for the purposes of economic development under limited conditions.

The implementation of a new Article XVIII following the 1954/55 revision of the GATT went some way towards easing the dissatisfaction of the developing countries. The new Article XVIII gave greater legitimacy to the needs of economic development. It authorised more widespread recourse to infant industry protection and relaxed the use of quantitative restrictions to safeguard the balance of payments.[38] It was not, however, until the publication of the report by a panel of experts, convened by the GATT, entitled *Trends in International Trade* in 1958[39] that the movement which culminated in the addition of a new section to the GATT in 1965 gathered momentum. The report stated unequivocally, '[the] prospects for exports of non-industrial countries are very sensitive to internal policies in the industrial countries and (that) on balance their development will probably fall short of the increase in world trade as a whole.'[40]

In February 1965 the Contracting Parties added a new chapter entitled 'Trade and Development'. The addition of Part IV was primarily in response to the pressure of the developing countries for change. The developing countries began to act as a coordinated group in GATT in 1959 and enhanced their bargaining power in the reform process initiated as a result of the Haberler Report. Moreover, pressures in the United Nations system for the reform of the international trade order persuaded the developed countries that their interests could best be safeguarded through reform of GATT. The alternative of the creation of an international trade organisation was anathema to the West. Reform of the GATT was the West's counter to the convening of the United Nations Conference on Trade and Development (UNCTAD). Although the developing countries were successful in establishing UNCTAD as a permanent organisation, Part IV ensured a continuing relevance for GATT in the battle for influence.

The importance of Part IV lay more in its symbolic value than any substantive changes it brought to trade relations between the developed and the developing countries. It gave legal sanction to the principle of special and differential treatment and provided the developing countries with a concrete reference point. Part IV represented a codification of the discussions which took place in the GATT following the publication of the Haberler Report. The commitments undertaken by the developed countries, under the new articles to grant improved market access and to give priority to products of export interest to developing countries in future trade liberalisation negotiations, were not binding obligations. Developed countries also agreed under Part IV to exempt the developing countries from making reciprocal tariff concessions.[41]

It was on the issue of non-reciprocity and specifically that of preferences that the developing countries mounted their next major campaign for the reform of the international trading system. The divisions among the developing countries, with serious differences emerging between countries already in receipt of selective preferences and those outside any schemes, conflict between those countries with a substantial manufacturing base and therefore likely to benefit from the conclusion of a Generalised System of Preferences (GSP) and those for whom any benefits would only be in the long run, made it difficult for the developing countries to present a united profile in the bargaining on preferences.[42]

Although the principle of non-reciprocity was conceded because of the 'development, financial and trade needs' of the developing countries, Part IV did not signal agreement on a generalised system of preferences. The long, and at times, acrimonious debate on preferences was, for the most part, conducted in UNCTAD. At its second conference in 1968 UNCTAD passed a resolution which recognised, 'unanimous agreement in favour of the early establishment of a mutually acceptable system of generalised non-reciprocal and non-discriminatory preferences'.[43] GSP which resulted from the ensuing negotiations was incorporated under GATT rules through a 10-year waiver granted in 1971 to set aside the MFN obligations under Article I. The Tokyo Round in 1979 extended the GSP unconditionally.

The GSP is designed to increase the exports of manufactures and semi-manufactures from Third World countries through the granting of preferential access to the markets of the industrialised countries. The schemes, which were concluded and implemented by the developed countries, varied in their product coverage and preference margins. The GSP as agreed is neither general nor systematic. Many products are excluded from GSP coverage if they become competitive with domestically produced goods.[44]

The developing countries used the Tokyo Round as a vehicle to enhance claims for special and differential treatment. Among the explicit goals of the Tokyo Round was the commitment to 'secure additional benefits' and to improve the participation of developing countries in international trade. Special and more favourable treatment for developing countries was selected as one of the priorities of the negotiations. The Tokyo Declaration which commenced the Multi-lateral Trade Negotiations (MTN) recognised, 'the importance of the application of differential measures to developing countries in ways which will provide special and more favourable treatment for them in areas of the negotiation where this is feasible and appropriate'.[45] Moreover, non-reciprocity for developing countries was declared to be the basis on which negotiations would proceed. In the words of the declaration, 'The developed countries do not expect reciprocity for commitments made by them in the negotiations to reduce or remove tariff and other barriers to the trade of developing countries.'[46]

The Tokyo Round results included four Framework Agreements.[47] Some of these agreements establish a new legal basis for the treatment of developing countries in the GATT but others are of a non-binding nature. The Framework Agreement entitled 'Differential and More Favourable Treatment, Reciprocity and Fuller Participation of Developing Countries', also known as the enabling clause, is the most important of the four understandings. It provides a legal basis for the GSP, preferential arrangements among developing countries and more favourable treatment for developing countries. It also recognises the need for special treatment for the least developed countries.

The 'Declaration on Trade Measures Taken for Balance-of-Payments Purposes' relaxed the circumstances under which developing countries could impose surcharges for balance of payments purposes. The 'Decision on Safeguard Action for Development Purposes' extended the scope for the imposition of surcharges beyond the previous infant industry definition. Finally, the 'Understanding Regarding Notification, Consultation, Dispute Settlement and Surveillance' envisages that in strengthening consultative procedures special attention will be given to the problems and interests of the developing countries.

The developing countries welcomed this advance in recognition of special and differential treatment but were less receptive to the graduation provision contained in the enabling clause. This declared that,

> Less-developed contracting parties expect that their capacity to make contributions or negotiated concessions or to take other mutually agreed action under the provisions and procedures of the General Agreement would improve with the progressive development of their economies and

improvement in their trade situation, and they would accordingly expect to participate more fully in the framework of rights and obligations under the General Agreement.[48]

The Ministerial Declaration adopted at Punta del Este in 1986 launching the Uruguay Round reaffirmed the commitment to differential and more favourable treatment. The developed countries repeated their support for the principle of non-reciprocity with respect to the developing countries. The Punta del Este Declaration also maintained the emphasis on the differentiation of the developing countries initiated at the conclusion of the MTNs. The principle of graduation was repeated and the problems of the least developed were given special mention.[49]

The campaign by the developing countries for special and differential treatment has been successful if judged solely on the basis of the formal recognition of this principle in the GATT framework. On the other hand, many critics have argued that the quest for different and more favourable treatment was misguided at best and harmful to the real interests of the developing countries at worst.

Liberal trade theorists are united in condemning special and differential treatment. They argue that the developing countries in opting for the protectionist policies symbolised by special and differential treatment have retarded their economic growth and supported protectionist forces in the developed world and therefore further reduced the potential benefits available from international trade.[50] The liberal case is based on the assumption that a positive correlation exists between economic liberalisation and economic development.[51] The liberal paradigm asserts that protectionist policies in developing countries result not only in an inefficient allocation of world resources but also in poor economic performance. Liberalisation improves economic performance in four ways. First, by exploiting comparative advantage it increases the employment in labour-intensive industries. Secondly, it relaxes the foreign exchange constraint on development by attracting foreign investment. Thirdly, it opens up the possibility of exploiting economies of scale. Finally, competition on the world market improves the efficiency of domestic firms and gains them access to information and technology.[52]

Furthermore, liberal economists attack the specific policies favoured under special and differential treatment. Trade policy measures are held to be of little value in achieving equilibrium in the balance of payments since they are both costly and ineffective in most circumstances.[53] The infant industry argument is rejected as a poor policy option.[54] One study found no empirical support for the infant industry argument.[55]

A further set of liberal arguments against special and differential treatment centre on the political impact of the acceptance of non-reciprocity and the granting of preferences. These critics argue that in the absence of reciprocity governments in developed countries will be reluctant to reduce trade barriers to the exports of the developing countries. An additional and more serious claim is often made to the effect that special treatment for developing countries has contributed to rising protectionism against them. Once an exception has been granted then it becomes easy to justify another exception. These writers also argue that in the absence of reciprocity the governments of developed countries find it difficult to resist the demands of domestic protectionist groups.[56] Some liberal theorists also argue that in giving legitimacy to protectionist measures this approach makes it more difficult for governments in the developing world to resist the pleas of special interest groups for protection. Thus governments without the discipline of an external constraint will be forced into implementing economically detrimental policies.[57]

From the standpoint of the left, special and differential treatment failed to live up to its promise. It produced few benefits and succeeded in marginalising the developing countries in GATT negotiations.[58] The sole concrete gain from special and differential treatment is the GSP, but liberal and radical critics have dissected its flaws.[59] Four main criticisms have been levelled against the GSP. In the first place, its overall impact on the developing countries is low because benefits are limited in size and skewed in favour of a small group of countries. A second problem with the GSP arises from the fact that the trade preferences have been eroded and outweighed by subsequent tariff reductions in the GATT and regional arrangements. Thirdly, the value of the GSP is reduced because of limited product coverage. The exclusion of so-called sensitive items, e.g. textiles, clothing and electronic products, reduces the benefits to the recipients. Finally, stringent rules-of-origin criteria reduce the quantity of developing country exports liable to gain from preferential access.

Agriculture

As previously noted, the agricultural sector has remained outside the GATT system. The attempt in the current Uruguay Round to liberalise trade in agricultural products is the first serious attack on this anomaly. The exclusion of agriculture from post-war trade liberalisation was the direct result of the interventionist farm sector policies followed by the major industrial countries. The United States, which is currently seeking an end to agricultural protectionism, was the main instigator of the interventionist policies responsible for agriculture's special status in world trade. The shift in US policy arises not from a new-found commitment to free trade but from the exorbitant costs of subsidising domestic production.

Protection in the North is justified in terms of domestic political and economic interests. Farm support prices are designed to support farm incomes, maintain food sufficiency and stabilise agricultural prices. The available evidence suggests that protectionism has signally failed to achieve these objectives. A number of studies have concluded that price support policies fail to maintain farmers' incomes or to stabilise prices.[60] Moreover, the goal of self-sufficiency was achieved in the 1960s and ceased to be a credible objective once overproduction became the norm in the industrial countries. The threat of a world food shortage and increased import demand from developing countries led policy-makers to support agricultural subsidies in the 1970s in the interests of global food security. By the 1980s these justifications no longer appeared relevant as the need to cut import bills in the wake of the debt crisis and increased self-sufficiency reduced import demand in the Third World.

The costly systems of protection maintained in the EC, US and Japan were not dismantled even though the economic rationale could no longer be sustained. Interventionist policies governed agricultural trade long after it had become apparent that they failed to achieve their objectives and were expensive to the state and detrimental to world welfare. Groups with vested interests in agricultural protection exercised political power far in excess of their numerical strength in the leading industrial countries.

It might be assumed that agricultural protection in the developed world is of minimal importance to developing countries since protection is only applied to temperate zone products. Such an assumption would be unwarranted on two grounds. First, it overlooks trade in competing products. Some Third World countries are producers of competing temperate zone products and some products, e.g. sugar, are produced in both tropical and temperate zones. It also omits consideration of the overall impact of agricultural protection on import and export prices. The effects of distortion in one commodity is not confined to that good. It has been noted that, 'The agricultural support policies of major developed countries have marked international consequences, affecting the level and variability of international prices and, as a consequence, the pattern of international trade in agricultural commodities.'[61]

Although measurement of the rate and level of protection and assessment of the trade-distorting effects of protection is difficult, the studies conducted to date arrive at broadly similar conclusions.[62] These analyses show that the agricultural policies of the industrial countries have an overall negative impact for both developed and developing countries. When protection leads to excess domestic production this results in lower world prices, hence reducing producers' incomes in third countries. Protection in the form of import levies and quotas, in removing a large part of agricultural trade from the world market increase the volatility of international prices. The insulation of domestic markets harms the export potential of foreign producers.

The developing countries have an interest in the agricultural policies of the developed world because of the negative overall impact of agricultural protection on their economies. The developing countries, therefore, should support agricultural liberalisation. However, the impact of liberalisation would not be uniform on all developing countries and depends on whether liberalisation takes place in both developed and developing countries or in developed countries alone.[63] Liberalisation of agriculture and the removal of protectionist barriers in developed and developing countries would increase trade, raise prices, and bring greater stability to prices. But, the net importers of cereals, meats and dairy products among the developing countries, currently benefiting from subsidised prices, would face higher prices as a result of the termination of farm support policies in the industrial countries. On the other hand, the developing countries which are net exporters of these products stand to benefit. These differences among developing countries correspond to broad regional categories. More than two-thirds of the benefits of agricultural trade liberalisation would go to Latin America and Southeast Asia. The African countries would be the major losers.[64] In short, food producing countries with a competitive export sector stand to gain but food importing countries will lose. The internal distributional impact in developing countries will favour producers over consumers.[65]

Textiles and clothing

The regime in textiles and clothing represents a sanctioned departure from normal GATT rules. A multilateral framework provides the ideological justification for what is in effect a selective, discriminatory and bilateral policy. As previously noted, trade in textiles and clothing have been regulated through a series of temporary agreements between the importing and exporting countries. The STA and LTA were established, principally, to regulate the import of textiles from Japan, but by the time the second LTA was negotiated in 1967 attention focused on exports from the developing countries. The MFA, in existence since 1974, confirmed that what began life as a temporary policy was transformed into a permanent feature of world trade. It increased product coverage from cotton textiles to cover wool and synthetic fibres. Furthermore, over the history of the MFA the controls used by the EC and the US were progressively tightened.[66]

The MFA is intended to prevent market disruption in importing countries. Market disruption arises when lower-priced imports from a particular source succeed in capturing a substantial share of the domestic market or a sharp rise in imports is registered. This definition is a rejection of comparative advantage, the very principle on which GATT is based! The rationale behind the MFA is the need to protect jobs in the developed countries. And, yet, the available evidence suggests that imports from developing countries have a small impact on unemployment in the textile and clothing industries in industrial countries.[67]

The conventional wisdom argues that this deviation from GATT's rules is attributable to 'the domestic political realities faced by the industrial country governments and their importance in shaping economic policy decisions'.[68] Declining labour-intensive industries are unable to compete with more competitive foreign firms and organise into protectionist lobbies. The geographic concentration of these industries increases their political importance and influence over governments worried about rising unemployment.

A more convincing explanation is provided by Diana Tussie.[69] She rejects the orthodox liberal viewpoint and argues instead that protection in the textile industry is the result of various structural forces. Successful trade liberalisation according to Tussie occurs for those goods and services that are organised internationally. The production of the textile sector is, primarily, organised nationally rather than internationally. A second factor arises from two aspects of production in developed countries: (i) domestic farm support prices in the US raised the cost of American textiles goods on the world market; (ii) in the switch from cotton to synthetic fibres the oligopolistic firms in the chemical industry supported protectionism and dragged along the clothing manufacturers. The expansion of Third World production was another structural factor contributing to the need for regulation. Here the influence of Japanese foreign investment in South Asia was crucial in expanding production in a number of countries. The competitive nature of the industry is the fourth structural feature which led to protection. According to Tussie, 'The fact that production was scattered among infinite factories dispersed in innumerable countries meant that trade management required a global solution.'[70]

The MFA is inherently discriminatory against Third World exporters. If trade in textiles and clothing were liberalised, exports from developing countries would increase significantly.[71] Moreover, for many developing countries textiles represent the first rung on the manufacturing ladder; protection not only denies comparative advantage it also damages economic growth.[72]

Discussion of the impact of the MFA on developing countries cannot be confined to the general level. The diversity of economic interests among developing countries precludes the adoption of a common position on the MFA apart from a commitment to right of market access. The MFA is not always seen by Third World exporters as negative. In some cases support is given to the MFA because it guarantees market share. Tussie distinguishes three different interest groups among the developing countries. The dominant suppliers, Hong Kong, South Korea and Taiwan have an interest in maintaining market shares. A controlled market helps in policing interventions of newly competitive countries and keeping prices high. The other Asian suppliers, who may not be able to compete with the dominant suppliers, benefit from the quota system which guarantees them a market and in certain cases provides the incentive for market growth. For the smaller marginal suppliers with a weaker inclination to export than East Asian producers quotas can remain unfulfilled.[73]

The view a Third World producer takes of the MFA depends on their competitive strength and quota allocation. Strongly competitive Third World producers with quotas below their export capacity will object to the MFA since it restricts their export potential. But exporters unable to compete in terms of price or organisation will welcome the protection provided by the MFA. These differences among developing countries should not obscure the fact that the overall impact of the MFA is to prevent developing countries from exploiting their comparative advantage.

Negotiations in GATT

The Uruguay Round is the first of the periodic GATT tariff-cutting exercises in which a large number of developing countries have taken an active role. But this is in keeping with the history of developing countries' participation in GATT. Each successive round of tariff negotiations since the Dillon Round has witnessed an increase in the number of developing countries taking part. In the first five rounds the developing countries took only a minimal part in proceedings. For example, at the time of the Dillon Round, 20 developing countries were members of the GATT but only Chile, Haiti, India, Israel, Nigeria,

Pakistan and Peru took part in the negotiations. Of some 20,000 tariff concessions, only 160 bindings or reductions of duties were on items of interest to the developing countries.[74]

There was increased participation in the Kennedy Round with 19 developing countries taking part in the negotiations. This reflected the desire of these countries to avail themselves of the possibilities of greater access to foreign markets which the Kennedy Round was offering. Two innovations in the negotiating rules enhanced the prospects for developing countries. In moving from an item-by-item to a linear approach all products were covered and the acceptance of the principle of non-reciprocity ensured that the export interests of developing countries would not be affected in the search for balance.[75] On the whole the results of the negotiations were disappointing to the developing countries. The round succeeded in achieving considerable tariff cuts on manufactures and semi-manufactures. Product groups in which developing countries have a special interest, e.g. iron and steel, either received less than average cuts or like agriculture were left untouched. And quantitative restrictions and other non-tariff barriers were hardly affected by the Kennedy Round agreements.[76]

Although 78 developing countries officially declared their participation in the MTN, active participation was limited to just over a quarter of that number. The middle-income developing countries with competitive manufacturing sectors, e.g. Argentina, Brazil, Egypt, India, Nigeria, South Korea and Yugoslavia, were the main developing country participants.[77] This shifted the developing countries from marginal status to a more active if limited negotiating role. But in the tariff negotiations the developing countries were divided. Some campaigned for preferential tariff cuts, and countries already in regional preferential agreements resisted this approach. Winham concluded that, 'Division in the developing-country ranks reduced the impact of their participation in the Tokyo Round tariff negotiation . . . .'[78] The results of the Tokyo Round for the developing countries were mixed. They achieved some success in negotiating special and differential treatment and some of the codes included clauses of economic significance. The framework negotiation contained some advances but crucially failed to impose obligations on developed countries with regard to the granting of preferences. And in the tariff negotiation tariff cuts on new trade amounting to $1.7 billion but the loss from GSP margins is estimated at almost $2.1 billion.[79]

This record of limited participation is the result of a number of factors. Developing countries' dissatisfaction with the international trading system, and the pursuit of outward-looking industrialisation policies are two of the reasons for their failure to be more active participants in the negotiating rounds. The high levels of protection in developing countries and their insistence on maintaining a range of protectionist devices reduced their interest in GATT negotiations. Developing countries were unwilling to accept many GATT obligations and whereas 80 to 90 per cent of the tariffs of industrial countries are bound, only a small percentage of developing country tariffs are bound.[80]

The success rates of GATT in liberalising trade in manufactures compared with its failure in agriculture is another reason for the traditional scepticism with which developing countries have approached GATT negotiations. GATT is perceived as a 'rich man's club', able to deal effectively with products of export interest to the major industrial countries but woefully inadequate in reducing barriers to goods in which the developing countries are competitive. Moreover, many minerals and tropical products enter the markets of developed countries at zero or under low tariff rates. Most developing countries are dependent on these products but the tariff negotiation does not cover them.

The relatively weak bargaining position of developing countries in GATT negotiations is a third reason for their poor participation rates. Even if all developing countries are prepared to assume a full and active role in the negotiations they lack the capabilities effectively to influence the outcomes. This is a result both of their poor economic power, the cost of participation and the absence of highly qualifed personnel to represent these countries in the technical discussions.

None of these factors in isolation can explain why developing countries have been unwilling participants in the GATT and marginal to the outcomes when they have participated. Self-exclusion, limited bargaining strength and the structure of world trade are all relevant to the answer.

The Uruguay Round

The Uruguay Round launched in 1986 is the most ambitious multilateral trade negotiation to date. In a seemingly permanent state of crisis since the end of 1990 because of a bitter and protracted dispute between the US and the EC over agricultural subsidies, the round is notable for the new subjects on the agenda and the active participation of developing countries. In this section I will not discuss the progress of the negotiations or detail the dispute between the EC and US. Instead this section will outline the structure of the negotiations, and the main issues with special emphasis on the interests of, and positions taken by the developing countries in these negotiations.

Organisatlon of the Uruguay Round

The Ministerial Declaration inaugurating the Uruguay Round established a Trade Negotiations Committee (TNC) to oversee the negotiations. All participating countries are members of this committee. Reporting to the TNC are two other committees: the Group of Negotiations on Goods (GNG) and the Group of Negotiations on Services (GNS).

The GNG is divided into fourteen negotiating sub-groups as follows:

1. Tariffs.
2. Non-tariff measures.
3. Natural resource-based products.
4. Textiles and clothing.
5. Agriculture.
6. Tropical products.
7. GATT articles.
8. MTN agreements and arrangements.
9. Safeguards.
10. Subsidies and countervailing measures.
11. Trade-related aspects of intellectual property rights (TRIPs).
12. Trade-related investment measures (TRIMs).
13. Dispute settlement.
14. Functioning of the GATT system (FOGs).

The GNS is of equal status with the GNG and reports directly to the TNC. It was not incorporated as a negotiating sub-group of the GNG because the developing countries insisted that negotiations on trade in services, a new area for GATT, should be kept on a 'separate track'. This was to ensure that concessions on services could not be traded for concessions on goods.

The main issues

The significance of the Uruguay Round lies in the attempt to bring agriculture and textiles under the aegis of the GATT and to conclude agreement on new issues. The agenda of the Uruguay Round reflects the interests of the AICs with the developing countries fighting the inclusion of the new issues.

A combination of the high cost of price support schemes and the existence of surplus stocks is responsible for the decision to place agriculture on the agenda of the Uruguay Round. The high cost to consumers and taxpayers of subsidies to agriculture threatened to defeat government budgetary controls. Textiles and clothing have been brought to the negotiating table despite the opposition of producer groups in the United States and the European Community. The developed countries are committed to dismantling the MFA and subjecting this trade to the discipline of the GATT. Trade liberalisation in this area is a political response to pressures from developing countries. In seeking liberalisation on a number of new issues in the face of strong opposition from the Third World the leading industrial nations agreed to abandon one of the oldest forms of discrimination against developing countries.

The three new issues – services, TRIPs and TRIMs cannot be treated in isolation. Action to liberalise trade in services entails discussions on trade-related investment matters and trade-related aspects of intellectual property rights. The growing importance of services in the economies of the developed countries and the growth of world trade in services created a need for multilateral surveillance over international service transactions.

Increased trade in services is the result of three main trends.[81] First, there has been a sharp rise in the 'tradeability' of services. The number and types of services traded internationally have increased because of the impact of new technologies. Second, the service element in traded goods has increased. This is because of the increased complexity and specialisation of manufacturing goods. Third, increasingly interdependent trade and capital markets have contributed to a rise in demand for services.

The desire of the United States (supported by other industrial countries) to regulate this growing area of world trade in order to eliminate various sectoral barriers to trade created a strong pressure for the inclusion of services in the Uruguay Round.[82] As Coote points out, developed countries see services, TRIPs and TRIMs

> as inter-related and complementary to one another in achieving their objectives of optimising the use of their new and emerging technologies, and maintaining their comparative advantage in this area of economic activity. Hence they want to be able to extend their service industries, increase their investment opportunities, and protect their technologies from adaptation or imitation.[83]

TRIMs have been included on the agenda because they create trade distorting effects, infringe Articles I and III of GATT and are opaque rather than transparent instruments of policy.[84] It can also be argued that the negotiations are an attempt to reduce constraints on the global

operations of transnational corporations through establishing investment rights.[85]

TRIPs have been included on the agenda because the non-
enforcement of property rights condones the theft of another's research
and development. It has been argued, on the other hand, that this is an
attempt to increase protection rather than liberalise trade. The creation
of a regime for intellectual property rights will maintain the dominant
position of transnational corporations from developed countries.[86]

Developing countries and the Uruguay Round

The developing countries initially resisted the suggestion that a new
round of trade negotiations be initiated. They flatly rejected the idea
that trade in services should be included in GATT talks. For the
developing countries the failure in the past to secure liberalisation in
agriculture, textiles and clothing, and tropical products, and the mush-
rooming of quantitative restrictions against their exports, revealed the
inequities in the international trading system. These countries were
fearful that negotiations on services would be used to extract concessions on trade in other products.

This initial scepticism was soon replaced with a positive attitude to the
Round and active participation in the negotiations. Three factors
account for this changed perspective. In the first place, the hetero-
geneous Third World became even more differentiated in the 1980s.
This made it increasingly difficult to maintain a common Third World
position. The relaxation of group discipline enabled a more accom-
modating dialogue to be established across the North–South divide. A
second important development is the increase in trade liberalisation in
the developing world.[87] Although there are country and regional
variations in the trend and pattern of trade liberalisation in Africa, Asia
and Latin America a strong movement towards export sector liberalisation is visible across these regions. The reasons for this move to liberal
trade policies are: recent thinking on trade policy and development
which documents the failure of import substitution strategies and
stresses the positive impact of maintaining open economies; IMF and
World Bank policy advice and the ability of the international financial
institutions to impose conditions favourable to liberal trade as part of
their lending policies; bilateral pressure from developed countries; and
the weakening of the foreign exchange ccnstraint as exports increased in
response to growth in the developed world.[88] A strong constituency
arose in the developing world in favour of strengthening the multilateral
regime. Another reason for the changed perspective towards the

Uruguay Round was the realisation that this time an attack would be made on agricultural protectionism.

No single developing country perspective exists on the Uruguay Round and coalitions across the North–South divide have been formed. The most important such grouping is the Cairns Group. The Cairns Group brings together countries from the Asia/Pacific region (Australia, Fiji, Indonesia, Malaysia, New Zealand, the Philippines and Thailand), Latin America (Argentina, Brazil, Chile, Colombia and Uruguay), and Canada and Hungary. Cairns Group members account for approximately a quarter of world trade. As major agricultural exporters they have a stake in the liberalisation of agriculture and have put forward proposals for the complete abolition of restrictions on agricultural trade.[89]

Southern negotiating positions have been more fluid than in previous GATT rounds and cross-cutting interests find developing countries on opposed sides on a number of issues. Moreover, South–South divisions have developed, particularly in relation to preferences. The African, Caribbean and Pacific (ACP) countries are keen to protect their preferential access to the EC market but the Latin American countries have been trying to erode these special preferences. The existence of selective preferences has been a source of tension since the early 1960s and erupts into conflict periodically.

On the 'new issues' agenda and on special and differential treatment, the developing countries have demonstrated greater solidarity. But as the negotiations progressed the developing countries have dropped many of their original positions and arrived at compromise with the industrial countries.

The developing countries from the outset took a negative view of the inclusion of services on the agenda and have articulated a position substantially at odds with the Northern countries. Developing countries view Northern proposals to liberalise trade in services as inherently discriminatory.[90] They objected to the inclusion of services in the Uruguay Round and although unsuccessful, the negotiations on services were placed in the GNS which is technically outside the framework of the GATT. They view free trade in services as a threat to economic sovereignty. They argue that the regulation of services is not fuelled by protectionist sentiments but by the desire to promote economic growth and development.

Developing countries have for a long time maintained interventionist regimes on foreign investment. The TRIMs proposals were seen as an onslaught on a government's freedom of action to regulate the domestic economy. Governments in the developing world have justified restricting foreign capital inflows for a number of reasons. These include local-content requirements, trade-balancing requirements, local-equity requirements and local-employment requirements.

The US demand for a liberal regime for intellectual property rights in effect seeks to grant protection to American, European and Japanese transnational corporations. From the perspective of the developing countries, extending patent protection privileges corporate interests at the expense of the public. It will, in areas like medicine and pharmaceuticals increase the price of drugs and prohibit the development of local industry since TNCs will in effect be granted monopoly rights.

Scheduled to end in 1990 the Uruguay Round has lurched from crisis to crisis. At the mid-term review in 1988 it was clear that sufficient progress would not be made by the agreed end date for a satisfactory conclusion to be reached. In December 1991, Arthur Dunkel, the then director-general of GATT submitted a draft Final Act which contains the basic shape of the conclusions of the Uruguay Round. Over one year later, the round is still not over. Peter Sutherland, the current director-general of GATT, has set December 1993 as the final deadline for completion of the Round. A final agreement cannot be reached until the deadlock between the United States and the European Community over agriculture is broken. The fact that a conclusion is dependent on the US and the EC highlights the continued inferior position of the developing countries in the international trading system.

Assessment of the results of the Uruguay Round as set out in the Dunkel Draft depends on the viewpoint of the analyst. From a liberal perspective the liberalisation of agriculture, phasing out of the MFA, the proposed General Agreement on Services and the rules on intellectual property rights will bring benefits to the developing countries. From a liberal perspective, the advantages of protection rarely outweigh the costs. Radical critics of the GATT system, while accepting that liberalisation in agriculture and the demise of the MFA represent modest gains, are likely to conclude that overall the developing countries will not benefit. This is because the new agreements will strengthen TNCs and weaken the ability of governments to intervene to protect the welfare of their citizens.

The reactions of the developing countries to the Dunkel Draft reflect the divisions apparent during the negotiations. The more advanced economies with liberal foreign trade regimes have been positive in their assessments. The members of the Cairns Group have also welcomed the results. Most developing countries show little enthusiasm but accept that this is the best deal available. The Jamaican Ambassador to the GATT is quoted as saying, 'The draft package is reflective of the distribution of negotiating power and whether or not we are prepared to accept it as a reasonable basis for the further phase is academic.'[91]

Conclusion

In the absence of a set of rules to govern world trade, the protectionist measures followed by the more economically powerful states are likely to hurt the economic interests of the poorer countries. If GATT did not exist, discrimination against Third World exports would be much greater than it has been. And yet, GATT is a weak international organisation which has not had much success in effecting change in its environment. The answer to the question concerning whether membership of GATT has been positive or negative for Third World countries depends not only on one's views of the benefits of free trade but also of the alternative institutional arrangements in the world trading system.

For most of the post-war period Third World governments adopted a sceptical attitude to the liberal international economic system. In so far as they were members of the GATT, they sought special measures to aid in the drive for economic development. Developing countries argued that the application of free trade principles was likely to damage rather than promote their economic development. The demand of the developing countries for special and differential treatment was granted by the mid-1960s but serious friction over trade issues continued between the North and South. During the 1980s many developing countries began to re-evaluate their trade strategy. Throughout the developing world governments have increasingly adopted more open, outward-oriented economic policies. This gave them a new perception of the importance of an open, liberal trade order.

A common Third World position on international trade is rapidly becoming a thing of the past. The economic differentiation among developing countries has dictated the appearance of divergent trade interests. The NICs, for example, have a clear interest in an open, trading system. Nevertheless, some semblance of the North–South split still remains, reflecting differences in priority and economic power between the two groups.

Notes

1. The conclusion of the Uruguay Round is likely to lead to the creation of a Multilateral Trade Organisation (MTO) which will subsume the GATT.
2. 'Proposals for Consideration by an international Conference on Trade and Employment'; also see 'Proposals for Expansion of World Trade and Employment', *United States Department of State Publications 2411, Commercial Policy Series 79* (November 1945).
3. ECOSOC Resolution of 18 February 1946, quoted in full in W. A. Brown, Jnr, *The United States and the Restoration of World Trade* (Washington DC: The Brookings Institution 1950) p. 59.

4. It contained six states we now class as developing countries – Brazil, Chile, China, Cuba, India and Lebanon (and South Africa).
5. Australia and Liberia were the only states formally to ratify the Charter.
6. See Clair Wilcox, *A Charter for World Trade* (New York: Macmillan 1949); Edward Dana Wilgress, *A New Attempt at Internationalism – The International Trade Conferences and the Charter. A Study of Ends and Means* (Paris: Société d'édition d'enseignement supérieur 1949); and J. E. C. Fawcett, 'International Trade Organisation', *British Yearbook of International Law* vol. XXIV (1947) pp. 376–382, for accounts of the Havana Conference, the Charter and the ITO.
7. This was largely at the instigation of the US. President Truman had been granted the power to negotiate tariff reductions, under the Reciprocal Trade Agreements Act, renewed in 1945 for a three-year period.
8. See Kenneth W. Damm, *The GATT: Law and International Economic Organization* (Chicago: University of Chicago Press 1970); Karin Kock, *International Trade Policy and the GATT, 1947–1967* (Stockholm : Almqvist & Wiksell 1969) and John H. Jackson, *World Trade and the Law of the GATT* (New York: Bobbs-Merrill 1969).
9. See Harry Shutt, *The Myth of Free Trade* (London: Basil Blackwell & The Economist Books 1985) pp. 16–21.
10. See D. Gale Johnson, K. Hemmi and P. Lardinois, *Agricultural Policy and Trade: A Report to the Trilateral Commission* (New York: New York University Press 1985); and Robert. L. Paarlberg, *Fixing Farm Trade* (Cambridge, Mass.: Ballinger 1988) for discussions of US farm policy.
11. Ivo van Bael, 'The GATT Dispute Settlement Procedure', *Journal of World Trade* vol. 22 no. 4 (1988) p. 69.
12. John H. Jackson, *Restructuring the GATT System* (London: Pinter for Royal Institute of International Affairs, 1990) p. 19.
13. Kevin Watkins, *Fixing the Rules: North–South Issues in International Trade and the GATT Uruguay Round* (London: Catholic Institute for International Relations 1992).
14. For non-technical expositions of the liberal argument see the essays in Ryan C. Amacher, Gottfied Haberler and Thomas D. Willett (eds), *Challenges to a Liberal International Economic Order* (Washington DC: American Enterprise Institute for Public Policy Research 1979).
15. Susan Strange, 'Protectionism and World Politics', *International Organization* (Spring 1985) p. 236.
16. See, for example, Anthony Brewer, *Marxist Theories of Imperialism: A Critical Survey* (London: Routledge & Kegan Paul 1980); Ranjit Sau, *Unequal Exchange, Imperilism and Development* (Calcutta: Oxford University Press 1978); and Arghiri Emmanuel, *Unequal Exchange: A Study in the Imperialism of Trade* (London: NLB 1972).
17. John Gerard Ruggie, 'International Regimes, Transactions, and Change: Embedded Liberalism in the Postwar Economic Order' in Stephen D. Krasner (ed.), *International Regimes* (Ithaca and London: Cornell University Press 1983). pp. 195–231.
18. David Greenaway, *International Trade Policy: From Tariffs to the New Protectionism* (London: Macmillan 1983) p. 90.
19. *Ibid.* p. 92.
20. See Gilbert R. Winham, *International Trade and the Tokyo Round Negotiation* (Princeton, NJ: Princeton University Press 1986).

21. *Ibid.* p. 17.
22. David Greenaway & Robert C. Hine, 'Introduction: Trends in World Trade and Protection' in David Greenaway, Robert C. Hine, Anthony P. O'Brien & Robert J. Thornton (eds), *Global Protectionism* (London: Macmillan 1991) p. 7.
23. Nigel Grimwade, *International Trade* (London: Routledge 1989) pp. 51–53.
24. Jock A. Finlayson & Mark W. Zacher, 'The GATT and the Regulation of Trade Barriers: Regime Dynamics and Functions', *International Organization* (Autumn 1981) pp. 561–602.
25. Strange, *op. cit.* p. 258.
26. See Grimwade, *op. cit.* pp. 178–192 for a summary of various studies.
27. John Stopford & Susan Strange, *Rival States, Rival Firms* (Cambridge: Cambridge University Press 1991) p. 42.
28. See Diana Tussie, 'Trading in Fear? U.S. Hegemony and the World Political Economy in Perspective', in Craig N. Murphy & Roger Tooze (eds), *The New International Political Economy* (Boulder: Lynne Reinner 1991) pp. 79–95.
29. Apart from studies previously cited see H. W. Singer, Neelamber Hatti & Rameshwar Tandon (eds), *New Protectionism and Restructuring* 2 vols (New Delhi: Ashish Publishing House 1988); Jagdish Bhagwati, *The World Trading System at Risk* (Hemel Hempstead: Harvester Wheatsheaf 1991).
30. *The Economist*, 'World Trade Survey' (September 1990) p. 11.
31. On US 301 policy see Jagdish Bhagwati & Hugh Patrick (eds), *Aggressive Unilateralism: America's 301 Trade Policy and the World Trading System* (Hemel Hempstead: Harvester Wheatsheaf 1990).
32. Herbert van der Wee, *Prosperity and Upheaval: The World Economy 1945– 1980* (London: Penguin 1987) p. 386.
33. Enzo Grilli, 'The Macroeconomic Determinants of Trade Protection in the 1970s and 1980s', *World Economy* (Sept 1988) pp. 313–326.
34. Fred Bergsten & John Williamson, 'Exchange Rates and Trade Policies in William R. Cline (ed.), *Trade Policies in the 1980s* (Washington DC: Institute for International Economics 1983) pp. 99–120.
35. Enrico Sassoon, 'Protectionism and International Trade Negotiations During the 1980s' in Enzo Grilli and Enrico Sassoon (eds), *The New Protectionist Wave* (London: Macmillan 1990) p. 11.
36. See Winham, *op. cit.* pp. 371–383.
37. This is also called different and more favourable treatment.
38. See UNCTAD Secretariat, 'The Developing Countries in GATT' pp. 432– 469 and GATT Secretariat, 'The Role of GATT in Relation to Trade and Development'; pp. 470–492 in *Proceedings of the United Nations Conference on Trade and Development, First Session, Geneva 1964, vol. V* for a history of the relationship between GATT and the developing countries in the 1950s and the impact of these changes.
39. Also known as the Haberler Report.
40. *Trends in International Trade. Report by a Panel of Experts* (Geneva: GATT 1958) p. 54.
41. Article 36:8.
42. See Marc Williams, *Third World Cooperation: The Group of 77 in UNCTAD* (London: Pinter 1991) ch. 6 for an analysis of conflicts among developing countries over preferences.
43. Conference Resolution 21 (II) in *Proceedings of the United Nations*

Conference on Trade and Development Second Session, New Delhi 1968 vol. I p. 38.
44. Craig MacPhee, 'Preferential vs. MFN Tariff Liberalization: Effects of the Tokyo Round on LDC Exports' in Khosrow Fatemi (ed.), *International Trade: Existing Problems and Prospective Solutions* (New York: Taylor & Francis 1989) pp. 89–105, however, argues that the GSP is beneficial to preference receiving countries.
45. GATT, 'The Tokyo Declaration', para. 5. in *GATT Activities 1973* (Geneva: GATT 1974).
46. *Ibid.*
47. See GATT, *Basic Instruments and Selected Documents* (1980) for the text of the agreements.
48. Para. 7 of the 'Enabling Clause'.
49. GATT, 'Ministerial Declaration on the Tokyo Round', paras. B (vi) and (vii) in *GATT Activities 1986* (Geneva: GATT 1987).
50. See Martin Wolf, 'Two-Edged Sword: Demands of Developing Countries and the Trading System' in Jagdish N. Bhagwati & John Gerard Ruggie (eds), *Power, Passions and Purpose* (Cambridge, Mass.: MIT Press 1984) pp. 201–230.
51. See T. N. Srinivasan, 'Why Developing Countries Should Participate in the GATT System', *World Economy* (March 1982) pp. 85–104.
52. Martin Wolf, 'Why Trade Liberalization is a Good Idea' in J. Michael Finger & Andrej Olechowski (eds), *The Uruguay Round: A Handbook on the Multilateral Trade Negotiations* (Washington DC: World Bank 1987) p. 19.
53. See Brian Hindley, 'Differential and More Favourable Treatment and Graduation' in Finger & Olechowski, *op. cit.* p. 70 for this point and the general argument against protection.
54. See J. N. Bhagwati & V. K. Ramaswami, 'Domestic Distortions, Tariffs and the Theory of Optimum Subsidy', *Journal of Political Economy* (February 1963) pp. 44–50.
55. Anne O. Krueger & Baran Tuncer, 'An Empirical Test of the Infant Industry Argument', *American Economic Review* (Dec 1982) pp. 1142–1152.
56. See Robert E. Hudec, *Developing Countries in the GATT Legal System* (Gower for Trade Policy Research Centre 1987) pp. 134–135.
57. *Ibid.* pp. 134–137.
58. Watkins, *op. cit.* pp. 33–34.
59. See, for example, Watkins, *op. cit.* p. 34; Belinda Coote, *The Trade Trap: Poverty and the Global, Commodity Markets* (Oxford: Oxfam 1992) p. 108; and Robert E. Baldwin & Tracy Murray, 'MFN Tariff Reductions and Developing Country Trade Benefits under the GSP', *Economic Journal* (March 1977) pp. 30–46.
60. See H. Don. B. H. Gunasekera, David Parsons & Michael G. Kirby, 'Liberalizing Agricultural Trade: Some Perspectives for Developing Countries' in John Whalley (ed.), *Developing Countries and the Global Trading System vol. 1* (London: Macmillan 1989) p. 238.
61. *Ibid.* p. 239.
62. See Bruce Gardner, 'Agricultural Protection in Industrial Countries' in Greenaway *et al.* (eds), *op. cit.* pp. 107–110 for a summary of recent studies.

63. *Ibid.* pp. 272–274.
64. Enzo Grilli, 'Protectionism and the Developing Countries' in Grilli & Sassoon (eds.) *op cit.* p. 133.
65. Gunasereka *et al.*, *op. cit.* p. 247.
66. For a brief history of the MFA see Diana Tussie, *The Less Developed Countries and the World Trading System* (London: Pinter 1987) ch. 4.; and Madhavi Majmudar, 'The Multi-Fibre Arrangement (MFA IV) 1986–1991: A Move towards a Liberalized System', *Journal of World Trade* vol. 22 no. 2 (1988) pp. 109–125.
67. Marcelo de Pavia Abreu & Winston Fritsch, 'Market Access for Manufactured Exports from Developing countries: Trends and Prospects' in Whalley (ed.), *op. cit.* p. 116; Greenaway, *op. cit.* p. 180.
68. Grilli, *op. cit.* p. 136.
69. Tussie, *The Less Developed op. cit.* pp. 75–98.
70. *Ibid.* p. 100.
71. Grilli, *op. cit.* p. 143.
72. See Watkins, *op. cit.* for an attack on the negative impact of the MFA on development.
73. See Tussie, *The Less Developed op. cit.* pp. 98–99.
74. 'The Developing Countries in GATT' *op. cit.* p. 449.
75. Ernest H. Preeg, *Traders and Diplomats* (Washington DC: Brookings Institution 1970) pp. 226–227.
76. *Ibid.* pp. 227–232; and Kock, *op. cit.* pp. 245–246.
77. Tigani E. Ibrahim, 'Developing Countries and the Tokyo Round', *Journal of World Trade Law* (Jan: Feb 1978) pp. 15–16.
78. Winham, *op. cit.* p. 273.
79. *Ibid.* pp. 275–280; also see Bela Balasaa, 'The Tokyo Round and the Developing Countries' *Journal of World Trade Law* (Mar:Apr 1980) pp. 93–118.
80. Alan Oxley, *The Challenge of Free Trade* (Hemel Hempstead: Harvester Wheatsheaf 1990) p. 106.
81. See Jeffrey J. Schott & Jacqueline Mazza, 'Trade in Services and Developing Countries', *Journal of World Trade Law* (May:June 1986) pp. 254–255.
82. See V. N. Balasubramanyam, 'International Trade in Services: the Real Issues' in Greenaway *et al.* (eds), *op. cit.* pp. 119–142; and Siegried Schultz, 'Services and the GATT', *Intereconomics* (Sept: Oct 1987) pp. 227–234 for the economic rationale behind the liberalisation of trade in services.
83. Coote, *op. cit.* p. 110.
84. See David Greenaway, 'Why Are We Negotiating on TRIMs?' in Greenaway & Hine (eds), *op. cit.* pp. 144–168.
85. Watkins, *op. cit.* pp. 89–91.
86. *Ibid.* pp. 91–97; and Coote, *op. cit.* pp. 112–113.
87. See John Whalley, 'Recent Trade Liberalisation in the Developing World: What is Behind it and Where is it Headed?' in Greenaway *et al.* (eds), *op. cit.* pp. 225–253.
88. See Barbara Stallings, 'International Influence on Economic Policy: Debt, Stabilization, and Structural Reform' in Stephan Haggard & Robert R. Kaufman (eds), *The Politics of Economic Adjustment* (Princeton, NJ: Princeton University Press 1992) pp. 41–88; and Thomas J. Biersteker, 'The Triumph of Neoclassical Economics in the Developing World: Policy

Convergence and Bases of Governance in the International Economic Order' in James N. Rosenau & Ernst-Otto Czempiel (eds), *Governance Without Government: Order and Change in World Politics* (Cambridge: Cambridge University Press 1992) pp. 102–131 for discussions of these themes.

89. See Oxley, *op. cit.* ch. 9 for a discussion of the Cairns Group.

90. See Deepak Nayyar, 'Some Reflections on the Uruguay Round and Trade in Services', *Journal of World Trade* vol. 22 no. 5 (1988) pp. 35–47; A. D. Koekkoek, 'Developing Countries and Services in the Uruguay Round', *Intereconomics* (Sept:Oct 1987) pp. 234–242; and Andre Sapir, 'North–South issues in Trade in Services' in Singer *et al.* (eds), *op. cit.* pp. 721–741.

91. Cited in Watkins, *op. cit.* p. 132.

7

The United Nations Conference on Trade and Development and the Third World

The United Nations Conference on Trade and Development (UNCTAD) created in 1964 is often seen as an organisation dominated by the developing countries. Unlike the previous international economic organisations discussed in this book, UNCTAD was not created by Western countries to serve their interests. UNCTAD was established in 1964 as a direct result of pressures in the UN system by the developing countries and they have remained its most important constituents. The developing countries created UNCTAD as an instrument to further their campaign for global economic justice. Their demands of UNCTAD are therefore qualitatively different from those addressed to the three international organisations previously analysed in this book. Given the different levels of development among the members of the G77 no single UNCTAD campaign can possibly benefit all developing countries equally. From the perspective of an individual country UNCTAD's importance and usefulness is a function of its ability to deliver concrete results, change the rules and norms of international economic relations and increase pressure on other international economic organisations for change.

The eighth UNCTAD Conference held in Cartagena, Colombia in February 1992 marked a turning point for the organisation. The Cartagena Conference initiated a reform process with widespread changes in UNCTAD's organisation and mandate. Until these recent changes UNCTAD could be viewed as a counter-hegemonic organisation resisting the dominance of the Bretton Woods institutions. The restructuring of the organisation has given it a less confrontational role in the North–South dialogue.[1] This is an attempt to improve UNCTAD's effectiveness. The desire to reform rather than abolish

UNCTAD comes from the recognition that it is the only international economic organisation that concentrates on trade and development and it is the only IEO that developing countries control.

Third World participation in UNCTAD evolved along fundamentally different lines from their involvement with the Bretton Woods institutions. In the Bretton Woods institutions the developing countries felt marginalised from decision-making and mounted campaigns to increase their level of participation and to make the organisations more receptive to the needs of development. From its inception UNCTAD's central concern has been to identify and analyse development problems. This chapter will examine the use that developing countries have made of UNCTAD and attempt to assess how useful UNCTAD has been as an instrument of Third World pressure in the global political economy. UNCTAD was created to serve the interests of the developing countries and this chapter will examine the extent to which UNCTAD has been successful in promoting these interests. It will concentrate on the period before the Cartagena Conference because the implementation of the new organisational structures and working methods only began in October 1992.

It was once observed that UNCTAD stood for Under No Circumstances Take Any Decisions and the most persistent line of criticism of UNCTAD accuses it of irrelevance. It is alleged that the organisation has achieved very little in its quest to transform the international political economy. Such critics frequently think that UNCTAD's quest is ill-advised, and are indeed pleased with its failure. This ineffectiveness is usually attributed to organisational deficiencies, in particular the unwieldy nature of UNCTAD conferences,[2] the group system[3] and the poor calibre of the staff and the economic illiteracy of UNCTAD's analyses.[4]

Writers sympathetic to UNCTAD's goals point to certain concrete successes and tend to place the blame for UNCTAD's failure to achieve more substantial gains on the lack of political will of the developed countries. They also argue that UNCTAD has made an important contribution to thinking on economic development. Moreover, its role in providing a forum where the Third World countries can articulate and aggregate their interests is seen as a positive achievement.[5]

This chapter will begin with an account of UNCTAD's origins. An account of the factors behind UNCTAD's creation is crucial for understanding the evolution of the organisation. It will then examine the importance of organisational variables in accounting for UNCTAD's successes and failures. Examination of the organisational infrastructure will highlight the importance of the recent changes in the organisation's working methods and goals. The third section will discuss UNCTAD's attempts to transform international economic relations.

The origins of UNCTAD

The establishment of UNCTAD arose from the dissatisfaction of the developing countries with the workings of the international economy and the lacunae in the institutional structure of world trade.[6] A growing awareness of common problems and the forging of a coalition to campaign for the redress of economic inequality were crucial factors in the transformation of inchoate expressions of disgruntlement into an effective movement for change. In this sense UNCTAD was, 'the first institutional response in the economic sphere to the entry of the Third World on to the international scene'.[7]

The emergence of a Third World coalition is one of the most striking features of post-war international politics. The coalition has its roots in the process of decolonisation, growing disillusionment with the workings of the liberal international economic order, dissatisfaction at the efforts of the Bretton Woods institutions to frame an adequate response to the problems of economic development and the role of international organisations in providing a forum in which developing countries could articulate and aggregate their interests.[8]

The process of decolonisation increased the representation of the Third World in the United Nations. In 1960 the entry of 17 African states and Cyprus swelled the ranks of the developing countries guaranteeing a decisive majority in the General Assembly. The independence revolution not only increased the number of developing countries in the UN system, it also gave voice to many countries at a lower level of development than the existing developing countries. The material standard of living in the new African states was, 'generally, lower than in Latin America or Asia. These countries perceived economic growth as one of the most important problems facing their regimes and at the international level infused a new intensity to the demands for reform of the international trading system.

Another consequence of decolonisation was the creation of the Non-Aligned Movement (NAM). The NAM was created at the first non-aligned summit conference in Belgrade in 1961. The roots of the movement, however, can be traced to the Afro-Asian Peoples Conference held in Bandung, Indonesia in 1955. This conference laid the basis for the embodiment of non-alignment in a multilateral framework. The Bandung Conference created the framework for the NAM through its articulation of the central goals of the movement, namely, economic development and decolonisation; and the demonstration of a cross-regional coalition based on broad common objectives. The Belgrade Conference marked the inception of the NAM, establishing the regional basis of the movement on a wider footing with delegations from Africa, Asia and Latin America, and through its exclusion of China and Pakistan attempting to forge a unity away from the Cold War blocs. In delinking economic development from the context of the Cold War the NAM provided not only a basis for increased cooperation among developing countries but helped to create the conditions under which economic development could be given attention in its own right.

In the 1950s the developing countries began to question the workings of the international economy. This was a result of the severe foreign exchange problems many developing countries experienced during this period. In order to finance economic development these countries needed to increase their capacity to import. However, in the 1950s their export receipts fell, thus leaving them unable to meet their import requirements. The developing countries experienced a slower expansion of exports and declining terms of trade. Between 1953 and 1961 the developing countries' share of world trade declined by 22 per cent.[9] The exports of the developing countries were concentrated in primary products while the major growth area in international trade was manufactures. Price and demand instability compounded the problems of declining terms of trade. Moreover, the flow of international capital although increasing during this period was inadequate to meet the demand for increased resources.

The international organisations established at the end of World War II reflected Northern interests and concerns. Furthermore, their decision-making processes effectively excluded the newly independent countries. The GATT's two basic principles – reciprocity and most-favoured treatment were held to be biased in favour of the developed countries. From the perspective of the developing countries GATT was inadequately equipped to cope with the problems of development. It hampered their efforts to achieve growth through import-substitution. The assumption of complete equality among GATT members in terms of rights and obligations was held to be discriminatory to developing countries. At this time neither the GATT nor the IMF appeared capable of meeting the demands of the developing countries. To counter declining terms of trade and falling export shares the developing countries requested the creation of international commodity agreements to stabilise export earnings and the provision of compensatory financing to remedy fluctuating export receipts. The developing countries lamented the failure to ratify the ITO. The absence of a central body to coordinate world trade, and the deficiencies of the existing organisations in addressing the problems of commodity trade fuelled the demands for a new organisation in the UN system to coordinate policy on trade and development.

The decision of the General Assembly in December 1962 to convene a conference on trade and development[10] was the culmination of a process of intense debate in the General Assembly and in the Economic and Social Council (ECOSOC) begun at the sixteenth session of the General Assembly. This decision was a triumph for Third World pressure over Western opposition. The Western states eventually gave up their opposition because of two factors. First, a perceived Soviet interest in the creation of an international trade organisation convinced the United States and its allies that they could not afford to let the developing countries and the communist bloc form an organisation without them.[11] Secondly, and perhaps most importantly, the increasing Third World majority in the UN left them no choice.

When the United Nations Conference on Trade and Development convened in Geneva in March 1964 it was not a certainty that a permanent organisation would be created.[12] The failure of the conference to achieve any progress on substantive issues contributed to the decision to establish it on a permanent basis. North–South differences on the institutional issue at the conference was instrumental in promoting solidarity among the developing countries. Although at the outset differences on future institutional arrangements existed among the developing countries the stalled negotiations on other issues contributed to a growing awareness that unless a new organisation was established the demand for changes in international economic relations would be ignored. UNCTAD was created by the developing countries with the grudging acceptance of the developed world. For the developing countries a new organisation was necessary in order to advance their interests in international economic reform. Throughout this period the developed states had insisted that existing organisations, in particular the GATT and the IMF could adequately incorporate Third World demands. They insisted that the creation of a separate organisation would fragment and dissipate efforts to tackle the problem of global poverty. In the words of Richard Gardner, the vice-chairman of the US delegation to the Geneva Conference,

> If we agree that the trade problems of the developing countries should be considered as an integral part of the problem of development, then the establishment of a separate institution for [trade] with a separate secretariat and budget would result in an artificial division between trade and development frustrating that very integration of effort which we are all seeking.[13]

The North's opposition to the creation of a new organisation is reflected in their attitudes to UNCTAD. For the developed countries UNCTAD is an unnecessary institution whose functions can be performed effectively by other international organisations. The developing countries demanded the creation of a new international organisation because they believed that unregulated market forces did not work to their advantage. Existing international organisations based on liberal principles failed adequately to reflect their interests. The developed countries, on the other hand, tended to support liberal arguments and were reluctant to support an organisation committed to the regulation of the international economy. This clash of ideologies pervaded UNCTAD's deliberations between 1964 and 1992.[14] It is too early to assess the extent to which the profound institutional changes in the organisation and the reorientation of its agenda will lead to increased positive participation by Northern countries in UNCTAD's deliberations.

UNCTAD: organisational structure and political process

Organisational infrastructure

UNCTAD was established by General Assembly resolution 1995 (XIX) and this created an organisational structure which with minor amendments remained unchanged until UNCTAD VIII in 1992. The principal organs of UNCTAD are the Conference, the Trade and Development Board and the secretariat. UNCTAD's membership is non-restrictive and it is open to all states that are members of the United Nations, or alternatively, members of the specialised agencies or of the International Atomic Energy Agency (IAEA). UNCTAD currently comprises 183 member states, including the 179 members of the United Nations. Many non-governmental and inter-governmental organisations have observer status.

The Conference, which bears the same name as UNCTAD itself, is the highest organ and is entrusted with the task of implementing the functions entrusted to it by the General Assembly. Initially, it was envisaged that it would meet every three years but in practice, apart from two exceptions, it has been convened in four-yearly cycles. Open to all member states this assembly at ministerial level is the highest decision-making body of the organisation. It establishes policy guidelines, reviews the work of the organisation and sets the priorities for future areas of work. Eight conferences have been held to date: UNCTAD I in Geneva, 23 March–16 June 1964; UNCTAD II in New Delhi, 1 February–29 March 1968; UNCTAD III in Santiago, 13 April–21 May 1972; UNCTAD IV in Nairobi, 5–31 May 1976; UNCTAD V in Manila, 6–29 May 1979; UNCTAD VI in Belgrade, 6 June–3 July 1983; UNCTAD VII in Geneva, 9 July–3 August 1987; and UNCTAD VIII in Cartagena, 8–25 February 1992.

The Trade and Development Board (TDB) normally meets once a year in regular session. It also holds special sessions periodically. At UNCTAD VIII it was decided to initiate executive sessions of the TDB. These would be half-day or one-day meetings, convened at the level of permanent representatives. The aim of these meetings is the strengthening of the policy functions of the Board. A more regular input from the Board will enhance the review of work programmes and priorities thus giving greater impetus to the continuing work of the Board's subsidiary bodies. The Board ensures continuity between conferences by carrying out all the functions entrusted to the conference. It is the task of the TDB to serve as a preparatory committee for the conference. It is responsible for selecting the agenda and providing relevant documentation. The TDB, furthermore, plays a role in the implementation of the conference's resolutions and decisions. The TDB's centrality in the UNCTAD organisational structure is enhanced by its competence to create subsidiary organs 'as may be necessary to the discharge of its functions'.

UNCTAD VIII effectively restructured the standing committees and other subsidiary organs. All existing committees of the Board, with the exception of the Special Committee on Preferences and the Inter-governmental Group of Experts on Restrictive Business Practices were suspended. The Board's main subsidiary organs are now the following four committees and five *ad hoc* working groups:

- The Committee on Commodities.
- The Committee on Poverty Alleviation.
- The Committee on Economic Co-operation Among Developing Countries.
- The Committee on Developing Service Sectors.
- The Ad Hoc Working Group on Investment and Financial Flows.
- The Ad Hoc Working Group on Trade Efficiency.
- The Ad Hoc Working Group on Privatisation.
- The Ad Hoc Working Group on Trading Opportunities for Developing Countries.
- The Ad Hoc Working Group on the Interrelationship between Investment and Technology Transfers.

The UNCTAD secretariat has two principal functions. First, the secretariat provides adequate servicing for the Conference, the TDB and its subsidiary organs. Secondly, it undertakes research requested by member states. At the head of the secretariat is the UNCTAD Secretary-General who has always been a national from a developing country. The Secretary-General plays a key role in the UNCTAD decisional process. S/he can attend any meeting and can submit statements to the deliberative bodies. Furthermore, s/he assists in the construction of the agenda and can convene commodity conferences in the UN system.

Decision-making

The recent changes in UNCTAD have had a profound impact on decision-making in the organisation. For most of the organisation's history the formal decision-making machinery has been less important than the informal methods and procedures. Decision-making in UNCTAD and the structure of influence is intimately related to the functions of the organisation and the perception of the organisation's role held by its members. The importance of the recent changes arise from the revisions in the functions agreed at Cartagena.[15]

The new approach confirms UNCTAD's original functions but specifies a precise sequencing in which they are to be implemented. UNCTAD fulfils four interrelated functions. These functions can be termed policy formulation, negotiation, implementation and technical assistance. Policy formulation refers to the creation of general and specific principles pertaining to international trade and development and includes policy analysis. The negotiation function is inclusive of all activities involving intergovernmental deliberation, consensus-building and negotiation aimed at arriving at concrete agreements through the decision-making process. The implementation function includes monitoring and follow-up procedures. Technical assistance pertains to the provision of technical services and technical cooperation for member governments.

Under the new arrangements in fulfilling its functions the organisation must conform to the following procedure: first, identification of a relevant set of issues; secondly, high-quality analytical work undertaken by the secretariat in consultation with external experts; thirdly, discussions with governments aimed at identifying areas of convergence. Finally, where appropriate, negotiations would be entered into on specific subjects when it was felt that the possibility of agreement existed.[16]

The significance of the reforms lies in the fact that a consensus now exists between developed and developing countries concerning the role of the organisation in the field of trade and development. Until 1992 UNCTAD was essentially a contested organisation. The developing countries and the developed countries had fundamentally different and conflicting conceptions of UNCTAD's role. The different premises from which each group conceived the nature of the organisation contributed to the persistence of the group system and the atmosphere of confrontation which characterised UNCTAD. The developing countries wanted UNCTAD to play an important role in norm creation and to serve as an effective negotiating instrument. In their view UNCTAD should be an institution empowered to make and implement decisions. The developed countries, in contrast, viewed UNCTAD solely as a deliberative forum in which the developing countries could express their demands and an exchange of views on North–South relations could take place. This was not a forum in which concrete agreements could be reached. UNCTAD could raise issues but negotiations were to be conducted elsewhere, i.e. in the GATT, IMF and World Bank. Ansari found a correlation between negativity to UNCTAD and a country's stake in the prevailing economic system. He claims that, 'The higher the GNP, the greater the voting power [in the post-war international economic organisations], the bigger the investment and aid contribution of a Group B country, the greater the likelihood that it opposed the passage of UNCTAD resolutions.'[17] This debate on whether UNCTAD should be merely a deliberative forum or, in contrast, an organisation empowered to formulate, negotiate and implement decisions created the basis for the emergence and persistence of the group system in UNCTAD. It was a conflict whose origins lay in the dispute at UNCTAD I concerning the permanent institutionalisation of the conference.

The attempt by the developing countries to widen UNCTAD's scope and mandate and the determination of the developed countries to restrict the organisation's role ensured that the group system became the central feature of UNCTAD's decisional process. For purposes of election to the Board and its main committees four groups were created. List A contained the African and Asian states and Yugoslavia, List B the OECD countries, List C the Latin American and Caribbean states and List D represented the socialist countries of Eastern Europe. Lists A and C merged to form the Group of 77. UNCTAD politics revolved around these groups. All deliberations in the organisation took place on the basis of the group system. UNCTAD was transformed into a forum in which intragroup consensus became more important than intergroup agreement.

Two conflicting interpretations of the group system and its impact on UNCTAD's ability to achieve change is discernible in the literature. Supporters of the group system defended it on two main grounds. First, its role in facilitating the decision-making process by providing for regular consultation and coordination of positions. The fact that the group system enables a large number of delegations to be represented by one spokesman is seen as a useful simplifying device.[18] Secondly, the group system is praised for its contribution to the formulation of principles and general policies aiming at structural change. The group system, by enabling the developing countries to articulate and aggregate their interests, increases their bargaining power. The unity of the G77 is imperative in order to legitimate their demands for change and to increase pressure on the Bretton Woods institutions.[19]

Critics claimed that although the group system might be useful in the context of pressure group activity it restricted UNCTAD's capacity to be a negotiating forum. Group discipline constrains and curtails the search for effective diplomatic compromise.[20] Thomas Weiss, for example, argues that although the group system permitted the start of the North–South dialogue, and led to the adoption of general principles governing international economic policy it turned out to be a source of stalemate in the dialogue, in so far as it is counter-productive for negotiating the details of binding international agreements.[21] The group system retards the pace of negotiations and contributes to the failure to achieve agreement since group unity is prized above compromise with opposing groups.

The effective demise of the group system at the end of 1991 arose from agreement between the developed and developing countries about the functions of a revitalised and restructured UNCTAD. In the new climate cross-group alliances and issue-oriented groups will be promoted. A number of factors are responsible for the adoption of a new work programme for UNCTAD and the beginning of a new era, i.e. one in which the main participants no longer dispute the objectives and role of the organisation. First, UNCTAD had become increasingly marginalised in the making of international economic policy. The organisation only flourished effectively when it was the venue for intense political North–South negotiations. This happened twice in its history; over the GSP negotiations and the attempt to create an integrated programme for commodities (IPC). No new initiative had emerged since the end of the IPC and Common Fund (CF) negotiations in 1980. Secondly, UNCTAD's approach to trade and development appeared out of step with the new orthodoxy of structural adjustment and liberalisation. Interventionist schemes to regulate commodity trade not only did not fit with current thinking but the absence of functioning International

Commodity Agreements (ICAs) contributed to a perception that such thinking was no longer relevant. Thirdly, the Western assault on UNCTAD was intensified in the 1980s. UNCTAD was a prime target of President Reagan's assault on the UN system. From its inception Western nations tried to undermine UNCTAD through opposition to items on its agenda; transferring substantive issues to more congenial agencies; and by attacking the secretariat for the absence of impartiality. These attacks were increased and served to reduce the already diminished influence exerted by UNCTAD. Fourthly, more developing countries lost interest in supporting an organisation that appeared to offer only minimal gains. The spread of neo-liberalism in the developing world and the shift in internal policies away from import-substitution to those with an export orientation called into question UNCTAD's relevance.

Organisational ideology

UNCTAD's traditional interventionist, anti-free trade stance placed it firmly at odds with the major international economic organisations. This heterodox position made it a favourite target of liberal economists who berated the organisation for alleged economic illiteracy and manifest incompetence. The recent changes in UNCTAD's direction appear to be based on a rejection of its previous organisational ideology. It is not apparent at the time of writing what the precise content of the new organisational ideology will be. This section will outline the traditional UNCTAD analysis of the international economy since it conditioned the organisation's behaviour during most of the period under review.

UNCTAD's campaign to restructure international trade and to foster international cooperation was based on an analysis which argued that the liberal international economic system increased the dependence of Third World countries on the developed countries to the detriment of the former. The basis for this approach lay in the thinking and writing of Raul Prebisch, the first secretary-general of the organisation. In his capacity as secretary-general of the Geneva Conference, Prebisch produced a report, *Towards a New Trade Policy for Development* [22] which provided the conceptual framework for the development of UNCTAD's economic analysis.

The Prebisch Report was based on four assumptions. First, it assumed that the countries of the world could be divided into two groups – the centre (developed countries) and the periphery (developing countries) – and that economic processes were different in each region. Related to this assumption was a denial of Ricardian comparative advantage theory. Instead Prebisch argued that the integrated capitalist world system tended to produce disparities between the centre and the periphery. Secondly, he argued that a widening trade gap would develop, mainly because of increased import costs and decreased export receipts. Thirdly, Prebisch assumed that the terms of trade of raw material producers tended to decline relative to those of manufactures. Deteriorating terms of trade were a major obstacle to Third World development and therefore the developed countries benefiting from this trend should provide some form of compensation. Finally, he assumed that there was a 'persistent tendency towards external imbalance associated with the development process'.[23] It followed from this that import needs in early industrialisation were different from later stages in the process.

UNCTAD focused on increasing the export earnings of the developing countries, whether the exports comprised primary commodities or manufactured or semi-manufactured goods. The UNCTAD analysis emphasised the various problems inherent in reliance on primary commodity exports as the major source of external revenue. The prices of primary commodites were more volatile than manufactures. Price (and revenue) instability affected development planning. The solution to this problem was market regulation. As Gamani Corea, the third Secretary-General of UNCTAD has written, 'The case for intervention, whether national or international, to regulate commodity markets stems from the special characteristics of primary commodities and their consequent vulnerability, in the context of the operation of market forces alone, to sharp fluctuations in prices'.[24] Furthermore, the prospects for increased revenue from the export of primary products is not very promising. Low-income elasticity of demand meant a relative decline in demand compared with manufactured goods. Technological progress resulted in a diminishing raw material content in manufactures and the increased substitution of synthetics for primary products. Agricultural protectionism in the developed countries compounds the problems faced by the exporters of raw materials. The favoured remedy was the conclusion of international commodity agreements to establish minimum prices or to improve the long-term trend. Where commodity agreements fail or are inappropriate, compensatory financing schemes should be instituted, over and above regular aid transfers to correct losses from the deterioration in the terms of trade.

UNCTAD supported action to increase the growth of manufactured and semi-manufactured exports from the developing countries. Manufactured exports from the South were inhibited by the deficiency of capital and industrial skill and the existence of protectionist barriers in Northern markets. UNCTAD promoted the creation of a universal non-

discriminatory, non-reciprocal system of tariff preferences for developing countries and the establishment of regional preferential arrangements among developing countries as a means to increase the Third
World's exports of manufactures.

This regulatory approach to the world economy was applied to other
areas such as shipping, technology transfer and investment. The central
concern of UNCTAD's analysis was development. UNCTAD's
approach started from the recognition that although free trade will
improve total global welfare it cannot ensure that the gains from trade
are distributed equally. Unlike the liberal theories underpinning the
work of the World Bank, IMF and GATT, the role of economic and
political power in shaping outcomes is prominent in the traditional
UNCTAD economic philosophy.

The 'traditional' UNCTAD organisational ideology was a mix of
global Keynesianism[25] and dependency theory. The use of centre–
periphery concepts was abandoned in the 1980s as the organisation
started to emphasise global interdependence. I have chosen to stress
continuity rather than discontinuity in the organisational ideology at this
stage because the central aspects concerned a commitment to market
intervention and a focus on the external conditions of development.

At this point it is difficult to give more than a sketch of the new
UNCTAD economic philosophy. It does appear, however, that the new
approach deviates from the old in three fundamental respects. In the
first place, much greater stress is placed on efficiency and the role of
market solutions. Secondly, the aggregative approach to developing
countries has been replaced by greater emphasis on the particular
experience of national economies. Thirdly, the near exclusive concentration on the external dimensions of development has been supplanted
by an approach which focuses on the importance of domestic policies. It
would, however, be premature at this stage to conclude that UNCTAD
has accepted the entire neo-liberal perspective, especially in the light of
its *Trade and Development Report 1992*[26] which calls for the application
of Keynesian policies to stimulate private consumption and investment
demand.

UNCTAD and international economic reform: 1964–92

The radical reorientation and revamping of UNCTAD's working
methods and focus of concern suggests that for many of its constituent
members UNCTAD had ceased to play an important role. One of
UNCTAD's main failings from the perspective of the developing
countries has been its inability to produce tangible economic gains. In

constructing UNCTAD, developing countries hoped that it would become the foremost IEO in the field of trade and development. Feeling alienated and marginalised from the IMF and the GATT the developing countries aspired to establish an organisation over which they exerted control. Negotiations in such an organisation would, it was hoped, lead to more equitable outcomes.

But, UNCTAD's reformist goals represented a direct challenge to the embedded liberalism of the post-war international economic order and its counter-hegemonic stance was never likely to go unchallenged. UNCTAD's ability to fulfil the aspirations of its founders was challenged from the outset by the developed countries who rejected it as an appropriate venue for negotiations. The organisation's highest profile came during the Third World's struggle for an NIEO.[27] This attempt, in the 1970s, to negotiate regime change on the basis of commodity power (particularly the oil weapon) foundered as the credibility of the Third World threat vanished. It was apparent by 1980 that NIEO demands were no longer being taken seriously by the AICs. With the demise of the NIEO, much of UNCTAD's rationale disappeared. The organisation spent the next 10 years searching for a role in a rapidly changing global political economy. The 1992 restructuring represents an attempt to save UNCTAD from complete irrelevance in international trade and development policy-making. And yet this harsh judgement should be tempered. If UNCTAD ultimately failed to live up to the expectations of its founders it, nevertheless, was not entirely devoid of positive accomplishments.

This section will examine UNCTAD's record and the extent to which it furthered the interests of the developing countries. First, however, it is necessary to explore the reasons which are usually advanced to account for UNCTAD's failure to yield more concrete results for the G77. No agreement exists on UNCTAD's failure to live up to the expectations of its founders. Although various writers proffer single factor explanations for the mixed results achieved by UNCTAD, the organisation's underachievement can best be explained in terms of a combination of structural and organisational factors.

A key constraint on UNCTAD's ability to transform the international political economy arose from the disparity between the voting power of the developing countries in UNCTAD and the structural power of the developed countries in the international system. This profound inconsistency between the distribution of voting power in UNCTAD and the structure of power in the general international environment in which the organisation is located created an unresolvable dilemma. In one sense the developing countries effectively controlled UNCTAD since they had overwhelmingly superior numbers and were instrumental in constructing UNCTAD's agenda and work programme. The active role taken by the G77 in shaping UNCTAD's agenda is clear from a consideration of the number of resolutions initiated by the various groups in the TDB. Between 1965 and 1979, G77 members co-sponsored 91.7 per cent of all the resolutions presented to the TDB.[28] But superiority of numbers and control over the agenda did not translate into effective control of the organisation. The AICs' power in the organisation is derived not from the voting provisions but from their position in the global political economy. Nye showed that between 1964 and 1969 the most influential countries in UNCTAD were the United States, Britain and France.[29]

The AICs formed an effective blocking coalition in UNCTAD. They were able to frustrate its efforts to achieve change because bargaining in UNCTAD is non-reciprocal. In effect the G77 could petition for change but the implementation of any decision depended on the willingness of Northern governments. The industrial countries' power in the external environment enables them to ignore any resolutions they dislike even if they did vote against it. One of UNCTAD's major achievements, for example, was the adoption of an official aid target of 0.7 per cent of GNP. But the organisation could not compel the AICs to honour this commitment. And, the developed countries were intent on maintaining UNCTAD as a forum organisation. If at all possible the Group B countries preferred substantive issues raised in UNCTAD be trans-ferred to another IEO. As one Western diplomat observed, 'no Group B country has made UNCTAD its chosen instrument of policy.'[30]

Moreover, UNCTAD's reforms were obstructed by the hegemonic discourse established by the Bretton Woods institutions. UNCTAD's reformist mission was blocked by the norms and principles of the existing liberal economic order. The industrial countries used neo-classical economic theory to counter UNCTAD's reformist efforts. The strength of the intellectual challenge to UNCTAD was a function not only of the technical superiority of the anti-UNCTAD critique but of the dominant position of those ideas in the international political economy.

The rigidity of the group system was a contributory factor in UNCTAD's failure to achieve more significant reform in the 1964–92 period. Two consequences of the group system inhibited the negotia-tions between the G77 and Group B. First, the imperative of maintain-ing unity within the G77 led to the adoption of a negotiating position which could not form the basis for serious bargaining. Group unity is preserved through the construction of a common position inclusive of the diverse interests of the membership.[31] These portmanteau resolu-tions were inappropriate since in effect they reduced the pressure on

Group B to enter into meaningful negotiations. Instead of looking for areas of agreement Group B could respond in a vague manner. The process of arriving at consensus in Group B also meant that their negotiating position reflected the minimum common denominator. Maximum demands from the G77 tended to induce minimal responses from Group B.[32] Secondly, by giving more importance to intragroup cohesion than intergroup negotiations the group system inhibited genuine dialogue and brought an unnecessary degree of rigidity to the bargaining process. This rigidity made the conferences seem like the end rather than the start of negotiations.[33]

It is possible to overstate the importance of the group system if it is viewed in isolation. The problems caused by the group system were real but it is important to recall that this system was a reflection of the contested nature of the organisation. And little evidence exists to support the claim that the AICs were prepared, during this period, to enter into meaningful discussions with the G77.

The conflicting and irreconcilable nature of the tasks imposed on it by the Third World was a third reason for UNCTAD's failure to achieve concrete results. The developing countries wanted UNCTAD to be both a pressure group and a negotiating forum. These activities are in conflict since as a pressure group the organisation is committed to supporting a particular viewpoint, but as a negotiating venue it is supposed to perform the role of honest broker.

Prebisch took an active role in defining UNCTAD as a pressure group and he did not think that there was a conflict between this role and others the organisation was required to fulfil. He argued that,

> there would . . . be no derogation from either the letter or the spirit of the Charter if the Secretary-General and his staff took due account that some nations were much weaker than others, and much less well equipped to argue their own case before the organs of the UN.[34]

The identification of the secretariat with the G77 was continued by Prebisch's successors.

Close identification between the G77 and the secretariat served to infuriate Group B and to further distance them from an organisation they viewed with suspicion. One of the major complaints voiced by developed countries in this period was the lack of impartiality by the secretariat. As one Western delegate exclaimed, 'This is not a secretariat – it's a sectariat.'[35]

These three factors are interrelated and explanation of UNCTAD's record should consider the impact of both structural and organisational constraints. UNCTAD's institutional framework was an expression of the North–South divide in the international economy. The group system developed because in 1964 it did appear to conform to an important aspect of contemporary reality. The continuation of the group system into the 1980s and 1990s may well have been detrimental to the functioning of the organisation and its capacity to respond effectively to the demands of the Third World. But it is worth recalling that the abandonment of the group system was in the control of the member states and not the organisation. And before its final demise the group system had become more flexible permitting some attempts to identify common interests and common tasks at UNCTAD VII.[36]

In depriving UNCTAD of legitimacy the developed countries succeeded in reducing its influence on international economic relations. The developed countries insisted that UNCTAD was an unsuitable venue for negotiations. Even when UNCTAD was acting as a negotiating venue the developed countries continued to insist that it was purely a forum for discussion. And in insisting that agreements negotiated in UNCTAD should be implemented in other fora the West undermined UNCTAD's legitimacy. The crisis of legitimacy in UNCTAD was one created by the developed countries who from its inception refused to see it as an organisation capable of serving Western interests. UNCTAD's dilemma lies in the fact that the realisation of its goals depends on the willingness of the developed countries to agree and implement redistributive strategies. The next part of this section examines how far UNCTAD has succeeded in fulfilling its goals.

During the first 28 years of its existence UNCTAD's activities spanned the entire field of international trade and development policy. In fulfilling the mandate set by the General Assembly it has attempted to (i) formulate and implement principles and policies on international trade and development; (ii) provide the venue for the negotiation of specific agreements; and (iii) coordinate the activities of the UN system in the field of international development policy.

In considering to what extent UNCTAD has responded to the demands of the developing countries and the impact of UNCTAD's policies it is necessary to consider the different roles played by the organisation. From the perspective of the developing countries, UNCTAD's usefulness can be calculated on the basis of its role as:

1. a forum for negotiation;
2. a forum for dialogue and discussion;
3. a generator of ideas and formulator of new thinking and policies on development;
4. a pressure group influencing the policies of other international organisations; and
5. the provision of technical assistance.

Most analysts would agree with Ansari that 'UNCTAD's substantive initiatives have had, at best only a marginal impact on the substance of North–South relations.'[37] But if UNCTAD has failed in its attempt to restructure the international economic system, it has, nevertheless, made valuable contributions in all five areas identified above. The organisation pioneered analysis and made policy recommendations in a number of related areas and has been the primary IEO focusing on trade and development.

It is as a forum for negotiations that UNCTAD most disappointed its founders. In a 28-year history few substantive agreements emerged from the UNCTAD framework and the value of these is debatable. Nevertheless, a number of agreements were concluded: the Generalised System of Preferences (1970), the Code of Conduct for Liner Conferences (1974), the Common Fund for Commodities (1980), the Set of Multilaterally Agreed Equitable Principles and Rules for the Control of Business Practices (1980), the Convention on International Multimodal Transport of Goods (1980), the Convention on Conditions for Registration of Ships (1986), the Global System of Trade Preferences (1988). The signing of an agreement is only the first stage of the process. Some of these agreements experienced problems of ratification and implementation.

One of UNCTAD's main contributions as a forum for discussion is the wide range of issues it has considered. It has explored, among others, commodity trade, trade in manufactures, shipping, money and finance, insurance, tourism, economic cooperation among developing countries, invisibles, technology transfer and the special problems of the most disadvantaged countries (the least developed, island and land-locked countries). In focusing on these wide ranging issues UNCTAD pioneered an approach which emphasised the interdependent nature of the world economy. On the other hand, as a forum UNCTAD sometimes gave the impression of conducting a dialogue of the deaf. Both North and South appeared more intent on striking postures than engaging in real dialogue. The organisation's role as a forum for North–South discussions has not been static. In certain periods the dialogue worked better than others.

UNCTAD also had an important role in this period in articulating a different approach to economic development. It stressed the inseparable link between the problems of trade, development finance and the international monetary system. UNCTAD pioneered studies on the problems of the most disadvantaged countries, the role of the invisible sector and economic cooperation among developing countries. The existence of an alternative viewpoint ensured that the international debate on economic development was not wholly controlled by organisations dominated by the industrialised countries. UNCTAD's dissident voice was frequently the target of vociferous criticism but it provided a position sympathetic to the aims of the developing countries.

UNCTAD provided a challenge in the early years of its existence to the IMF and the GATT and both organisations gave more attention to the special needs of the developing countries because of pressure exerted in UNCTAD. The creation of UNCTAD and its espousal of a competing perspective spurred a new concern within already existing IEOs for the interests of the developing countries. The IMF and the GATT both responded to the new pressure by instituting measures demanded by the developing countries. For example, Part IV of GATT was a response to the creation of UNCTAD and increased participation of the developing countries in the negotiations on reform of the international monetary system (C-20) came about as a result of pressure exerted through UNCTAD.

Although not specified in the resolution creating UNCTAD, technical assistance has been an essential aspect of UNCTAD's work programme from its early days. UNCTAD became a participating and executing agency of UNDP in 1968, and technical assistance assumed an increasingly important role in the organisation's work. The technical assistance provided by UNCTAD has been one of the organisation's positive achievements. This was recognised at UNCTAD VIII and technical assistance is an important part of the restructured UNCTAD. Trade and market access for manufactures and semi-manufactures exported by developing countries were the central concerns of UNCTAD in this period.

In all five areas the record is mixed but one is unlikely to find a national or international organisation which did not have both positive and negative outcomes. If emphasis is placed on UNCTAD's catalytic and proselytising roles the organisation has achieved a reasonable measure of success. On the other hand, if emphasis is placed on UNCTAD as a forum in which agreements are negotiated the organisation emerges a failure.

From the perspective of the developing countries UNCTAD's importance was not restricted to its constitutional roles. It could be argued that UNCTAD's most significant achievement in this period was as a forum in which the developing countries could aggregate their interests and articulate an alternative paradigm of economic development. Robert Walters defines interest aggregation as 'the process of combining demands to reduce inter-unit inconsistencies and collectively advocating these demands as a single package'.[38] UNCTAD succeeded in providing the institutional venue conducive to intragroup cohesion in the G77. In this period UNCTAD 'provided an organisational framework in which the pressures for group conformity and group solidarity acted as effective bulwarks against the centrifugal tendencies in the G77'.[39]

The two most important issues for UNCTAD in this period were commodity trade and market access for manufactured exports from the developing countries. An examination of these two issues will now be undertaken in order to assess the impact of UNCTAD on its developing country constituents. Each section will look at the attempt to change international norms but will not focus on the detailed negotiations.

A commodity policy for development?

The importance of mining and agriculture in the economies of developing countries and a heavy export concentration on primary commodities provided the basis for the demands by the developing countries for the reform of international commodity policy. Since for many developing countries the major share of export earnings are generated by primary commodities, much of UNCTAD's work has been concerned with stabilising the prices of primary commodities. The political economy of international commodity trade does not support a simple division of the world into developed and developing countries. Individual countries have specific interests arising from their positions as producers and consumers of particular commodities. The developing countries nevertheless identified a common interest based on their heavy dependence on commodity exports, the fluctuations in market prices, the prevailing 'rules of the game' and the weak institutional arrangements in existence. Their major aim was a complete revision of the principles which governed action in this area.

Until the creation of UNCTAD, the principles guiding commodity trade were those embodied in the Havana Charter,[40] especially Chapter VI entitled 'Inter-Governmental Commodity Agreements'. Firmly grounded in market principles the Charter provided for the control of production only in exceptional circumstances, i.e. 'when a burdensome surplus has developed' or where there is 'widespread unemployment or under-employment' (Article 62). In pursuit of price stability around the long-term trend, international commodity agreements could be created but would have to provide equal representation for producer and consumer governments, although the costs of financing the ICA would fall solely on the producers.

The developing countries through UNCTAD sought to relax the conditions under which ICAs could be established, to ensure equal financing by both producer and consumer governments and to use ICAs to raise prices above the long-term trend.[41] The debate and resolutions adopted at UNCTAD I provided the framework for UNCTAD's attempt to create a commodity policy for development. Four different types of objectives were established in 1964. First, the revision of existing international law and the creation of new rules and norms to govern international commodity policy. These new principles included commitment to intergovernmental cooperation and intervention as an integral part of development planning. Secondly, the proliferation of ICAs to secure remunerative, equitable and stable prices for commodities. Thirdly, autonomous and collective action by developed countries to dismantle protectionist devices against developing countries' commodity exports and to prevent the erection of any new barriers. Finally, the developing countries wanted UNCTAD to initiate analytical research on individual commodity markets and the problems faced by developing countries as exporters of commodities.[42]

Between Geneva and New Delhi very little was accomplished either in creating new principles or in the negotiation of specific commodity agreements. The Committee on Commodities soon decided that the attempt to devise universal solutions for commodity problems was futile and although not abandoned completely it was integrated with a new pragmatic commodity-by-commodity approach. In this period no new commodity agreements were negotiated but three existing arrangements were successfully renegotiated. The Third International Tin Agreement was negotiated in April 1965. The 1963 Olive Oil Agreement (but this included no provisions for the regulation of price or supplies) was extended by protocol until September 1969. The International Wheat Agreement (outside UNCTAD auspices) adopted an International Grains Agreement in August 1967 comprising a Wheat Trade Convention and a Food Aid Convention. Informal market share agreements were also concluded for sisal and henequen (1967) and abaca (1968).

UNCTAD II meeting in New Delhi adopted five resolutions on commodity problems and policies.[43] Resolution 16 (II) was the most important and detailed specific courses of action to be taken on some 20 commodities and commodity groups.[44] In collating these individual commodities together this resolution recognised both common problems and the need for an integrated approach and the different problems facing each commodity and therefore the necessity for specific remedial measures for particular commodities. This was the first international recognition of the need for an integrated approach to international commodity policy.[45]

Some noticeable progress in norm creation was made between the New Delhi and Santiago Conferences. In the Committee on Commodities two decisions were reached in 1968 and 1969 which represented significant advances on the consensus achieved at UNCTAD II. In November 1968 it was agreed that buffer stocks should be financed by both producers and consumers.[46] The lack of symmetry between principles and practice was starkly revealed, however, by the failure of the consuming countries to assist in the financing of the buffer stock provisions of the fourth International Tin Agreement concluded in 1970.[47] In May 1969 agreement was reached on a text which *inter alia* called on the developed countries to reduce trade barriers on natural products facing competition from synthetics.[48]

Additionally, progress was made in the establishment of ICAs. Between 1968 and 1972 four international commodity agreements were concluded and one informal arrangement. A new International Sugar Agreement with innovative provisions relating to national stocks, supply commitments and special measures for developing countries was agreed in 1968. The 1962 International Coffee Agreement was successfully renegotiated in 1968 but was experiencing serious difficulties by the time UNCTAD III convened.[49] The fourth International Tin Agreement was concluded in 1970 and the 1967 International Grains Agreement was replaced in 1971 by an International Wheat Agreement. Under the auspices of the FAO informal export quota schemes were agreed by tea producers in 1969.

When UNCTAD III convened in 1972 the developed countries were preoccupied with the collapse of the fixed exchange rate regime and problems arising from monetary instability. They were unprepared to advance on the minimal concessions made since the New Delhi Conference. Although five resolutions were passed they hardly represented a consensus and could not really be taken as indicators of future action.[50] Moreover, the necessity for resolutions on price stabilisation measures, access to markets, pricing policy and the mechanism and effectiveness of existing ICAs revealed the limited progress made since 1964.

The developing countries' attempt to create a new international commodity policy through UNCTAD culminated with the Integrated Programme for Commodities and CF negotiations. The IPC was the centrepiece of the efforts to construct a New International Economic Order and its failure provides an excellent illustration of UNCTAD's limitations as an instrument for change.

Resolution 93(IV) Integrated Programme for Commodities adopted without dissent at UNCTAD IV in 1976 set in motion a series of negotiations on the CF and individual commodities linked under the umbrella of the IPC. McMahon asserts, 'The passing of Resolution 93(IV) finally brought about a new commodity policy for development, displacing the policy agreed at Havana in 1947.'[51] In the period between UNCTAD I and UNCTAD IV, few ICAs had been concluded but analysis and policy recommendations had made an impact on the international debate on commodity policy. During this period many studies and reviews had been implemented, increasing knowledge of the workings of individual commodity markets and of the problems connected with commodity trade. A minimal revision of international law had taken place and some new principles had been accepted. Pressure exerted in UNCTAD had been responsible for the IMF's decision to establish a BSFF in 1969.

The principal aim of the IPC was to increase the gains which developing countries derive from international trade. The IPC was based on the premise that deteriorating terms of trade and excessive price fluctuations harmed the development prospects of the developing countries. The two main objectives of the IPC were price stabilisation and price increases above the long-term trend. The IPC also included five subsidiary objectives: (i) improvements of access to supply for importing countries; (ii) improved market access for producers; (iii) improved competitiveness of natural products *vis-à-vis* synthetics; (iv) expanded processing of commodities in developing countries; (v) improved food aid.[52]

The commodity coverage of the Integrated Programme included foodstuffs, minerals and agricultural raw materials. Resolution 93(IV) mentioned 18 commodities of export interest to developing countries and left open the possibility that other commodities could be added at a later stage. The 'Nairobi 18' included 10 'core commodities' (cocoa, coffee, copper, cotton and cotton yarns, hard fibres, jute, rubber, tea, tin and sugar) and 8 'other' primary products (bananas, bauxite, iron ore, manganese, meat, phosphates, tropical timber and vegetable oils including olive oil and oilseeds).

Five kinds of international measures were outlined in pursuit of the aims of the Integrated Programme. The two most important were the setting up of international buffer stocks and the establishment of a Common Fund to finance the programme. Other measures included the negotiation of multilateral long-term purchase and supply commitments; the improvement of compensatory financing facilities; and the expansion of processing in developing countries. It was envisaged that two separate accounts would be opened in the Fund. The first account, or 'First Window' would finance buffer stocking operations. The second account, or 'Second Window' would finance other measures, for example, research and development, and improvements in marketing, transport and distribution undertaken by the Common Fund.

Gamani Corea, the UNCTAD Secretary-General during this period claims that, 'The story of the Common Fund is the story of a negotiating success.'[53] It is indeed correct that despite a long, bitter, controversial and heated dispute between the developed and developing countries agreement was finally reached on the creation of a Common Fund in June 1980.[54] The compromise that was finally arrived at while meeting some of the important demands of the developing countries established an organisation with restricted competence. For the developing countries the Common Fund negotiations were successful because in the first place a CF was created, secondly, the fund includes a 'Second Window' to finance measures other than stocking and thirdly, although they will not control the voting in the new organisation the voting procedures make it difficult for any one group to assume a dominant role. This is an advance on the Bretton Woods institutions. On the other hand, the CF as negotiated has a much less important role to play in regulating international commodity trade. First, it is dependent on ICAs rather than being able to perform an independent catalytic role. Secondly, the financial base of the CF is much less than originally envisaged. And even if this is not an impediment for First Window, i.e. stocking activities,[55] it severely restricts Second Window activities. When the Common Fund Agreement was opened for signature in October 1980 it was hoped that it would achieve sufficient signatures representing the necessary capital subscription for it to enter into force in 1981. Pleas were made at UNCTAD VI, and UNCTAD VII, for the ratification of the Agreement but it only came into force on 19 June 1989.

The story of the CF encapsulates the dilemma of the developing countries in UNCTAD in this period. A great deal of time and energy was expended and political importance attached to a negotiating process from which the benefit was negligible.

Whereas the CF negotiations produced a result, however unsatisfactory, under the Integrated Programme only one new ICA, the International Natural Rubber Agreement (1979) was established. New agreements were created for jute and jute products (1982) and tropical timber (1983) but they did not include price stabilisation mechanisms. A number of existing agreements were renegotiated, e.g. olive oil, tin, sugar, cocoa and wheat but these organisations were of limited influence as instruments of market regulation. The spectacular collapse of the International Tin Agreement in 1985 encapsulated the problems faced by ICAs in the 1980s.

The bold objective of the Integrated Programme to create a linked set of ICAs failed to materialise for a number of reasons. The institutional venue was considered unsuitable by both producers and consumers. The highly political atmosphere of UNCTAD, the commitment of the secretariat to the IPC and the decision-making structure all inhibited negotiations on individual commodities.[56] Secondly, the link between the CF and the IPC created an air of uncertainty which pervaded the negotiations on individual commodities. The failure to complete the CF negotiations at an early date contributed to stalling tactics in commodity negotiations. Governments were reluctant to conclude agreement without some idea of what the integrating mechanism would look like.

A third reason for the failure to conclude individual commodity agreements arose from the opposition of the major developed countries. The negative response of the advanced industrial countries (apart from France) arose not only from opposition to market intervention on doctrinal grounds but also from the existence of conflicting theoretical perspectives on the merits of pursuing price stabilisation through ICAs. The failure of the UNCTAD secretariat to provide a convincing intellectual case for the IPC and CF is another reason for the limited progress in commodity negotiations.[57] Finally, the negotiation of ICAs is an inherently difficult and conflictual process. The resolution of producer–consumer conflicts and producer–producer disputes is complex and as likely to end in failure as in success.[58]

Market access for manufactures from developing countries

One of UNCTAD's earliest concerns was the subject of tariff preferences for the developing countries. The adoption of the Generalised System of Preferences was a testament to the organisation's ability to fulfil the functions of interest aggregation, interest articulation and negotiation. The idea of a scheme under which the manufactured and semi-manufactured exports of developing countries would be granted preferential access to the markets of the developed countries first surfaced in GATT.[59] It was in UNCTAD, however, that the scheme was debated and negotiated, even if implementation required a GATT waiver.

The case for preferences rests on a variant of the infant industry argument. Firms in developing countries are unable to compete with producers in the developed countries because of high initial costs. Preferential access to the markets of the industrial countries improves the competitiveness of the developing countries' exports because producing for the larger market results in economies of scale and the development of technical, organisational and managerial skills. Another line of reasoning behind the case for preferences arises from the tariff structures of most industrial countries. In operating a sliding scale of tariffs with duties low on unprocessed goods but increasing with the degree of processing, developed countries inhibit manufactured exports from developing countries. A third argument in favour of preferences stresses the welfare implications. Increased production and exports is likely to provide opportunities for increased use of previously unemployed or underemployed factors.[60]

The quest for a general system of preferences came into conflict with existing schemes of selective preferences. The Yaoundé Convention linking the EEC and its 18 African associates and the Commonwealth preference system of the United Kingdom provided benefits for its members that might be eroded in the event of the creation of a general preferential scheme. On the other hand, those countries not benefiting from selective preferences were concerned that the retention of these schemes would devalue any general scheme. These conflicting interests among the intended beneficiaries was an important aspect of the bargaining process.[61]

The demand by the developing countries for improved market access and the commitment of the UNCTAD secretariat[62] to the issue made preferences the pivotal issue in UNCTAD's early years. The subject of preferences was an important part of the discussions at the first UNCTAD conference. The developed countries rejected the idea of a general system of preferences but agreed to the creation of a committee to consider the question of preferences. By the time UNCTAD II convened the United States and other developed countries had dropped their opposition to a general system of preferences. The US decided to support a general scheme as a counter to the demands of Latin American countries for selective preferences and because the Johnson administration was concerned that the EEC should not create more selective schemes.[63]

Resolution 21(11) passed at the New Delhi Conference recognised, 'the unanimous agreement in favour of the early establishment of a mutually acceptable system of generalised non-reciprocal and non-discriminatory preferences' and established a Special Committee on Preferences to elaborate the details of the scheme. The Special Committee on Preferences adopted 'Agreed Conclusions' in respect of a GSP in October 1970,[64] bringing to an end the first successful negotiations conducted in UNCTAD. The agreement on preferences represented a significant symbolic achievement for the developing countries. It signalled the end of reciprocity and non-discrimination as applied to developing countries in the GATT. The GSP was important in the campaign for special and differential treatment in GATT. The GSP was allowed by a 10-year waiver in the GATT, thus further enhancing the developing countries' campaign for special treatment in that organisation.

The successful conclusion of the GSP and the implementation of national preference schemes did not constitute the end of the campaign for improved market access. UNCTAD has continued to monitor the implementation and effectiveness of the GSP.[65] The benefits from the GSP are curtailed through limited product coverage, the withdrawal of preferential status if exports become too competitive and the erosion of preferential markets through the success of trade liberalisation in the MTN. Nevertheless, the GSP has been beneficial to some developing countries.

UNCTAD has also been concerned with restrictive business practices. The third session of the conference established an *ad hoc* group of experts to study restrictive business practices. This put in motion a series of studies which led to the adoption of a Set of Multilaterally Agreed Equitable Principles and Rules for the Control of Business Practices. In 1980, the General Assembly adopted the set and an Intergovernmental Group of Experts on Restrictive Business Practices was established in UNCTAD to monitor the application and implementation. The set is not binding and implementation has not progressed beyond information-gathering and the analysis of data.[66]

Conclusion

If UNCTAD has failed to fulfil the high hopes of its founders, it nevertheless has not been the abject failure its detractors portray. Looked at from an historical perspective UNCTAD has made an important contribution to development diplomacy. UNCTAD's main value lies in its role as a pressure group. From the perspective of the developing countries, UNCTAD's role in articulating a vision of development different from that proposed by the Bretton Woods institutions was important in the 1960s and 1970s. UNCTAD's main failure has been as a negotiating forum, where despite the conclusion of some agreements, the overall record is very disappointing.

The conventional explanation of UNCTAD's failure to produce more tangible gains emphasises the rigidity of the group system and the unrealistic nature of the demands made by developing countries. The need to maintain the unity of the G77 is given as the main cause of the espousal of maximalist demands. There is an element of truth in this viewpoint but it is only partially correct. In failing to give closer attention to the attitude and behaviour of the industrial countries the entire blame for stalemate in North–South negotiations is placed on the G77. This approach assumes that the Northern countries are willing and prepared to enter into the sort of negotiations likely to effect a major change in international economic relations. This is an unwarranted assumption. The industrial countries took a negative response to UNCTAD from the outset and were never willing to see it as more than a forum for discussions. Even when they were engaged in negotiations they argued that the process was not proper negotiation.

It is not unsurprising that UNCTAD failed to effect the sort of system change which its Third World members hoped for when they created the organisation. The Third World lacked the economic and political power to negotiate regime change. The brief period following the quadrupling of oil prices in 1979/74 appeared to herald a shift in North–South bargaining power but this turned out to be a temporary and reversible phenomenon.

The G77 and the UNCTAD secretariat turned UNCTAD into the chief instrument through which a NIEO would be negotiated. The failure of the NIEO negotiations left UNCTAD in a vacuum. Moreover, the triumph of neo-liberal economic thinking in the 1980s further marginalised the organisation. The emphasis in neo-liberal analyses on the importance of domestic policies contrasted sharply with UNCTAD's stress on the external environment. UNCTAD's failure to pay more attention to domestic factors made its economic analysis and advice seem outdated and irrelevant.

The increasing differentiation among the developing countries made it more difficult to maintain the unity of the G77. Third World leaders, while maintaining interest in an organisation which despite its shortcomings was nevertheless identified as one which they controlled, began to feel that the Bretton Woods institutions were likely to provide increased resource flows. UNCTAD appeared to be incapable of providing solutions to the debt crisis, global recession and falling commodity prices. Increasing economic hardship and the absence of tangible gains from UNCTAD prompted many developing countries to abandon rhetoric in favour of seeking accommodation with the IMF, World Bank and the GATT. The recent organisational changes and shift in focus is an attempt to make UNCTAD more relevant to development diplomacy.

Notes

1. Sarita Kendall, 'UNCTAD catches the free-market bug', *Financial Times* (27 February 1992) p. 3.
2. Michael Lipton, 'UNCTAD. SCMUNCTAD? Why Not Start Again From Scratch', *Round Table* (July 1972) pp. 297–308.
3. Thomas G. Weiss, *Multilateral Development Diplomacy in UNCTAD* (London: Macmillan 1987).
4. Robert Ramsay, 'UNCTAD's Failure: The Rich Get Richer', *International Organization* (Spring 1984) pp. 387–397; Harry G. Johnson, 'Commodities: Less Developed Countries' Demands and Developed Countries' Response'

in Jagdish N. Bhagwati (ed.), *The New International Economic Order: The North–South Debate* (Cambridge, Mass.: MIT Press 1977) pp. 240–251.

5. See, for example, Michael Zammit Cutajar (ed.), *UNCTAD and the North–South Dialogue: The First Twenty Years* (Oxford: Pergamon Press 1985); Autar Krishan Koul, *The Legal Framework of UNCTAD in World Trade* (Leyden: A. W. Sitjhoff 1977).

6. See Branislav Gosovic, *UNCTAD: Conflict and Compromise* (Leyden: A. W. Sitjhoff 1971) ch. 1.

7. Michael Zammit Cutajar 'Editor's Note' in Cutajar (ed.) *op. cit* p. vii.

8. See Marc Williams, *Third World Cooperation: The Group of 77 in UNCTAD* (London: Pinter 1991) ch. 2.

9. *Ibid.* p. 29; Gosovic, *op. cit.* pp. 6–7.

10. UNGA Resolution 1785 (XVII), 8 December 1962.

11. See Charles L. Robertson, 'The Creation of UNCTAD' in Robert W. Cox (ed.), *International Organisation: World Politics* (London: Macmillan 1969) pp. 258–274; M. Lavichenko & I. Ornatsky, 'Barometer of Interstate Relations', *International Affairs (Moscow)* (January 1964) pp. 62–68; Jozsef Bognar 'The World Trade Conference', *Co-Existence* (November 1964) pp. 89–98.

12. Isaiah Frank, 'Aid, Trade and Economic Development: Issues Before the U.N. Conference', *Foreign Affairs* (January 1964) pp. 210–226 argues that the creation of some institutional arrangement was an inevitability.

13. Richard N. Gardner, 'The United Nations Conference on Trade and Development', *International Organization* (Winter 1968) p. 122.

14. Alfred Maizels, 'A Clash of Ideologies', *IDS Bulletin* (July 1984) pp. 18–23.

15. See TD (VIII)/Misc. 4 for the results of UNCTAD VIII.

16. *UNCTAD Bulletin No. 13* (Jan–Apr 1992) p. 3.

17. Javed Ansari, *The Political Economy of International Economic Organisation* (Hemel Hempstead: Harvester Wheatsheaf 1986) pp. 198–199.

18. Diego Cordovez, *UNCTAD and Development Diplomacy: From Confrontation to Strategy* (Journal of World Trade Law 1972) p. 172; B. Gosovic, 'UNCTAD: North–South Encounter', *International Conciliation* (May 1968) pp. 29–30.

19. Gosovic, *op. cit.* p. 15; Robert S. Walters, 'International Organizations and Political Communication. The Use of UNCTAD by Less Developed Countries', *International Organization* (Autumn 1971) pp. 828 & 830; Mahqub ul Haq, *The Poverty Curtain* (New York: Columbia University Press 1976) p. 182; Koul, *op. cit.* p. 67.

20. Robert W. Gregg, 'Negotiating A New International Economic Order: The Issue of Venue' in R. Jutte & A. Gross-Jutte (eds), *The Future of International Organization* (London: Frances Pinter 1981) pp. 62–63; Robert L. Rothstein, *Global Bargaining: UNCTAD and the Quest for a New International Economic Order* (Princeton, N.J.: Princeton University Press 1979) pp. 195–203; Gosovic, 'UNCTAD: North–South' *op. cit.* p. 29.

21. Weiss, *op. cit.* pp. 6 & 42.

22. Raul Prebisch, 'Towards a New Trade Policy for Development', Report by the Secretary-General of the UNCTAD (New York: United Nations 1964).

23. *Ibid.* p .3.

24. Gamani Corea, *Taming Commodity Markets: The Integrated Programme and the Common Fund in UNCTAD* (Manchester: Manchester University Press 1992) p. 6.

25. See Hans Singer, 'Ideas and Policy: the Sources of UNCTAD' *IDS Bulletin* (July 1984) pp. 14–17.
26. UNCTAD, *Trade and Development Report 1992* (New York: United Nations 1992).
27. See Gamani Corea, 'UNCTAD and the New International Economic Order', *International Affairs* (April 1977) pp. 177–187; Geoffrey Goodwin & James Mayall (eds), *A New International Commodity Regime* (London: Croom Helm 1980).
28. If resolutions co-sponsored by the G77 and other groups are excluded. See Williams, *op. cit.* p. 64.
29. Joseph S. Nye Jr, 'UNCTAD: Poor Nations Pressure Group' in R. W. Cox & H. K. Jacobson (eds), *The Anatomy of Influence* (New Haven: Yale University Press 1974) p. 358.
30. *Ibid.* p. 346.
31. Cordovez, *op. cit.* p. 152; Weiss, *op. cit.* pp. 48–49. Gosovic, *UNCTAD: Conflict and Compromise op. cit.* p. 290.
32. Gosovic, *op. cit.* pp. 297–298; Gardner, *op. cit.* p. 115; Rothstein, *op. cit.* p. 130.
33. Marc Williams, 'UNCTAD and International Economic Reform: A Note on Organisational Characteristics and the Political Process' in Paul Taylor & A. J. R. Groom (eds), *Global Issues in the United Nations' Framework* (London: Macmillan 1989) p. 277.
34. Quoted in Sidney Dell, 'The Origins of UNCTAD' in Cutajar (ed.), *op. cit.* p. 28.
35. Quoted in Gardner, *op. cit.* p. 107.
36. See C. B. Boucher & W. E. Siebeck, 'UNCTAD VII: New Spirit in North–South Relations', *Finance and Development* (April 1987) pp. 14–16.
37. Ansari, *op. cit.* p. 296.
38. Walters, *op. cit.* p. 824.
39. Williams, *Third World Cooperation op. cit.* p. 73.
40. C. P. Brown, *The Political and Social Economy of Commodity Control* (London: Macmillan 1980) pp. 288–289 fn. 2 argues that several aspects of the Havana Charter were altered in spirit during the 1950s in the UN system.
41. This objective was stated as early as 1966. See TD/B./C.1/26 – 'The Development of International Commodity Policy' and S. D. Metger, 'Developments in the Law and Institutions of International Economic Relations. UNCTAD', *American Journal of International Law* (July 1967) p. 762.
42. See Recommendations A II.1 to A II.9 in *Proceedings of the United Nations Conference on Trade and Development, First Session, Geneva 1964* vol. I, pp. 26–34.
43. Resolutions 16 (II) to 20 (II). See *Proceedings of the United Nations Conference on Trade and Development, Second Session, New Delhi 1968* vol. I. pp. 34/35.
44. L. N. Rangarajan, *Commodity Conflict* (London: Croom Helm 1978) p. 23 comments that, 'This plethora of draft resolutions created the impression that, by 1968, the international community had succeeded in (i) identifying the specific commodities for which international agreement were possible and (ii) devising an appropriate mix of techniques for regulating each one.'
45. See Joseph A. McMahon, *Agricultural Trade, Protectionism and the*

Problems of Development: A Legal Perspective (Leicester: Leicester University Press 1992) pp. 39–42 for a discussion of the integrated approach reached at UNCTAD II.

46. See TD/B/202, Annex 1 (14 November 1968).
47. See Kerstin Barkman, 'Costs and Finance of the Tin Buffer Stock', *Journal of World Trade Law* (Nov–Dec 1976) for a calculation of the costs of financing the International Tin Agreement.
48. See TD/B/248, Annex 1 (16 June 1969).
49. See Cheryl Payer, 'Coffee' in Cheryl Payer (ed.), *Commodity Trade of the Third World* (London: Macmillan 1975) p. 165.
50. See Resolutions 49 (III) 'International Cocoa Agreement', 50 (III) 'Competitiveness of natural products, synthetics and substitutes', 54 (III) 'The stabilization of commodity prices and, in particular the role of the International Bank for Reconstruction and Development', 78 (III) 'Marketing and distribution systems', and 83 (III) 'Intergovernmental consultations on commodities in connection with access to markets and pricing policy' in *Proceedings of the United Nations Conference on Trade and Development, Third Session, Santiago 1972* vol. I pp. 77–81.
51. McMahon, *op. cit.* pp. 49–50.
52. The objectives of the IPC were outlined in a number of UNCTAD documents. The original source is TD/B/498 – 'An Overall Integrated Programme for Commodities' (8 August 1974).
53. Corea, *The Taming of Commodity Markets, op. cit.* p. 69.
54. See TD/IPC/CF/CONF/L. 15 – 'Draft Agreement establishing the Common Fund for Commodities'. The Final Text is contained in TD/IPC/CF/CONF/ 24 (29 July 1980) – 'Agreement establishing the Common Fund for Commodities'. The real breakthrough had taken place during the Third Negotiating Conference on the Common Fund (12–19 March 1979). See TD/IPC/CF/CONF/18 (21 March 1979) – 'Fundamental Elements of the Common Fund'.
55. Corea, *Taming op. cit.* pp. 112–114.
56. See Rothstein, *op. cit.* ch. 4.
57. See Brown, *op. cit.* ch. 8.
58. On the problems faced by ICAs see, for example, E. Ernst, *International Commodity Agreements* (The Hague: Martinus Nijhoff 1982); Fiona Gordon-Ashworth, *International Commodity Control: A Contemporary History and Appraisal* (London: Croom Helm 1984); Rangarajan *op. cit.*
59. See Peter Tulloch, *The Politics of Preferences* (London: Croom Helm 1975) p. 37; Press Release GATT/750, 17 May 1963.
60. See Tracy Murray, *Trade Preferences for Developing Countries* (London: Macmillan 1971) pp. 18–20; K. S. Sundar Rajan, 'Tariff Preferences and Developing Countries', *Proceedings of the American Society of International Law* (1966) pp. 87–88.
61. See Williams, *Third World Cooperation op. cit.* pp. 112–116 for an analysis of the cleavages among the developing countries.
62. See A. K. Bhattacharya, 'The Influence of the International Secretariat: UNCTAD and Generalized Tariff Preferences', *International Organization* (Winter 1976) pp. 75–90.
63. See Ronald I. Meltzer, 'The Politics of Policy Reversal: the U.S. Response to Developing Countries and Linkages Between International Organizations

and National Policy Making', *International Organization* (Autumn 1976) pp. 649–668.

64. See TD/B/329 (12 October 1970).

65. The Special Committee on Preferences conducts an annual review of the operation of the GSP.

66. See Gautam Sen, 'UNCTAD and International Economic Reform' in Taylor & Groom (eds), *op. cit.* pp. 255–258; Colin Greenhill, 'Manufactures and Semi-Manufactures: Twenty Years of Work in UNCTAD', *IDS Bulletin* (July 1984) pp. 40–41.

8

Justice, efficiency and international economic organisations

The Third World's campaign for the reform of the international political economy is, in large measure, a demand for global redistributive justice. Decolonisation, with the attendant advent of over 100 new states at levels of economic development substantially below that of the old members of international society, created the conditions from which the problem of global distributive justice emerged in contemporary world politics. And the developing countries, collectively and individually, in raising the issue of underdevelopment and the need for redress gave effective voice to the demand for global distributive justice. However, although these states can place global distributive justice on the international agenda they lack the political and economic power to implement the necessary changes.

The demand that the rich countries transfer resources to the poor ones and the response to it is embodied into existing concepts and developed in the frameworks of theories of international relations and economics. Considerations of justice are problematic in both international relations and economics.

Writers and practitioners of international relations have traditionally asserted the existence of a conflict between order and justice.[1] In the development of international political theory, with its focus on a system of states, the claims of order tended to be given priority over those of justice. The key requirement of a given international arrangement was its contribution to stable and orderly patterns of conduct among the members of international society. Demands for justice were inimical to international order since they posed a potential threat to the balance of power.

Economic theory is concerned with the allocation of scarce resources to productive ends. A number of values – efficiency, justice, security and stability – intrude, as it were, on the processes of production, distribution and consumption. These goals are not always compatible and a conflict between the goals of efficiency and justice is recognised as unavoidable. People will possess different views concerning the notions of fairness and justice making solutions to questions of distributive justice and equity very difficult to resolve. Moreover, the fact that a more equal division of resources may be at the expense of efficiency and productivity increases the likelihood that disputes will arise between proponents of efficiency and supporters of greater economic justice.

Do international economic organisations promote justice and efficiency? Before an answer can be given to this question another question has to be answered. And that is, should the promotion of justice be the concern of international economic organisations in the first place? Few economists or international relations theorists would query the pursuit of efficiency as a legitimate objective of international economic organisations. It is likely that we would find a large measure of agreement that the efficient allocation and use of resources is a good thing. But the same cannot be said about social justice. It will, therefore, be necessary to establish whether the promotion of justice should be a legitimate concern of international economic organisations before assessing their performance. The second part of this chapter will discuss the concept of distributive justice. My intention is to see whether a basis exists for applying considerations of justice to the operations of IEOs. The first part of the chapter will begin on more familiar territory by looking at the issue of efficiency.

International economic organisations and efficiency

Most of this book has been addressed to answering this question and this section will merely review the evidence without adding to it. Economists recognise two types of efficiency: technical efficiency and economic efficiency. Technical efficiency simply means the most effective use of resources in a particular tasks, i.e. no waste. There are two kinds of economic efficiency, standard and Pareto optimal. Standard efficiency includes technical efficiency and is attained through choosing among scarce resources so that the best allocation of resources is made. In other words, economic efficiency is obtained when the output produced cannot be increased without at the same time decreasing the output of some other good. Pareto optimality refers to a situation where no one can be made better off without making someone else worse off. I think we can conclude without any hint of controversy that the world is not in a Pareto optimal state. Pareto optimality as a measure of welfare could be used as the criterion by which to assess whether economic justice had been attained. But since Pareto optimality can attain in conditions of gross inequality it is not an appropriate measure.

The debate about the impact of the IEOs on the developing world has concentrated on the extent to which they have promoted the efficient allocation of resources necessary to stimulate growth and development. As we have argued throughout, the answer to this question is far from straightforward and depends on the analytical framework of the analyst. It is also a question to which different answers can be given depending on whether a systemic perspective is employed or the subject is being viewed from the standpoint of a particular economy. This book has argued that a systemic evaluation is possible but that it is incorrect to extrapolate the results for a particular economy from the conclusions arrived at concerning the impact of the IEO's policies and prescriptions on another economy. To put this in a stark manner: IMF policies implemented by, say, Peru will not have the same impact as similar policies undertaken by Zimbabwe. The results may well be similar but this can only be discovered through comparative analysis of the separate programmes and not from general propositions about the consequences and effectiveness of IMF programmes. With that proviso in mind, I shall now summarise the evidence on the performance of the four IEOs in meeting the test of efficiency.

The discussion of the IMF's role in the developing countries tends to revolve around the issue of Fund conditionality. The Fund and its supporters contend that it has a flexible approach to balance of payments stabilisation which is ultimately successful in most cases in returning the debtor country to external equilibrium. The assertion of the correctness of Fund policies is based on recognition of the desperate economic crisis facing countries who apply for IMF loans. The Fund insists that countries tend to delay their requests for assistance thus exacerbating an already bad economic situation. Moreover, Fund sources assert that without its programmes countries would be worse off. On the positive side, the IMF insists that its medium-to-long-term strategy is successful. Its interventions are aimed at increasing the efficiency of the local economy and in so far as its policies are followed this goal is achieved. Borrowing countries usually have a number of policies which create waste and inefficiency. These include overvalued exchange rates, food subsidies and import restrictions. Fund policies promote increased competitiveness and improve efficiency by removing restrictions to the operation of market forces.

Critics of the IMF accuse it of pursuing policies which fail to alleviate the economic distress faced by debtor nations. Radical critics argue that

Fund policies are deflationary and increase inequality.[2] They lead to 'contraction in per capita incomes, rising unemployment, rising urban poverty, reduced government expenditure per head of population, rising malnutrition among children, stagnant or falling levels of real investment and no improvement in the current account of the balance of payments'.[3] Other writers on the Fund's relationship with the developing countries who reject some of these accusations, nevertheless arrive at negative assessments of impact of Fund-supported programmes. Killick and his collaborators in a wide ranging study of Fund stabilisation programmes concluded that the programmes do not generally have strong deflationary impacts and have little impact on inequality. Nevertheless, their findings suggest that Fund-supported programmes have 'limited effectiveness'. Their survey showed that,

> With regard to the balance of payments, the test results suggest that programmes are associated with a modest short-term improvement in the current account (but this is of low statistical significance). There is a slightly stronger tendency for the basic or overall balances to be improved (but again the statistical significance was found to be low). The tests indicated that Fund programmes do result in inflows of capital from other sources but that the effect is not large, Finally, no systematic association was found to exist between Fund programmes and sustained liberalisation.[4]

Critics and supporters of the Fund cannot agree on the impact of IMF policies on Third World states.

As with its twin institution, assessment of the World Bank's performance is open to dispute. The focus of the Bank on the provision of development assistance immediately places any judgement of the Bank's ability to fulfil the efficiency criterion in the context of debates on the efficacy of foreign aid. Critics from both the left and right of the political spectrum condemn aid and allege that it is a wasteful use of resources. These general critiques are based more on supposition than examination of the evidence, and although forming a backdrop to analysis of the World Bank and the financing of economic development they cannot in themselves provide an answer to the question posed. The evidence on changing World Bank approaches to, and priorities in development finance – trickle-down to basic needs to adjustment lending – is inconclusive. The closer cooperation between the Bank and the IMF since the early 1980s has led many observers to question the policies proposed by the Bank.

Unlike the IMF and World Bank the GATT is not a provider of financial assistance and therefore is more of a forum than an actor. Any assessment of GATT's contribution to the promotion of economic efficiency in developing countries is dependent on the view taken of the benefits and/or costs flowing from free trade. As I have tried to suggest, this is a somewhat irrelevant dispute since GATT is a managed trade organisation and not one promoting free trade. From this perspective GATT's contribution to the efficient allocation of resources is a limited one for two reasons. First, GATT's acquiescence in agricultural protectionism and sanctioning of the Multi-Fibre Agreement represents a failure to halt the inefficient use of resources on a global scale. Secondly, in granting special and differential treatment to developing countries GATT has explicitly promoted nationalist objectives over efficiency.

UNCTAD, like GATT is largely a forum organisation. Of the IEOs examined in this book, UNCTAD has exercised the least influence over the international economy. Its *raison d'être* is the promotion of the interests of the developing countries and it has been unable to turn many of its proposals into concrete agreements. From the perspective of liberal political economy UNCTAD's failures are a positive development since UNCTAD's approach is held to be illiberal and hence inefficient. Supporters of UNCTAD would not claim that the organisation was seeking an inefficient allocation of global resources but would insist that economic justice was a greater priority.

Three of the four IEOs examined in this book would place economic efficiency above economic justice. Their goals are stability and efficiency, and justice, in so far as it is given any attention, is a second order issue. Only UNCTAD, created by the developing countries in their quest for a more just international economic order, would reverse the priorities of the Bretton Woods institutions. The prioritising of stability and economic efficiency over justice is by no means accidental. It is the logical consequence of the views on world order held by the architects of the post-war international economic organisations. International justice is a subject on which a great deal of scepticism exists. In the next section I will examine the objections that have been made to consideration of justice in international relations and then assess several arguments that have been made for international distributive justice.

Justice and international society

The denial of the relevance of morality to international affairs is made from a variety of theoretical perspectives.[5] Here I will only discuss the realist objection to considerations of ethical issues in world politics. Realism, the dominant approach to international relations, takes a pessimistic view about the applicability of morality to foreign policy. For realists, international relations is the arena of necessity and morality is an impediment to the preservation of the nation-state. Statesmen and stateswomen act in the name of the national interest. They owe allegiance to their constituents and not a fictive international society. World politics unlike domestic politics lacks a sovereign and in this state of nature justice cannot be a priority. For realists,

> The international system is not to any appreciable extent a society united by common rules, but simply an aggregate of separate societies each pursuing its own purposes, and linked with one another in ways that are essentially ad hoc, unstable, and transitory.[6]

In the absence of a sovereign, ethical action by any one state is inherently risky if not reciprocated. In the words of Stanley Hoffman,

> in a domestic system which functions well, individuals and groups can behave morally because there is a framework of social order – in which they have a stake. *A contrario,* when that framework disappears, and survival or basic needs become the obsession of all, individuals and groups start behaving in an immoral way.[7]

The world of the realists is one in which conflict and the possibility of being implicated in a generalised war, as Raymond Aron put it, are the general conditions of international relations.[8] In the absence of a world community realists reject the possibility of international justice.[9]

This view can be, and has been, challenged by many writers on international relations. The English School of International Relations with its focus on international society rejects this Hobbesian conception of international relations and posits a world order in which a morality of states is a possibility. In this tradition moral norms pertain to the framework of international society but are derived from the existence of states and not individuals. The principles of international justice derived from a conception of a society of nation-states include sovereign equality, self-determination, non-intervention, the right of self-defence, fulfilling international legal obligations and so on. In this tradition states can and do act morally but only in keeping with the special conditions of international society.[10]

This conception of international justice has a number of limitations.[11] It is inherently conservative and legitimises the *status quo*, is state-centric and so excludes the activities of international organisations and is incapable of dealing with international inequalities. As Thompson concludes, 'a theory of justice based on the entitlement of sovereign states seems inadequate to deal with questions of justice which inevitably arise in world affairs.'[12] Nigel Dower, while sharing Thompson's reservations about a state-centric theory of international justice, nevertheless suggests that a right to development can be derived from this approach.[13] But as Dower indicates, this is an unsatisfactory basis on which to construct an international obligation. Theories of global distributive justice attempt to go beyond a theory of justice based in the entitlement of states to one constructed on the rights of individuals.

Global distributive justice

A number of attempts have been made to construct a model of global distributive justice. The most well-known attempts have as their source John Rawls' *A Theory of Justice*.[14] Rawls describes justice as fairness, and he argues that rational individuals would choose two basic principles of social cooperation if they were starting from an 'original position' in which they were unaware of the position they will occupy in society. Behind this 'veil of ignorance' the two principles of justice chosen by individuals are: the equal liberty principle and the difference principle. According to the equal liberty principle each person is guaranteed the most extensive liberty compatible with similar liberties for all. The difference principle is concerned with the existence of social and economic inequalities. Such inequalities are tolerated if they benefit the least advantaged and provided the offices and positions to which they attach are open to all.[15]

Rawls constructed his theory of justice for a national society and assumed that since states are relatively self-contained units the contracting parties in the original position represent different nations. The two principles of justice are not applicable beyond national borders but minimal principles of international justice, i.e. the liberal principles of sovereign equality, self-determination and self-defense do apply in the international realm.[16]

Rawls' failure to apply his theory to international relations has not deterred other scholars from so doing. The most widely discussed application of Rawlsian principles to international relations is that undertaken by Charles Beitz.[17] He contends that there is no reason why the two principles of justice should not be globalised. The facts of economic interdependence are sufficient to make the concept of international society a reality. In other words, 'international relations is coming more and more to resemble domestic society in several respects relevant to the justification of principles of [domestic justice].'[18] It follows that if a world society exists there is no reason why the Rawlsian approach is not applicable. Beitz argues that if everyone in the world was placed in the original position but unaware of which state they would inhabit (i.e. dropping the limiting assumption that contractors in the original position are aware of their nationality) it is likely that they would choose the two principles of justice. Adoption of the difference principle would lead to increased interstate transfers. For Beitz, the failure to extend the Rawlsian argument to international relations results in a position whereby global inequalities and injustices appear to be condoned. If the facts of interdependence are correct and we do live in a world society then the unit of analysis should be the world and not the state.

The argument in favour of global distributive justice made by Beitz has encountered a number of objections. One line of criticism focuses on the claim that interdependence has created the basis of a world community. Brian Barry argues that interdependence conceived as an extended network of international trade cannot create the basis for justice since it is not the relevant type of cooperative scheme; that is, 'justice as fair play arises not from simple exchange but either from the provision of public goods that are collectively enjoyed . . . or from quasi-insurance schemes for mutual aid.'[19] This denial that international society meets Rawls' definition of society is echoed by other writers. The interstate system is still one of self-interest and interdependence can foster hostility as well as cooperation.[20] The difference principle is inapplicable to international relations because the assumption of co-operation made by Beitz is false. International relations still approximates the condition of self-help; interdependence does not and cannot create the basis of community.

Critics also allege that Beitz's proposals are impracticable. The gap between political theory and practical reality is a yawning chasm. How, it is asked, are these principles to be implemented? In the absence of a world government or some central authority it is inconceivable that the necessary tranfers from rich to poor could take place. Principles of justice need a civil authority for their implementation and Beitz is silent on this point.[21]

A third objection concerns the difficulties involved in securing agreement on how the difference principle is to be operationalised. It is far from obvious in a multicultural and diverse international society what social inequalities should be taken into consideration, and what further transfers can be legitimately demanded.[22] Different climatic conditions and levels of development will bring about different needs. As Sen points out, 'a person in the rich country with a higher real income than a person in a poor country must not automatically be taken to be more advantaged.'[23]

These objections at first glance appear to be compelling but their robustness will depend on the view taken of the counter-attack. Beitz argues that the objections to the practicality of his suggestions are not persuasive because,

> they misunderstand the relation between ideal theory and the real world. Ideal theory prescribes standards that serve as goals of political change . . . the ideal cannot be undermined by simply pointing out that it cannot be achieved at present. One needs to distinguish two classes of reasons for which it may be impossible to implement an ideal. One class includes impediments to change that are themselves capable of modification over time; the other includes impediments that are unalterable. . . . Only in the second case can one appeal to the claim of impossibility in arguing against an ideal.[24]

The debate between Beitz and his critics therefore hinges on one's perception of the durability of the state system and the possibilities of its transformation. It can be pointed out that since the nation-state is an historical construct there is still a place for an 'ideal theory' of justice. On the other hand, if the cosmopolitanism immanent in Beitz's theory can be shown to be misplaced in any possible set of alternative futures (within a reasonable time period), then the criticism still has force.

The objection concerning interdependence and the creation of a global society is essentially a conflict of interpretation. Indeed it is possible to go beyond Beitz's limited formulation of the conditions under which global society is brought into being. Andrew Collier in a recent article asserted that,

> Today, [however], we have become one world in two ways: economically, in that we are massively dependent on goods produced all over the world; and ecologically, in that we are all threatened by the ecological irresponsibility of all. The whole planet has become a shared world, even for those who never leave their village. Thus a tie which is both real and universal has arrived; not yet in the form of a real collectivity embracing humankind, but of real relations of mutual dependence through the sharing of the world; and it is from just such relations, I have suggested, that values and obligations arise.[25]

The perspective of Collier and Beitz on the existence of global society is just as relevant as those who insist that the barriers between nations are far greater than links of commonality. Moreover, an approach to international relations which focuses on the structure and dynamics of international social life reorients our conception of the world system.[26]

The 'international' becomes an explanatory rather than a residual category. Such an approach is supportive of arguments which stress the many linkages in contemporary global society.

The final objection is difficult but not impossible to overcome. Similar problems beset basic needs approaches to development in the 1970s. These differences point to the need for extended research and analysis into how the primary goods will be distributed but do not foreclose the possibility of finding a distributional formula.

The argument for global distributive justice presented by Beitz is a powerful one. It is difficult to deny that at least an emerging world society exists. The existence of global injustice and the inability of contemporary mechanisms to provide redress is equally correct. If Rawls' model of justice is correct there should be no reason why we cannot apply distributive justice to international relations. Theorists who reject the Kantian basis of Rawls' approach, or cosmopolitan accounts of international obligation would, however, not accept these conclusions. I will now examine one influential critique of Rawls' theory of justice before concluding this section with a brief examination of other attempts to establish a basis for global distributive justice.

The entitlement theory of Robert Nozick attacks the basis of Rawlsian approaches to justice.[27] He argues that Rawls' theory is a patterned theory and hence fundamentally defective. For Nozick, Rawls' theory and others like it fixes end-state principles to which the actual distribution should conform and therefore overdetermines the system. According to Nozick, principles should lead to whatever outcomes will emerge but the difference principle only leads to certain outcomes and thus the end-state is determined in advance. In rejecting consequentialist rights-based theories Nozick also rejects redistributive obligations. According to Nozick, individuals have rights which cannot be abrogated by any higher authority. Individuals have entitlements to the property s/he has acquired, either through their own efforts or through transfers from others, including ancestors. If holdings have been acquired justly then an individual cannot be coerced into giving them up for some common good. In this conception redistribution has first to be justified rather than the existence of inequalities. Justice arises from the application of the principles of acquisition and transfer.

The major problem with Nozick's entitlement theory lies in the difficulty in showing that existing holdings were derived from the operation of the principles of acquisition and transfer. There is of course a major debate concerning the role of imperialism in the current unequal relations between the developed and developing countries. It would be almost impossible to show that current holdings in world politics are just. But according to entitlement theory this is not distributive justice but rectification for past wrongs. Entitlement theory leads to a never-ending argument concerning past exploitation and its impact and provides no realistic basis on which transfers could be made. Another important critique of entitlement theory concerns the arbitrary nature of its assumptions. Why should the starting point be property rights and not some other right(s)? There is no reason why entitlements and justice should be confined to property.

Entitlement theory provides a counter to theories of distributive justice but fails to produce strong enough arguments to undermine them. Moreover, entitlement theory is itself open to serious objections. Many contemporary philosophers and political theorists have developed theories of global distributive justice, and arguably, the idea of global distributive justice even if no agreement exists on a single approach is sufficient for us to conclude that it is possible to apply principles of global distributive justice to North–South relations.

The various theories of global distributive justice start from different positions. Some are rights-based, some take interests as the starting point and others begin with needs.[28] But they all share the central assumption that the transfer of resources internationally should be governed not only by humanitarian considerations but by the application of principles of justice.

Barry rejects the application of justice as reciprocity and replaces it with a conception of justice as equal rights. If we assume that natural resources are the possession of the human race as a whole and justice is defined as equal rights then the present unequal distribution of resources provides a starting point for a theory of distributive justice.[29]

Other recent theories of global distributive justice include Janna Thompson's attempt to combine the cosmopolitan and communitarian traditions. In her model, global inequalities will be bridged in two ways. First, transnational communities consisting of individuals from rich and poor regions will form and the internal distribution in these groups will reflect principles that all members can endorse. Secondly, the existence of these communities will create a new pattern of relationships at the global level. These new relationships will 'make it more likely that the activities and relationships which in our world tend to cause or exacerbate poverty and oppression do not occur and that past injustices can be remedied'.[30]

International economic organisations and global distributive justice

If the arguments presented above are accepted, the Third World's demands can be conceived as appeals for justice and not charity. And international organisations are legitimate instruments to achieve economic justice. The distinction between charity and justice is important.[31] Barry encapsulates the difference neatly, 'the obligations of humanity are goal-based, whereas those of justice are right-based.'[32] This distinction is important both for the donor and the recipient, and changes the basis of their relationship.

I have so far demonstrated that the Third World can legitimately couch their demands in the language of justice. But no agreement exists on the methods by which international redistribution will take place. One key issue that remains unresolved is whether justice refers to individuals or states.[33] It is not my intention to look at various schemes to transfer resources from North to South. The more limited question of this chapter concerns the record of IEOs in promoting justice. Two issues are of importance in this connection. The first pertains to the actual performance of IEOs and the second refers to the limitations of IEOs as suitable instruments.

If economic justice is defined as the implementation of policies which reduce disparities in income and allocate increased wealth so that the most disadvantaged gain and the more privileged do not increase their gains merely as a result of original inequalities, the organisations examined in this book have a poor performance record. The asymmetrical adjustment mechanism of the IMF penalises deficit countries but is unable to enforce obligations on surplus countries. The World Bank, especially through the IDA, can conceivably be construed as enhancing economic justice. But the domination of the Fund and the Bank by the donor countries and the international adjustment process over which they preside is not conducive to the promotion of justice. The GATT suffers from similar problems in that it too is an organisation dominated by the interests of the powerful trading states. GATT has not been able to deliver the kind of market access to Third World products commensurate with increased economic justice. On the other hand, if GATT had operated according to its stated principles, the tendency for free trade regimes to work to the benefit of the strongest economies leads to the conclusion that it would have failed to promote justice. UNCTAD failed to secure its stated goals of changing the terms of trade and improving the positions of the developing countries in the international political economy but did register some minor successes.

The above evaluation needs to be placed in the context of the goals of the four organisations. The interests of the Bretton Woods institutions are system maintenance and stability. They were not designed to promote economic justice and accusations that they have failed in this task can therefore seem irrelevant. From the perspective of the majority of their membership this is not a pointless question since it is not the original purpose of the organisations but their ability to adapt to change which is of most importance.

Sen outlines two basic approaches to international income distribution: 'evasion' and 'fantasie'. The conservative belief that the *status quo* does not need alteration gives rise to 'evasion', i.e. 'entitlement valid for all substances I own now'. The approach to the transfer of resources which fails to take account of internal income distribution gives rise to 'fantasie', i.e. 'fiction of all nations throbbing as symbolic individuals in existence'.[34] This chapter has argued that the basis exists to go beyond 'evasion'. I think that it follows from what has been said above that a state-centric approach to international relations, and by implication international justice, is too restrictive. This chapter is only concerned with trying to establish if efficiency and justice are relevant criteria to be applied to international economic organisations. The precise formulation of principles and the design of a system whereby the impact of IEOs can be tested is beyond the scope of this chapter.

Notes

1. Hedley Bull, *The Anarchical Society* (London: Macmillan 1977).
2. E. A. Brett, *The World Economy Since The War* (London: Macmillan 1985) pp. 219–226.
3. Frances Stewart, 'Should Conditionality Change?' in Kjell Havnevik (ed.), *The IMF And The World Bank In Africa* (Uppsala: Scandinavian Institute of African Studies 1987) pp. 32–33.
4. Mary Sutton, 'Introduction and summary of companion volume' in Tony Killick (ed.), *The IMF and Stabilisation: Developing Country Experiences* (London: Heinemann 1984) p. 5; and Tony Killick, 'The Impact of Fund Stabilisation Programmes' in Tony Killick (ed.), *The Quest for Economic Stabilisation: The IMF and the Third World* (London: Heinemann 1984) pp. 227–269.
5. See Janna Thompson, *Justice And World Order* (London: Routledge 1992) pp. 2–9.
6. Terry Nardin, *Law, Morality and the Relations Of States* (Princeton, NJ: Princeton University Press 1983) p. 36.
7. Stanley Hoffman, *Duties Beyond Borders* (New York: Syracuse University Press 1981) p. 17.
8. Raymond Aron, *Peace and War: A Theory of International Relations* (London: Weidenfeld & Nicolson 1966).
9. For an effective demolition of the national interest and Hobbesian state of nature arguments see Brian Barry, 'Can States Be Moral?' in Brian Barry, *Liberty and Justice: Essays in Political Theory 2* (Oxford: Clarendon Press 1991) pp. 159–181.
10. See Bull, *op. cit.* passim.
11. See Thompson, *op. cit.* pp. 12–13.
12. *Ibid.* p. 13.

13. Nigel Dower, 'Sustainability and the Right to Development' in Robin Attfield & Barry Wilkins (eds), *International Justice and the Third World: Studies in the Philosophy of Development* (London: Routledge 1992) p. 104.
14. John Rawls, *A Theory of Justice* (London: Oxford University Press 1973).
15. *Ibid.* pp. 60–62.
16. *Ibid.* p. 378.
17. See Charles Beitz, *Political Theory and International Relations* (Princeton, NJ: Princeton University Press 1979); David Richards, *A Theory of Reasons for Action* (Oxford: Oxford University Press 1971); Brian Barry, *The Liberal Theory of Justice* (Oxford: Clarendon Press 1973); Thomas Pogge, *Realizing Rawls* (Ithaca: Cornell University Press 1989).
18. Beitz, *op. cit.* pp. 125–176.
19. Brian Barry, 'Humanity and Justice' in Barry, *Liberty and Justice op. cit.* p. 194.
20. See, for example, Robert Tucker, *The Inequality of Nations* (London: Martin Robinson & Co. 1977).
21. Thompson, *op. cit.* p. 15; Hoffman, *op. cit.* pp. 4–5.
22. Thompson, *op. cit.* p. 15.
23. Amartya Sen, 'Ethical Issues in Income Distribution: National and International' in Amartya Sen, *Resources, Values and Development* (Oxford: Basil Blackwell 1984) p. 294.
24. Beitz, *op. cit.* p. 156.
25. Andrew Collier, 'Marxism and Universalism: Group Interests or a Shared World?' in Attfield & Wilkins, *op. cit.* p. 87.
26. See Jan Aart Scholte, 'From Power Politics to Social Change: an Alternative Focus for International Studies', *Review of International Studies* (January 1993) pp. 3–21.
27. Robert Nozick, *Anarchy, the State and Utopia* (Oxford: Clarendon Press 1974).
28. See the following essays in Attfield & Wilkins, *op. cit.* Kai Nielsen, 'Global Justice, Capitalism and the Third World' pp. 17–34; Andrew Belsey, 'World Poverty, Justice and Equality' pp. 35–49; Dower, *op. cit.* pp. 93–116; and Collier, *op. cit.* pp. 77–92.
29. See Barry, 'Humanity and Justice' *op. cit.* pp. 187–203 for an elaboration of this argument.
30. Thompson, *op. cit.* p. 191.
31. See Ali Mazrui, 'Panel Discussion on the New International Economic Order' in Jagdish N. Bhagwati (ed.), *The New International Economic Order: The North–South Debate* (Cambridge, Mass.: MIT Press 1977) pp. 371–374.
32. Barry, 'Humanity and Justice', *op. cit.* p. 204.
33. See John Toye, *Dilemmas of Development* (London: Basil Blackwell 1987) pp. 142–145 for a discussion of this issue.
34. Sen, *op. cit.* pp. 292–293.

Index